Shooting the Pilot

SHOOTING THE PILOT

Laurence Marks
& Maurice Gran

First published in 2021 by Fantom Publishing, an imprint of Fantom Films.

www.fantompublishing.co.uk

Copyright © Laurence Marks and Maurice Gran 2021

Laurence Marks and Maurice Gran have asserted their moral right to be identified as the authors of this work in accordance with the Copyright, Designs and Patents Act 1988.

All rights reserved.

A catalogue record for this book is available from the British Library.

Hardback edition ISBN: 978-1-78196-364-7

Typeset by Phil Reynolds Media Services, Leamington Spa
Printed and bound by CPI Group (UK) Ltd, Croydon, CR0 4YY
Jacket design by Aaron William Lowe

Contents

Dedication and Acknowledgements — vii

Foreword by David Renwick — ix

Introduction — 1

1 *Holding the Fort* — 3

2 *Shine On Harvey Moon* — 42

3 *The New Statesman* — 81

4 *Birds of a Feather* — 114

5 *Love Hurts* — 153

6 *Goodnight Sweetheart* — 212

7 *Lady Ottoline Pierpoint's Guide to Intimate Behaviour for Gentlewomen* — 247

Afterword — 285

Dedication and Acknowledgements

THIS BOOK IS DEDICATED to Barry and Lyn Took who believed in us more than perhaps we believed in ourselves. They both were always so encouraging and never stopped telling us that we *would* make it. How do you ever repay that confidence? A dedication?

But there are other amazingly kind and generous friends and acquaintances who deserve to be acknowledged and so we shall:

Don West, Joe Green and Ernest Andrews, three 'old timers' from our old Monday nights at Player Playwrights, which we attended when we were very young. These three gentlemen taught us more about drama than any critic, university or writing course could ever have managed.

And then there is Gary Brannan and Christopher Taylor from the Borthwick Library, the University of York, where is kept our archive. During the most locked-down of 2020 they managed to retrieve long-lost scripts and other fading documents that jogged our memories.

As for everyone else, well, you had such a large part to play in our success and the success of these scripts:

Emma Amos, Roger Andrews, Humphrey Barclay, Liz Carling, Esta Charkham, Tony Charles, Dick Clement, Kenneth Cranham, Peter Davison, Christopher Ettridge, Alan Field, Marsha Fitzalan Howard, Michael Grade, Sally Gran, David Harsent, Clare Hinson, Pauline Hoare, Patricia Hodge, Michelle Holmes, Frankie Howerd, Micheál Jacob, Carol

James, Lesley Joseph, Matthew Kelly, Dervla Kirwan, Ian La Frenais, Vernon Lawrence, Gary Lawson, Nick Lyndhurst, Paul Makin, Brigitte Marks, Sue Marks, Vic McGuire, Allan McKeown, Robin Nash, Susie Parriss, Geoffrey Perkins, John Phelps, Michael Pilsworth, Nigel Planer, Michael Portillo, Jonathan Powell, Pauline Quirke, David Reynolds, Linda Robson, Geoff Rowley, Linda Seifert, Renee Short, Guy Slater, Maggie Steed, Baz Taylor, Sue Teddern, Peter Tilbury, Michael Troughton, Zoë Wanamaker, Jo Willett.

Foreword

HALF A CENTURY AGO, when I first dipped my toes into radio, David Jason – or Sir David Jason as he then wasn't – had a reputation as the king of the kamikaze pilots. A national treasure still waiting to be dug up, he was the obvious choice for all us rookie writers trying to get our own projects off the ground. But once cleared for take-off most of these pilots promptly took a nosedive, and it was down to producers like Humphrey Barclay in television to give him his first big break. In truth I suspect the scripts were not up to much, though I have fond memories of the mad Gothic sketch show that Andrew Marshall and I penned called *The Curse of the Jasons*, which twice got to the recording studio but alas no further. This was a bitter blow as we were more than pleased with our efforts. But the channel controllers – then, as now – were all-seeing, all-knowing, so it was back to the drawing board.

In 1975 the veteran writer David McKellar suggested the two of us teamed up to write a vehicle for the late, great Peter Jones. (He was, of course, not late at the time, though I'm not sure that would have been much of a handicap on Radio Four.) And so we duly set to work and produced a rather surreally mordant half hour called *Things Could Be Worse*; about, well, a character for whom things couldn't be worse if they tried. To our surprise the BBC loved it, subject to one minor tweak. We were thrilled. And wasn't Peter Jones – yet to be canonised as the eponymous *Hitchhiker's Guide to the Galaxy* – the funniest, most perfectly gloomy candidate for the role? We were never to find out, as the "minor tweak" went by the name of Harry Worth, whose career the BBC bigwigs were trying to revive, and would take to our script like a duck to cement. Now Harry was the loveliest, sweetest of souls, but I can't say writing that series was the happiest time of my life. Far from using the pilot to iron out the faults, this became an exercise in weeding out its strengths; so that by show thirteen the project was a very far cry from the one we'd envisaged.

So while the piloting process may have its pluses, to road-test your premise and characters, and especially your casting, I've always believed you should trust your first instincts. And don't be gulled into all sorts of bright ideas that might tickle the programme commissioners, who won't have expended a fraction of the blood, toil, tears and sweat that you have, getting it right. Objectivity has its place, but know when to object to it.

Within these pages you'll learn of the intricate engineering performed by two of our most prolific and peerless screenwriters as they steered their work from the page to the screen. To a one – or maybe two-and-a-half – trick pony like myself their output is formidable, the quality speaks for itself, and its genesis makes for fascinating reading.

When they asked me to chip in with some thoughts I wasn't sure how much I could add. Looking back over my own career, and the half dozen or so original series that made it to the air, I'm struck by how little was changed in the scripts as originally submitted. Strictly speaking, only two were ever recorded as pilots, i.e., on the basis that the broadcaster reserved the right to throw them away. One was a sketch show for Thames called *The Steam Video Company*, so instantly forgettable it was shot on camera obscura; the other was a slightly more memorable outing titled *Whoops Apocalypse*. The seeds of the latter were sown at the BBC, where it was commissioned by John Howard Davies, only to fall on stony ground. To our relief it was rescued by the aforementioned Humphrey Barclay at ITV, who declared JHD "completely mad" (discuss) and managed to persuade his boss Michael Grade to cough up the money for a try-out. And here, I do recall, Andrew Marshall and I effected a major overhaul. Our first draft I think may have taken its cue more from *War and Peace* than World War Three and was vastly unwieldy. We cut out no end of indulgent waffle to streamline it into the regulation two twelve-minute chunks format for ITV, and still had plenty left over for subsequent episodes. After the recording we reshot a few scenes that hadn't quite worked, and this was enough to convince the network. Guidance from Humphrey was invaluable though not intrusive, and in those days interference from suits was unknown. For better or worse the series emerged as a personal project, not a corporate one.

One Foot in the Grave hung around for a while on someone's desk at the BBC (all right, Gareth Gwenlan's desk), before I managed to prise out a response. But once they'd decided they liked it the rest was a lot more painless than it would be today. There was some early resistance to my choice of Richard Wilson to play Victor ("a second banana, not a lead"), but in those days you could still have an argument about such things, and in this case, prevail. The producer Susan Belbin and I were left to our own devices, and at Richard's suggestion I added one more scene to show his character moping about the house, but that was it. Two other shows of mine, *Jonathan Creek* and *Love Soup*, survived the journey from spec script to screen entirely pilot-less. Whether this was a good thing I suppose depends on whether you trust driverless cars.

If I have learned anything in the past fifty years of comedy writing it's that there's almost nothing to be learned about comedy writing. Of course, there's masses of stuff you can teach about technique and characterisation and story arcs and structure, but none of that makes your work funny. You can't teach funny, and you can't say where on earth it comes from, you just know when it's arrived. You know because something suddenly pops into your head, a line or an idea or an image, that makes you chuckle.

But there's no way you can force this: unlike every other form of writing it doesn't respond to any kind of logic or reason. Of course, most people in the media, who are used to arriving at things intellectually, can't accept the idea of something that's purely intuitive. With *One Foot in the Grave* for example, the programme's success was all down to its central conceit… a man in tune with the frustrations of our age… a spokesman for the zeitgeist of the nineties… and so on and so on. But of course, it could be all of those things and still not be funny. Victor's attitude, his whole take on life, could have been presented in a purely dramatic way that was not remotely amusing.

Comedy, for its practitioners, is never a matter of "What approach shall I try?" or "Which demographic should I skew towards here?" It's something much deeper and more organic, that can't be quantified or qualified, and can merely be felt. And the short answer to "How do you make something funny?" is "Whatever works." But don't ask me *why* it works because I can't tell you.

Ultimately it defies both analysis and synthesis. A well-known television executive once took me to lunch and said: "Do you think there's a comedy series set in a working men's cafe?" Well, what do you say to that? (I actually said "*The Larkins*?") Only someone who doesn't create comedy for a living would come up with that little nugget, because it betrays a complete misconception of how we go about it.

I think my earliest insight into the nature of comedy was in 1971 when I was contributing to the late-night radio series *Week Ending*. Like all the other writers I would slave away each week producing sketches full of "clever" puns and political allusions; then I'd go along to the studio, where the funniest thing in a sketch about the Cod War was David Jason standing on a chair making seagull noises. It taught me the one infallible rule about broadcast comedy: that you're only as funny as your performers.

When we talk of sitcoms not working it's traditional to blame the script. Often with good reason. But the script is just one part of a complex process, and I think too many producers and commissioners concentrate their energies on getting the text right, then blow the whole thing by just casting some jolly good actors and assuming they'll make it work. Not if they're not funny they won't. Why was Paul Eddington funny? I have absolutely no idea, he just was. The bottom line, I'm afraid, is that audiences don't laugh at scripts, they laugh at people. I mentioned this once to the two Ronnies, pointing out that even the news desk only worked because it was the two of them delivering the lines. Ronnie Corbett expressed surprise at this theory, claiming it was the most formal thing they did with not a hint of personality. But, I said, I could sit there and read those exact same jokes, with exactly the same timing and rhythm and die a hundred deaths. Whatever we writers like to think, the material always takes a back seat to the actors.

To summarise then:

Unfunny script plus unfunny performers equals unfunny show.

Funny script plus unfunny performers equals unfunny show.

Unfunny script plus funny performers equals unfunny show.

Funny script plus funny performers plus unsympathetic direction equals unfunny show.

Funny script plus funny performers plus sympathetic direction equals funny show (sometimes).

Execution is all: the final fence at which many well-intentioned projects still fail. Never assume that giving funny people funny things to say and do will make it work like a dream. Every piece of business, every prop, every camera angle, every cut is critical. And in short, the most useful advice I would personally give to any fledgling writer is: never forget how unlikely you are to succeed. And don't imagine there's some universal scientific formula that will guide your hand.

Schopenhauer once said that what makes us laugh is the sudden, unexpected incongruity between concept and percept.

But then he never saw David Jason standing on a chair making seagull noises.

David Renwick
January 2021

<u>Notes from production executive:</u>
- *Why was he standing on a chair?*
- *Would it be funnier if he'd made the seagull noises as Del Boy?*
- *Why would you need a cast member to do this, when there's a perfectly good sound effects library that can be accessed through the BBC's intranet using a designated username and passcode?*
- *Who's Schopenhauer?*

Introduction

REVISITING THESE PILOT SCRIPTS – six which led to successful series, one that was never produced – brought us on a nostalgic journey, to a time when we were young and hopeful, and the world of television was a much simpler place. Our first script, *Holding the Fort*, was commissioned by one man at a meeting. We wrote a script, he read it, gave us his thoughts, we wrote a second draft and that was the script that was produced.

Life is more complicated now, as increasing numbers of television people have opinions, sometimes contradictory, which have to be taken into account. It was a golden age.

Often, in rereading the pilots, we've discovered that they differ significantly from the show that was actually recorded, because much can change during rehearsals and editing. Hearing actors interpreting our lines is very different to what we heard in our heads when we wrote the script. Episodes have to conform to a running time, so material can disappear during editing. But these are the building blocks on which the series were constructed.

People often ask where we get our ideas from. We tell them, "There's a little shop in Macclesfield," but there is no secret. Everyone has good ideas. But most people don't realise they've had a good idea because they don't know how to recognise that they've had one.

Inspiration seldom arrives unbidden. Great ideas arise when a writer is alert and open to the little wisps of creative potential as they drift by. It might be a newspaper headline, a photograph, a cartoon, a casual observation or even an overheard remark; anything can flick a switch in your brain and make you say, "Now *that's* interesting!"

For example, one day Maurice saw two overdressed women lunching in a smart hotel and thought they looked like gangsters' molls. He mentioned them *en passant* to Laurence, who instantly saw the comedy potential, and *Birds of a Feather* was born.

Later, Maurice returned the compliment when Laurence mused, apropos of very little, that there were some East End back streets that hadn't really changed since World War II. Immediately Maurice saw the dramatic possibilities of a world where past and present coexist, seen through the eyes of a character who can move between those two eras.

The existence of these two shows demonstrates the value of having a writing partner. In each case writer A wasn't aware that he had found a good idea until writer B pointed it out. Where solo writers go for their creative fuel is a mystery to us since our way is the only way we know. Of course, not all inspirations turn into long-running TV series. Some become short-running series. Some fail at the pilot stage. Some evaporate as soon as you try to explore them in depth. And some fall by the wayside because other people don't see the possibilities.

Fortunately for us, enough people did to bring us a career and the joy of making millions laugh. Which, after all, is the point of comedy.

1
Holding the Fort

In late November 1978 the Boomtown Rats were top of the pop charts with 'Rat Trap' and it was playing on the car radio as we pulled into a parking bay opposite London Weekend Television's South Bank skyscraper. We were just so excited having been invited in to meet Humphrey Barclay, the network's head of comedy. We had heard his name many times and now we were being summoned to see him and discuss any ideas we may have for a new sitcom.

What brought us to Humphrey Barclay's attention was the success of our six-minute monologue for Frankie Howerd at the Royal Command Performance just a couple of weeks earlier. The show was televised on the BBC and the "surprise unannounced" guest was none other than the man with the worst toupee in showbiz. We had worked on his latest radio show, so he had asked us to write him six minutes of patter – as he referred to it – which had gone down a storm with the guest of honour, Queen Elizabeth The Queen Mother. It was commonly agreed that Mr Howerd stole the show. The next morning, so we were later told, everyone in "the business" wanted to know who wrote his monologue.

It was us and, on the strength of our success, our first and new agent managed to wangle us through the revolving doors of LWT and into Humphrey Barclay's office. What we were going to pitch to the esteemed Mr Barclay was an idea that arrived quite by accident. It was a chance remark that came up in conversation in, of all places, Corfu. We were convalescing after the brutal experience of writing Frank's radio series, and Sally, Maurice's wife, said, "I think if we have children, Maurice would make a much better mother than me." The words would have floated away into the blue Corfu sky had not Maurice plucked them out of the air and said, "I think that just might make our first television series."

In the years leading up to our fateful meeting with Humphrey Barclay, we had written four sitcom scripts, each better than the last, but none "better enough" to be commissioned. We'd received some vaguely encouraging rejection letters of the "we quite like this but not enough" variety. We had even met the heads of comedy at the BBC and Thames Television, who both encouraged us to "keep at it". And so we kept at it, but after our fourth rejection we wondered whether it was worth the bother. Then along came Frankie Howerd.

By the time we were climbing the stairs to Humphrey Barclay's office, we had developed Sally's stray observation into a proper pitch about Russell and Vicky, a young couple trying to cope with the challenges of a new baby. Vicky has given up her job, as most wives still seemed to back then, leaving Russell as the sole breadwinner. Money is tight but one evening he comes home with good news. He's been offered a new and better position by the über-brewery for whom he works. The only problem is it entails moving to Cumbria. Russell tries to sell Vicky on the higher salary, detached house, health insurance and company car. She isn't buying this pitch. She doesn't want to leave London, her mother, her friends, their lovely shambolic terraced house or the job she plans to return to when their baby is old enough.

It's a simple enough set-up, but where was the "kicker", as poker players refer to the surprise? Well… what if she goes back to work and leaves him at home holding the baby? Now there's a good title, we thought: *Holding the Baby*. We discussed how she always earned more than he so it would make financial sense for her to return to work. Now we had something to work with. It was a very novel idea back in 1978.

At this stage we weren't sure what "Vicky's job" was, but we knew Russell was a brewer, though all we knew about beer was downing pints at our local. However, we had read about a young guy called David Bruce, who had just opened his first independent pub called the Goose & Firkin, with its very own microbrewery in the basement. He kindly let us spend the day with him and watch the bare bones of how to brew a barrel of ale. We realised Russell and Vicky's house was going to need a substantial cellar. At the end of our visit to his first pub, David, with phenomenal kindness, offered to become our "brewing adviser" *and* supply Russell's brewery in the studio with the necessary equipment… should we sell our idea.

Humphrey Barclay listened to our pitch with interest. We thought we might have him hooked.

"I like the set-up," said Humphrey, "but you say she goes back to work. So what does she do? What's her career?" We still hadn't really thought about that. At least not enough.

One of us ventured, "She could be in advertising?"

"But isn't that boring? And besides, I've seen it before."

"What about if she was in PR?" the other suggested desperately.

Humphrey looked unmoved. We sensed that we were running rapidly out of capital in the head of comedy's office.

As it happened, some weeks earlier we had read another article, this time about a young mother who had returned to work when her child was young. The reason this minor story made it into print was that her job was as a major in the United States Air Force, based in East Anglia. And so with *Holding the Baby* in mind we were intrigued enough to actually drive to Mildenhall to meet her and her husband… and baby too. On our way back to London we agreed that the idea of a brewer married to an army officer was just too wacky for mainstream television. But not now. In Humphrey's office. In sheer desperation.

One of us said, "She could be in the army?"

Humphrey smiled and said, "Now *that's* interesting." Later we wondered why we hadn't followed our instincts in the first place. The answer, and one every new writer should learn from, is that it was because rather than being original, we were trying to second-guess the market.

As soon as we redeployed Vicky as an army captain, Humphrey uttered the magic words: "All right, I'll commission a script." It's difficult to express how we both felt. Excited? Delirious Terrified? Now we had been handed our big chance. Get it right and perhaps, only *perhaps*, we could become professional television comedy writers. Get it wrong and we would have blown a once-in-a-lifetime opportunity. We both knew there was no room for failure.

As we hurried back to the car park we discussed when we'd start writing. We were both holding down "day jobs": Maurice was due back behind his Civil Service desk that very afternoon, while Laurence was expected back behind his typewriter at the *North London Weekly Herald*. We knew we would have to work late into the night and all weekend to write *Holding the Baby* – the gruelling schedule that had almost wrecked our health on the *Frankie Howerd Show*. Being a journalist, Laurence was unofficially on 24-hour call (headline stories don't always occur between nine and five), so Maurice suggested it might be better if we each applied for a week's leave. Then the National Union of Journalists called a strike and suddenly Laurence had all the time in the world. Maurice took that week's leave and we really got stuck in to *Holding the Baby*, except that on our first morning we realised that as Vicky was an army captain, wouldn't a better title be *Holding the Fort*?

We sat in one of the rooms of Laurence's council flat that he had turned into a sort of home office, inasmuch as it possessed a desk, on which sat a typewriter, a telephone, a bottle of Tipp-Ex (a white fluid used to paint out typing errors, and there were many), and a box of A4 paper. This was the age when there were no home computers; besides, a computer in those days was the size of a small home. Everything had to be written in longhand, then typed up, and any corrections meant the entire script being retyped… and perhaps even typed again. Looking back it isn't any wonder that a script took such a long time to deliver.

One of the first things we realised was that if Vicky was going "off to war" every morning we couldn't have Russell at home alone with only his six-month-old baby to talk to. He needed a mate, a confidant, someone perhaps to "assist" him with both his brewing and his deliveries. Enter Fitz. Where the name "Fitz" came from, neither of us can remember. He didn't possess a proper name. Indeed, he didn't seem to possess very much, not even an address. He was a long-distance lorry driver who slept over at the house of whichever woman he knew in whatever port.

Fitz was an essential component of the series. He was both Russell's and Vicky's sounding board, and, so we thought, could be the natural funnel for laughter. We portrayed him as something of a clown, which all too often sent the complications of the Milburns' situation off-beam. Yet as a character he worked for us, perhaps because he had known Russell and Vicky for ever and could be trusted by both parties.

If Russell needed a character with whom to share his scenes, then so did Vicky. When she returns to the Royal Signals Regiment, she comes up against Captain Hector Quilley, an old colleague and rival. There was no love lost between the two captains. Indeed, Quilley supplied most of the friction in the series. He clearly had gone to public school and Sandhurst and wasn't at all comfortable around women… and, in his view, the army was no place for a woman. She should be at home bringing up baby and looking after her husband. We enjoyed great fun at the expense of Hector Quilley and, perhaps most important of all, he afforded us comedy in the military setting.

So with our four central characters in place, we sat down to work out this first story; the scene breakdown, as we call it. Our principle is never to begin a script without knowing where it's going to end and how we're going to get there. An ITV pilot in those days ran to around 24 minutes: not very much time to cram everything in. These days an ITV half hour can be as short as 20 minutes, so the writer's task has become even more difficult.

We managed to write the first draft of this pilot during Maurice's week-long leave of absence and then handed it – by hand – to Mr Barclay. We weren't going to risk it getting lost in the post. No attaching it to an email in those days. Humphrey read it. It made him laugh. Quite a lot. Which was fantastic.

Then he said, "I like it… but I have some thoughts." We waited with bated breath. "You told me that she returns to her job in the army, yet you don't show or mention it in the script." He was dead right. Why hadn't it occurred to us to send Vicky off to her job interview in the British army? The answer, with hindsight, was "inexperience", or perhaps stupidity. Somehow we'd have to shoehorn that scene into the second draft.

Humphrey carefully marked his thoughts on the script and made it tighter, better, more playable. He sent us off to write the second draft. Nevertheless we were elated. We had made the great Humphrey Barclay laugh and we still believe, in our old-fashioned way, that laughter is the essence of all comedy. Reading the script now, for the first time in decades, we can see that we were trying too hard. There are gags where there should be witty dialogue, with characters saying things they probably wouldn't say in real life. But at the time we just wanted to be funny. Luckily Humphrey indulged us, and so, later on, did the TV audience.

We know that the script we created that week in the spare room of Laurence's council flat was far from perfect, but that's the draft we're presenting here, with all its over-enthusiastic shortcomings. *Holding the Fort* was one of seven scripts Humphrey commissioned for an on-screen showcase he called *Comedy Tonight*. This script, or at least the second draft, was the last of the seven, scheduled to be recorded in front of a studio audience on the night of August 10, 1979. What actually happened on that day warrants a book of its own. But eventually, of those seven pilots, *Holding the Fort* was the one chosen to go into series, and the reason you're reading this book.

HOLDING THE FORT by LAURENCE MARKS & MAURICE GRAN

"OVER A BARREL"

CAST.

VICKY MILBURN
RUSSELL MILBURN
FITZ
LADY ON TELEPHONE

LOCATIONS.

THE MILBURNS' KITCHEN/DINER. (INT)
THE M4 MOTORWAY AND THE BACK STREETS OF ACTON. (EXT)

January 1979

SCENE ONE. INT. DAY.

OPEN IN A FAIRLY LARGE KITCHEN OF THE MILBURNS' EDWARDIAN HOUSE IN ACTON, WEST LONDON. IT IS QUITE WELL APPOINTED, BUT NEVERTHELESS UNTIDY. WE SEE LOTS OF DIRTY DISHES AND CUPS ON THE DRAINING BOARD. THE CUPBOARDS AND DRAWERS ALL LEFT OPEN. IN THE CENTRE OF THE KITCHEN IS A HABITAT-STYLE PINE TABLE WHICH CARRIES A CARRY COT. NEXT TO THE TABLE WE SEE A CONCERTINA CLOTHES DRYER BEARING SHEETS, BABY ATTIRE, JEANS, SHIRTS ETC.

WE PAN IN ON A PAIR OF BOOTED FEET EMERGING FROM DIRTY DUNGAREES, WHICH IN TURN ARE EMERGING FROM THE CUPBOARD SPACE UNDER THE SINK. ON THE FLOOR, THE TORSO OF THE LEGS' OWNER IS HIDDEN BY THE SPACE UNDER THE SINK. ON THE FLOOR BY ONE LEG IS A BIG BOX OF TOOLS AND A DO-IT-YOURSELF MANUAL.

BANGING AND MUTTERED OATHS EMERGE FROM TIME TO TIME. THEN VOICES, BUT WE SEE NO PEOPLE.

VICKY: (FROM UNDER THE SINK, IN CHILD'S VOICE) Mummy, do all mummies have hands as soft as yours? (IN HER OWN VOICE, TO THE TUNE OF THE FAIRY SNOW ADVERT) 'Now hands that clear U bends can be crusted in gunge...'

THE LEGS WRIGGLE OUT FROM UNDER THE SINK, TO BE FOLLOWED BY THE REST OF VICKY. HER HAIR IS TUCKED INTO A BERET, AND SHE IS VERY MUCKY. ESPECIALLY HER HANDS WHICH SHE HOLDS IN FRONT OF HER LIKE A SURGEON.

VICKY: (IN CHILD'S VOICE) Why aren't Daddy's hands crusted in gunge, Mummy? (IN HER OWN VOICE) You may well ask.

VICKY TURNS ON THE TAPS AND NOTHING HAPPENS. SO SHE STARTS TAPPING THEM WITH A WRENCH. THE TAPPING BECOMES PROGRESSIVELY HARDER.

VICKY: Come on you swine. Push. Come on out of there you drip. Yes, you. You've been driving me round the bend for three months. You can't leave me standing here, oozing like the Beast from Ten Thousand Fathoms. (BANGS TAP) I've just unblocked your bloody U bend for you. That's got to be worth a trickle. (SHE GRITS HER TEETH) Right, you've asked for this (SHE GIVES THE TAP ONE HELL OF A WALLOP, AND WITH THAT THE BABY STARTS CRYING) Oh, no! (SHE MOVES OVER TO THE CARRY COT) Oh, you're not wet again, are you, darling? I wasn't asking you for a trickle.

VICKY GOES TO PICK BABY UP, BUT REALISES THAT HER HANDS ARE CAKED IN MUCK AND SLIME. SO SHE ATTEMPTS TO PICK UP BABY BY WRAPPING HER ELBOWS AROUND IT WHILE KEEPING HER HANDS AT SHOULDER LEVEL. SHE REALISES THAT THIS IS IMPOSSIBLE, SO SHE RUMMAGES IN A DRAWER AND PRODUCES A PAIR OF OVEN GLOVES OF THE SORT WHICH ARE JOINED BY A STRIP OF MATERIAL. AS SHE IS PUTTING THE GLOVES ON, THE TELEPHONE STARTS RINGING. THE CHILD'S CRIES GET MORE FRANTIC, BUT VICKY, EXASPERATED, LEAVES THE CHILD CRYING AND GOES AND ANSWERS THE WALL-MOUNTED PHONE IN THE KITCHEN.

SHE WEDGES THE PHONE BETWEEN SHOULDER AND EAR, AND WHILE SHE'S TALKING, SHE TAKES OFF HER OVEN GLOVES AND WIPES HER HAND ON A SHEET OF NEWSPAPER.

VICKY: (SCREAMS) Help!!

WE HEAR A WELL SPOKEN, MIDDLE AGED LADY'S VOICE ON THE OTHER END OF THE PHONE.

LADY: (DUBIOUSLY) Hello?

VICKY: Thank God you've phoned, mother. It's no good, you've got to come over. You remember me telling you about that dripping tap? Well, it's stopped and I can't get it started again. The plumbing has dried up completely. Russell's car's gone kaput, that's more expense we can ill afford. Emma needs changing... she's the only thing in this house that hasn't dried up. And if you don't come around straight away, a dreadful fate may overtake your only grandchild. (LETS OUT A GREAT BREATH)

LADY: But I don't have any grandchildren.

VICKY: The entire house is falling about my ears and.... what?

LADY: This is 2374, isn't it?

VICKY: No.

LADY: So you're not Maison Doris, hair artistes?

VICKY: No. And you aren't my mother, are you?

LADY: I'm sorry.

VICKY: (HESITANTLY) Does that mean you aren't coming round?

LADY: I'm sorry.

VICKY: But what about my taps?

LADY: Well I don't know anything about plumbing, but whenever my husband changes a washer, he goes around muttering 'stop-it-cock', if that's any help.

VICKY: Stop-it-cock. Yes, thank you. Goodbye. (HANGS UP)

SHE CROSSES QUICKLY TO THE SINK AND PUTS HER HAND DOWN THE SPACE BETWEEN SINK UNIT AND CUPBOARD AND TRIES TURNING SOMETHING. SO DOING,

THE WATER SUDDENLY HURLS ITSELF IN A TORRENT OUT OF THE COLD TAP, BOUNCES OFF THE BOTTOM OF THE SINK, AND SOAKS HER. SHE TURNS THE TAP OFF, BUT CANNOT STOP IT DRIPPING. WE LEAVE ON DRIPS RUNNING FROM THE TAP.

SCENE TWO. EXT. DAY

CUT TO A SEQUENCE WHEREBY CARS ARE TRAVELLING ALONG THE M4 DURING RUSH HOUR. AS TRAFFIC IS GOING REASONABLY SMOOTHLY, WE FOCUS ON A BRIGHT YELLOW SPORTS SALOON COMING UP IN THE FAST LANE, WITH HEADLIGHTS FLASHING. IT ZOOMS PAST ITS NEAREST RIVALS IN THE CENTRE LANE, AND FROM THE REAR WE SEE ITS EMERGENCY FLASHING LIGHTS GOING ON AND OFF. IT'S GOING SO FAST THAT IT DISAPPEARS OUT OF SHOT.

CUT TO THE SAME YELLOW CAR WHIZZING AROUND THE STREETS OF SUBURBIA, TAKING CORNERS IN RALLY FASHION. WE CLOSE IN AND NOTICE WHILE THIS LUNATIC IS DRIVING AS IF HE WERE ON THE CIRCUIT AT BRANDS HATCH, HE NONETHELESS STILL HAS TIME TO FLASH HIS HEADLIGHTS, PUT ON WIPERS (EVEN THOUGH IT IS NOT RAINING), AND WE NOTICE AN ELECTRONIC AERIAL GOING UP AND DOWN.

WE CLOSE UP TO DRIVER, WHO HAPPENS TO BE RUSSELL MILBURN. HE IS BEHAVING LIKE A CHILD WITH A NEW TOY. HE PULLS UP IN A SUBURBAN STREET, TURNS THE ENGINE OFF, BUT CONTINUES PLAYING WITH GADGETS ON DASH PANEL.

SCENE THREE. INT. DAY.

THE MILBURNS' KITCHEN. IT IS NOW AS TIDY AS IT WILL EVER BE – MEANING IT IS TIDIER THAN BEFORE, BUT FAR FROM BEING SPOTLESS.

WE SEE VICKY SITTING BY THE KITCHEN TABLE WITH HER FEET UP. HER FEET ARE IN TRAINING SHOES AND

SHE HAS ON HOOPED FOOTBALL SOX WITH HER JEANS TUCKED INTO THEM. SHE ALSO SPORTS A HOOPED RUGBY SHIRT, POSSIBLY THE SAME COLOURS AS THE SOX. SHE ALSO WEARS A FLAT CAP. SHE IS SMOKING A CIGARETTE.

THE RADIO IS PLAYING IN THE BACKGROUND. SHE IS READING A MAGAZINE, AND THE TAP IS STILL DRIPPING.

RUSSELL SNEAKS IN THROUGH THE KITCHEN DOOR. HE CREEPS UP BEHIND HER AND KISSES HER ON THE CHEEK. SHE QUICKLY TWISTS AROUND IN HER CHAIR.

RUSSELL: (NOTICING HER ATTIRE) Match rained off, was it?

VICKY: You're home early. You made me jump.

RUSSELL: (TAKING OFF HIS COAT AND BRAND NEW PAIR OF CAR GLOVES) Who did you think it was, the milkman?

VICKY: No, I knew it wasn't the milkman. He doesn't waste time with foreplay.

RUSSELL: Any tea?

VICKY: There's some in the caddy. I'll have a cup if you're making.

RUSSLL: It's alright for you, lounging about all day.

VICKY: Don't provoke me, Russell. I've had a pig of a day. If you really want to know, I have spent the best part of this afternoon stretched out on my back on this very kitchen floor.

RUSSELL: (FILLS KETTLE UP) So that's how you knew I wasn't the milkman. He's been and gone, has he? (CROSSES TO FRIDGE) Only one pint? You must be losing your touch. No, what's this? I can see we're well stocked up with yoghurts.

VICKY: I made those.

RUSSELL:	Oh, we are cultured. Where's Emma?
VICKY:	She's run off with the milkman.
RUSSELL:	(SITS AT KITCHEN TABLE) So why were you stretched out on the floor?
VICKY:	Well, it was raining, and there was nothing on the box, and I had nothing to do, so I thought I'd while away the afternoon under the sink and appreciate the classically simple curve of the U bend. And then I got bored, so I decided to unblock it.
RUSSELL:	(MAKES TEA) I'll let this brew and pop upstairs and see if I can get any more sense out of Emma.
VICKY:	What do you mean 'brew'? Those are 'Quick On The Draw' tea bags, not your Extra Strong Home Made Bitter. Anyway, don't go up there, it's taken me three quarters of an hour to get the child to sleep.
RUSSELL:	Huh. I never have any trouble.
VICKY:	We know. You just tell her a couple of your awful jokes and she's off. Mind you, they're enough to send an adult to sleep.
RUSSELL:	I tell her fairy stories.
VICKY:	How Grimm. There, you got me at it now.
RUSSELL:	Old Barrington called me up to his office for a chat today.
VICKY:	(REMOVES CRUMPLED ENVELOPES FROM THE BACK POCKET OF HER JEANS AND HOLDS THEM OUT) Oh, these came today.
RUSSELL:	Don't tell me, let me guess.
VICKY:	They feel like bills.

RUSSELL: How do you know?! You've never felt Bill's. Have you?

VICKY: (SHAKES HER HEAD SADLY) I cannot for the life of me understand why you find our increasing poverty so hilarious.

RUSSELL: (OPENS FIRST ENVELOPE) But I paid the annual insurance premium last year. (OPENS NEXT) Oh, what! Another rise in the mortgage?

VICKY: (MOCK CHINESE) Confucius he say, mortgage go up as fast as house fall down. Got that, Milburn?

RUSSELL: (TEARS OPEN NEXT ENVELOPE) Ah, water rates. My favourite.

VICKY: They've got a nerve sending that one today.

RUSSELL: No, I never begrudge my contribution to the water rates. They do a lot for charity.

VICKY: Charity?

RUSSELL: Yes, you know, The Grand Order of the Water Rates. Arthur Askey. Max Bygraves... Sorry.

VICKY: Give me strength.

RUSSELL: (COLLECTS THE BILLS TOGETHER AND STUFFS THEM IN DRAWER) Out of sight, out of cash. Oh, well, what's for supper? Something smells interesting.

VICKY: That's the U bend. And it's not supper, it's dinner.

RUSSELL: All right. What's for dinner, then?

VICKY: Nothing.

RUSSELL: Nothing! There must be something in the freezer.

VICKY: There is. Ice. There's so much of it in there, Robin Cousins has asked if he can come over later to practise his triple salchows.

RUSSELL: Look, there must be something to eat. Aren't you having anything?

VICKY: (NONCHALANTLY) I've eaten.

RUSSELL: Oh, I'm all right, Jack.

VICKY: Yes, I shared Emma's strained mutton casserole with prunes.

RUSSELL: So you'll both need changing tonight.

VICKY: If you're hungry go out and get yourself a Chinese takeaway.

RUSSELL: Vicky, you're not taking your housewifely role very seriously lately, are you? The rules are, man wins bread, hence breadwinner; woman <u>prepares</u> bread, so....

VICKY: Look, if you want toast you know where the breadbin is.

RUSSELL: (SLIGHT ANNOYANCE) I don't want toast. I want my meat and two veg. Where's <u>my</u> strained mutton casserole with prunes?

VICKY: Look, Russell. We've only got your salary coming in now, and I've told you before we've got to cut back on some of the luxuries we've been used to; things like food, clothing, and heat.

RUSSELL: (SCRAMBLING AROUND FRIDGE IN SEARCH OF FOOD) Hello, what are these?

VICKY: The chops are for Sunday.

RUSSELL: (TAKES BISCUIT BARREL OUT OF CUPBOARD AND LOOKS FOR CHOCOLATE ONES) I remember the days, not so long ago, when you couldn't close the fridge for food.

VICKY: You remember the days when I went to work. You know I'm only too keen to get back in uniform. God knows I'm not Acton's answer to Mrs Beeton.

RUSSELL: You can say that again.

VICKY: Normally, when a baby's born and the mother stops work it's the lesser wagepacket that's lost. But...

RUSSELL: Alright, don't start that again.

VICKY: Whereas, if I was back in harness, we could easily afford a full-time...

RUSSELL: No nannies! My daughter has every right to be brought up by her own parents.

VICKY: And something else. If I was working we could get that heap of metal you call a car repaired. Did you find out how much it is going to cost?

RUSSELL: Chap at the garage reckons at least seventy quid.

VICKY: Oh, well, you may as well cash in your tax disc, then.

RUSSELL: It's out of date. Anyway, we can't do without wheels.

VICKY: Russell, we've just agreed that our budget is tighter than Rod Stewart's Y fronts. We'll just <u>have</u> to do without the car.

RUSSELL: Fair enough, then. If you say so.

VICKY: (CURIOUSLY) Even though that car is the most important thing in your life?

RUSSELL: (PUTTING HIS ARMS AROUND HER) My family is the most important thing in my life.

VICKY: (PULLS BACK) Russell, have you been drinking?

RUSSELL: Of course I've been drinking. It's my job.

VICKY: I mean <u>drinking</u> drinking?

RUSSELL: At five in the afternoon?

VICKY: It has been known to happen.

RUSSELL: True. But not when I'm driving.

VICKY: (TAKES OFF HER CAP AND SCRATCHES HER HEAD) Driving?

RUSSELL: (SIPS TEA) I told you I had coffee with Barrington today?

VICKY: Driving what?

RUSSELL: Do you remember me telling you the brewery might be expanding out of London?

VICKY: I won't ask you again.

RUSSELL: All right, Mrs Vicky Milburn, let's go and look at tonight's <u>star</u> prize ....

<u>SCENE FOUR. EXT. DAY.</u>

SHOT OF GLEAMING NEW YELLOW SPORTS SALOON. BACK TO AN ASTONISHED VICKY. THE CAR IS STANDING OUTSIDE THEIR FRONT DOOR. BEYOND THIS NEW MONSTER CAN BE SEEN THEIR OLD HEAP.

RUSSELL LEADS VICKY BY THE HAND TO THE NEW CAR. HE OPENS THE PASSENGER DOOR LIKE A CHAUFFEUR, AND THEN GOES AROUND TO THE DRIVER'S SIDE AND GETS IN.

<u>SCENE FIVE. INT OF CAR. DAY</u>

RUSSELL: Tasty little motor isn't she? (HE SWITCHES ON A FINELY TUNED ENGINE AND REVS UP TO IMPRESS)

VICKY: (UNIMPRESSED) When's it going back?

RUSSELL: What do you mean?

VICKY:	Well either it's hired which we cannot afford. Or you are testing it with a view to purchase, which is ludicrous, or you've nicked it...
RUSSELL:	(IGNORING HER. ENGROSSED IN PANEL GADGETS) Five speed gearbox. Electronic ignition...
VICKY:	In which case you can almost certainly plead insanity.
RUSSELL:	Nought to sixty in ten seconds.
VICKY:	Emma and I would of course visit you in the padded cell.
RUSSELL:	And best of all, the brewery would pay all the running costs.
VICKY:	(STOPS IN SURPRISE) You mean it's a company car?
RUSSELL:	Could be.
VICKY:	(SHE FLINGS HER ARMS AROUND HIM AND STARTS KISSING HIM. AS SHE DOES THIS HE PRESSES A BUTTON AND LETS BACK RECLINING SEATS. HE BECOMES A LITTLE NAUGHTY) You cunning old, old – brewer.
RUSSELL:	(SMUG) Nothing new to the Milburn dynasty. Grandpa Horace was given a company dray horse.
VICKY:	So they've promoted you, then?
RUSSELL:	Possibly. How about this? (HE RETURNS, AT THE PRESS OF A BUTTON, THE SEATS TO UPRIGHT, AND TURNS WINDSCREEN WIPERS ON) Three speed wipers, including a special slow one for when it's not raining. But best of all. (PRESSES BUTTON AND AERIAL GROWS OUT OF FRONT WING)
VICKY:	Is that the aerial?

RUSSELL:	Could be. But in fact it's also an anti-traffic warden device. You see, this windscreen is sensitive to parking tickets. As soon as the polythene touches the glass, the aerial rises swiftly and silently right up the warden's nostril. (DEMONSTRATES WITH FINGER UP VICKY'S NOSE)
VICKY:	Russell!
RUSSELL:	Not bad though, is it?
VICKY:	It's super. What make is it?
RUSSELL:	You could call it a De Luxe Inducement GT. How about a run?
VICKY:	We can't leave Emma.
RUSSELL:	Well go and fetch her.

SCENE FIVE. INT. DAY.

CUT TO THEM WALKING IN THROUGH THEIR KITCHEN DOOR. RUSSELL GOES TO THE TABLE TO GET HIS GLOVES, VICKY GOES TOWARDS INTERNAL DOOR, BUT SUDDENLY STOPS WITH HAND ON HANDLE.

VICKY:	Russell? What did you mean 'possibly'?
RUSSELL:	What?
VICKY:	I asked you if you'd been promoted and you said 'possibly'. Why possibly? What's the catch?
RUSSELL:	Why should there be a catch? It's just that I might need a nippier little runner when I have a longer journey to work. Why don't you fetch Emma down, and we'll give it a spin.
VICKY:	(MOVES AWAY FROM DOOR AND COMES TOWARDS CENTRE OF ROOM) They're not sending you to head office, are they?

RUSSELL: Don't be daft. They don't make beer at Moorgate. They drink a lot, but they don't make any.

VICKY: Well where then?

RUSSELL: I told you they were building a new lager plant? Well, they want me to be Chief Technician.

VICKY: What's wrong with the old plant?

RUSSELL: Gone to seed, hasn't it.

VICKY: I'm being serious.

RUSSELL: Well it has. It's too small and old fashioned. I mean, lager is the drink of tomorrow. We can't make enough of it. And our new line, 'Brandenburg'.

VICKY: (LAUGHS) Brandenburg?!

RUSSELL: Don't laugh. According to marketing, it's a concerto on the tongue. And it will need a new plant all to itself. So the company are moving north where land is cheaper. The Board made the final decision this week.

VICKY: (LIGHTS A CIGARETTE) How far north?

RUSSELL: (HESITANTLY) Outside Greater London.

VICKY: Luton?

RUSSELL: Bit further west.

VICKY: Reading?

RUSSELL: Little bit further north.

VICKY: Further than Reading!! Well you are going to have a long drive to work.

RUSSELL: It'll be worth it for another fifteen hundred a year, private medical plan, enhanced pension, use

	of the executive loo, including soft toilet paper. And a generous relocation assistance.
VICKY:	(PAUSES) Relocation? As in 'move of house'?
RUSSELL:	Aren't you supposed to be getting Emma?
VICKY:	Russell, there is no way I'm moving out to Reading.
RUSSELL:	I've told you, it's not Reading.
VICKY:	Where then?
RUSSELL:	(GRITTING HIS TEETH) Workington.
VICKY:	I didn't hear that, Russell.
RUSSELL:	(MUMBLES) Workington.
VICKY:	I'm in no mood for your silly jokes.
RUSSELL:	It's not a joke. The brewery's moving to Workington. (TAKES A PAMPHLET FROM HIS POCKET, BEGINS READING FROM IT) "Workington offers a bracing environment. Clean air. First rate school. Modern low-cost housing...
	VICKY LEAVES HIM READING, AND RETURNS MOMENTS LATER STUDYING AN ATLAS.
RUSSELL:	"....Friendly people and only a short drive from world famous beauty spots. League football...." League football! When was this written?
VICKY:	Russell, I can't even find Workington on the map. (SHOWS HIM PAGE IN ATLAS)
RUSSELL:	Look, there it is.
VICKY:	(TAKES MAGNIFYING GLASS ATTACHED TO MAP AND PEERS THROUGH IT) That's Scotland!

RUSSELL: No it's not. There's Scotland. This is border country. Great sheep farming area.

VICKY: (SHUTS THE ATLAS WITH A BANG AND PUTS IT ON TABLE) Well I'm not moving up there. You'll have to commute.

RUSSELL: Commute! It's an eight hundred mile round trip. I can't commute.

VICKY: (UNINTERESTED) Then you'd better give the car back and ask for a company Lynx.

RUSSELL: A Lynx?

VICKY: A helicopter.

RUSSELL: Oh, that's right. I knew I'd heard of it. I remember one of your colour supplements doing a piece about a squadron of them disappearing while on a routine flight over Manchester.

VICKY: (AS IF KNOWING WHAT'S COMING NEXT) And what did the headline say, Russell.

RUSSELL: Missing Lynx Over Lancs.

VICKY: Right, now you've got that out of your system, you take that bright yellow bribe back and tell Mr Barrington he can keep his promotion. You're staying in London with your family.

RUSSELL: But I can't.

VICKY: How can you be so selfish? You know I want to get back to work as soon as Emma is at school. What sort of job am I likely to get up there? Watching my flocks by night?

RUSSELL: Be reasonable. Workington must have its advantages.

VICKY: What, besides its distance from your appalling father?

RUSSELL: Anyway, they're closing my brewery down completely. The simple fact is, it's Workington or redundancy.

VICKY: You're exaggerating. You're a qualified technician, you'll easily find another appointment.

RUSSELL: Where? All the big brewers are moving out of London. Either I go with, and float to the top, or stay behind like the sediment in the bottom of a barrel.

VICKY: How long have you to make up your mind?

RUSSELL: Barrington told me to think it over this weekend. (HE GOES OVER TO THE SERVING HATCH AND POURS HIMSELF A TANKARD OF ALE FROM BARREL. HE DRINKS APPRECIATIVELY) Ah. Now that's what ale should taste like. Not that pressurised pasteurised piddle we make. (DRINKS MORE) Good drop of beer, that.

VICKY: Russell? If you hate what you're making, why do you want to go 400 miles to keep the damn job?

RUSSELL: That's what brewing's about these days, and like it or not, it's my trade. Brewing's a craft. My grandfather was a brewer. My father was a brewer.

VICKY: Your father was an old piss artist.

RUSSELL: Only because he took his work home with him. At least he wasn't a quitter. He didn't throw it all up.

VICKY: He did at our wedding reception.

RUSSELL: He got carried away.

Shooting the Pilot

VICKY: He got carried <u>out</u>.

RUSSELL: You don't understand, do you? He's had a very hard life and I don't want to finish up like him.

VICKY: Thank heavens for that.

RUSSELL: (INDIGNANT) What I mean is, he was laid off and never got another job when his brewery moved.

VICKY: Russell, your father's brewery only moved from East Ham to West Ham. He could have moved with them had he been sober enough to have found his way to their new premises.

RUSSELL: It's still a warning not to turn your back on a secure job.

VICKY: Well I'll tell you one thing, Russell, either you give up this promotion or your wife and daughter give you up. Because I can tell you now, we're not leaving London.

RUSSELL: So it's you or Workington, is it?

VICKY: Precisely.

RUSSELL: You've got me over a barrel, then. (REALISES WHAT HE'S SAID) Joke.

VICKY: I'm warning you. I'm serious. (SHE WALKS OUT AND SLAMS THE DOOR BEHIND HER. THE BABY STARTS CRYING.)

RUSSELL TAKES OFF HIS DRIVING GLOVES AND THROWS THE KEYS OF HIS NEW TOY ON THE TABLE.

<u>END OF PART ONE.</u>

PART TWO

SCENE SIX. INT. NIGHT.

WE OPEN IN THE MILBURNS' KITCHEN SOMETIME DURING THE NIGHT. IT IS ALMOST PITCH BLACK, EXCEPT FOR A SHAFT OF LIGHT COMING THROUGH THE GLAZED KITCHEN DOOR.

WE CLOSE UP ON THE KITCHEN DOOR, AND SUDDENLY WE SEE A SHADOWY FIGURE APPEAR IN A DUFFLE COAT, WITH A HOOD UP AND A DUFFLE BAG OVER HIS SHOULDER. WE SEE HIM RUMMAGE THROUGH HIS POCKETS AND PRODUCE A BUNCH OF KEYS. HE TRIES A COUPLE OF THEM IN THE LOCK, BUT WITHOUT SUCCESS. HE TRIES SOME MORE KEYS AND EVENTUALLY OPENS THE DOOR.

HE TIPTOES IN, PUTS HIS DUFFLE BAG ON THE KITCHEN TABLE, SHUTS THE DOOR VERY QUIETLY AND CROSSES TO THE BARREL OF BEER IN THE SERVING HATCH AND POURS HIMSELF SOME INTO THE TANKARD BY THE BARREL. HE SITS DOWN BY THE KITCHEN TABLE, DRINKS THE BEER APPRECIATIVELY AND LIGHTS HIMSELF A CIGARETTE. HE FINISHES THE BEER. HE THEN LOOKS AT HIS WATCH, GETS UP, CROSSES TO THE FRIDGE AND OPENS IT. THE LIGHT FROM THE FRIDGE BRIGHTENS UP THE ROOM. FROM THE FRIDGE HE REMOVES EGGS, MILK, BACON AND PUTS THEM ON THE TABLE. HE LEAVES THE FRIDGE OPEN FOR NECESSARY LIGHT. HE TAKES OUT OF A BASE CUPBOARD NEXT TO THE COOKER A FRYING PAN, AND FROM A WALL CUPBOARD HE REMOVES A BOX OF TEA BAGS, SALT, PEPPER AND SAUCES. FROM THE DRAINER HE TAKES PLATES AND MUG. HE THEN PUTS BACON INTO PAN, TURNS ON THE COOKER, FILLS THE KETTLE, AND AS HE TURNS ON THE TAP THE PLUMBING MAKES A LOUD, REVOLTING BELCHING NOISE WHICH DOESN'T SEEM TO BOTHER HIM. WHILE HIS BREAKFAST IS COOKING, HE SEARCHES NOISILY IN CUTLERY TRAY.

HE PUSHES THE BACON AROUND THE PAN WITH A FORK AND THEN CRACKS EGGS VERY PROFESSIONALLY (ONE-HANDED). WHILE HE IS DOING THIS, WE HEAR THE URGENT WHISPERED VOICES OF RUSSELL AND VICKY COMING FROM JUST OUTSIDE THE KITCHEN. THEY DON'T APPEAR TO DISTURB THE INTERLOPER.

VICKY: You don't expect me to go in there, do you?

RUSSELL: Why not? You're trained in unarmed combat.

VICKY: Don't you care about my safety?

RUSSELL: He won't eat you.

VICKY: No? He eats everything else!

RUSSELL: All right. We'll both go in.... you first.

KITCHEN DOOR FROM THE HALL BURSTS OPEN. LIGHTS GO ON AS INTERLOPER CONTINUES TO MAKE HIMSELF A CUP OF TEA AS THOUGH NOTHING SURPRISING HAS HAPPENED.

HE IS CONFRONTED BY RUSSELL, IN DRESSING GOWN UNDER WHICH HE IS WEARING PYJAMAS, AND VICKY, IN LONG KHAKI OFFICER'S SWEATER AND OLD BERET. SHE HAS NOTHING ELSE ON, THE SWEATER COMING TO ABOUT MID-THIGH.

FITZ: It's a fair cop, guvnor. You've caught me bang to rights. Just finish me eggs and bacon while you call the Old Bill.

VICKY: What on earth is he talking about?

FITZ: (TO VICKY) I do like the negligee. Very Dirty Dozen. (HE PUTS BREAKFAST ON THE TABLE. THE KETTLE BOILS) Staying for tea?

VICKY: Russell, it's just not good enough!

FITZ: They're *your* tea bags. Two sugars, Vicky?

VICKY:	No, I don't take sug.... You realise that's our breakfast you're eating? This isn't a transport cafe, Fitzroy.
FITZ:	You ain't joking. Bacon's fatty. Sausages off. No tomatoes. Out of bubble and squeak.
VICKY:	You _can_ take your custom elsewhere.
FITZ:	Nowhere else open this time of the morning.

FITZ PUTS PLATE ON THE TABLE AND THREE MUGS OF TEA DOWN WITH TEA BAGS STILL FLOATING IN THEM. HE SITS DOWN, WHILE VICKY GETS SAUCER AND BEGINS FISHING TEA BAGS OUT OF MUGS. FITZ BEGINS GETTING STUCK INTO BREAKFAST. VICKY COMES AND SITS DOWN.

RUSSELL:	What are you doing back at....?
FITZ:	(LOOKING AT WATCH) I make it half past two.
RUSSELL:	But you weren't due back until tonight.
FITZ:	Yeah, but when you're a Knight of the Road, well, you know how it is? I'd planned to stay over in Birkenhead till morning. Little guest house I sometimes use. Modest, but dirty. A three-cockroach establishment in the Michelin guide.
VICKY:	Well?
FITZ:	Her old man's ship docked a day early, so I had to weigh anchor a bit sharpish.
RUSSELL:	(GRINNING) So you didn't get any slap and tickle?
FITZ:	I didn't even get any bubble and squeak.
RUSSELL:	So where's the artic?
FITZ:	(STUFFING HIS FACE) You just keep going due North and you can't miss it.

VICKY: He means the pantechnicon?

FITZ: Ain't that in Athens, near the Acropolis? What is this, Mastermind?

RUSSELL: The lorry?

FITZ: Oh, that! Yeah, I parked that outside behind that yellow motor.

RUSSELL: (PROUDLY) Tasty, isn't it?

FITZ: Not bad for a souped-up AA van.

VICKY: It's an inducement.

FITZ: Oh, Italian, is it? Very nice.

RUSSELL: It's mine.

VICKY: But it's going back.

FITZ: Stuck in reverse, is it? Trouble with these Italian jobs. Like their tanks in the war. Three reverse gears and one forward, just in case the enemy attacked from the rear.

VICKY: Thank you General Montgomery.

FITZ: Sorry. I forgot I was talking to an expert. So they've promoted you at last, have they, Russ? Out of the sediment, into the froth, so to speak?

VICKY: He's not taking it.

RUSSELL: Don't start that again, Vicky.

FITZ: Having trouble, are we?

VICKY: We? It's personal. Family business.

FITZ: And I'm not family? What's yours is mine, and what's mine is mine. (THINKS) No, that's wrong.

RUSSELL: Let's tell him. See what Fitz says. He's impartial.

VICKY:	I don't see our private life has anything to do with him.
RUSSELL:	It's simple. Either I take promotion: company car, extra money, the full bit, which means moving house at the company's expense; or, I stay here and take redundancy.
FITZ:	Where's the move to?
RUSSELL:	(MUMBLES) Workington.
FITZ:	Where?
VICKY:	He said Workington. It's a word he has trouble pronouncing.
FITZ:	Let's get this straight. New house? More money? Company wheels?
RUSSELL:	And free life insurance. And six weeks' paid holiday a year.
FITZ:	But you have to go to Workington. Right?
RUSSELL:	Tempting, isn't it?
FITZ:	(NON-COMMITTALLY) Mmm.
VICKY:	I'm going back to bed.
FITZ:	(FINISHES HIS TEA) Yeah, I think I'll come with you. No, seriously, hang on a tick, Vick. So what do you get if you choose redundancy?
RUSSELL:	Well. Oh, I don't know... About... It could be... There again...
VICKY:	Two thousand, three hundred and forty seven pounds, eighty six pence.
RUSSELL:	Yes, about that.

FITZ: (NODS) And you can't seriously make up your mind between two thousand readies in redundancy...

RUSSELL: Tax free.

FITZ: Or a new life in Workington with all the trappings of a rising young executive?

RUSSELL: Well, it's not an easy decision.

FITZ: It's a piece of cake, mate.

VICKY: I knew we shouldn't have told him. (SHE MOVES TOWARDS THE DOOR)

RUSSELL: (HOPEFULLY) Workington?

FITZ: Redundancy, Russell, any day of the week.

VICKY: (STOPS IN MID-STRIDE BY THE DOOR. TURNS AROUND) Good Lord! Thank you, Fitz.

FITZ: That's all right, darling. Got any biscuits?

VICKY: (BRINGS A LARGE TIN OF BISCUITS OVER) The chocolate ones are at the bottom.

RUSSELL: You told me we didn't have any chocolate ones.

VICKY: They're for special guests. (POKES HER TONGUE OUT AT RUSSELL)

RUSSELL: But, Fitz, if I chuck it in, I won't get another job, you know.

FITZ: (GOES ACROSS TO POUR ANOTHER BEER) Cor blimey, you've changed your tune, ain't you? Last time I was down, you were slagging off that firm of yours something rotten. What lousy beer they make and how fizzy and overpriced it is and how you had half a mind to go into business on your own. 'If I had a couple of grand behind me, Fitz', you said, 'I could start my own home brewery...'

VICKY:	Russell said that, did he?
RUSSELL:	It was the beer talking.
FITZ:	(DUNKING HIS CHOCOLATE BISCUIT INTO HIS BEER, MUCH TO BOTH VICKY AND RUSSELL'S HORROR) Exactly. Because you brew an eloquent drop of ale. Now look, how many barrels do you turn over a month?
RUSSELL:	Let's see. They have two down at the clubhouse. Mr Turner takes one. And the Vicar puts away a barrel...
FITZ:	There you go. You're sitting on a little gold mine. There's nothing the pubs around here serve that can hold a candle to your Jupiter Bitter.
VICKY:	Russell, purely out of interest, why did you call it Jupiter Bitter?
FITZ:	I christened that.
RUSSELL:	Because it's got the highest gravity in the solar system.
VICKY:	Is that good, then?
FITZ:	Good? Talk about close encounters of the slurred kind. It's psychedelic. It's so good, it should be illegal. Still, Russ, as you say, it was the beer talking. It's one thing to brew a couple of hundred pints a month for your mates, but it's something else to go into business on your own. I mean, selling to pubs. Keeping books. VAT. Customs and Excise. No, you're not the sort of bloke to launch out...
VICKY:	No, wait a minute. Why shouldn't he make a go of it?
RUSSELL:	(DETERMINEDLY) Yes, she's right. Why shouldn't I?

FITZ:	Why? Because you ain't got the bottle.
RUSSELL:	Very funny. You had me going there. I thought you were serious.
FITZ:	It's you what's got to be serious, my son. CLOSE UP ON RUSSELL, THINKING ABOUT WHAT FITZ HAS JUST SAID. FITZ PEERS INTO RUSSELL'S EAR. WITH THAT BABY'S CRIES COME FROM UPSTAIRS. THEY GET CONTINUALLY LOUDER.
FITZ:	Here, Vick, want to see how the inside of a brain works.
RUSSELL:	(GETS UP) Emma's crying. (MOVES TO DOOR)
VICKY:	But you only changed her before we went to bed.
RUSSELL:	Probably that tooth cutting through. I'll go and give her oral support. (EXITS)
FITZ:	He'll make someone a lovely wife.
VICKY:	He already has. Me. You're a surprising ally.
FITZ:	Why?
VICKY:	Well you know, this Workington lunacy he's got into his head. You usually take his side in all this family's problems.
FITZ:	Yeah, but I'm only trying to save him from himself. Does he know Workington?
VICKY:	I don't think so.
FITZ:	No, I didn't think he did. I've been through it a few times in the jug.
VICKY:	Jug!
FITZ:	Juggernaut. (CROSSES TO BEER BARREL) Fancy one?
VICKY:	No, I'm trying to give it up, thanks.

FITZ:	(POURING BEER) I mean, nothing wrong with the people. Very affable. Always stop you in the street for a chat. Keen to hear the latest news from the world outside. I remember how amazed they were the day I told them that we'd all converted to decimal currency.
VICKY:	Yes? When was that?
FITZ:	Week ago last Wednesday.
VICKY:	Funny, it seems longer.
FITZ:	What? Oh, yeah. Very funny. Here, do you know, thinking about it, that's the first joke you've ever cracked since I've known you. It was a joke, wasn't it?
VICKY:	I suppose it was.
FITZ:	I mean, I know you don't reckon me. It hasn't escaped my notice that you've never really warmed to me. Clasped me to your bosom – metamorphously speaking. Class, innit? I mean, you come from a long line of professional soldiers, while I only come from a short line of professional deserters.

BABY STOPS CRYING. |
VICKY:	Thank heavens she's stopped. Dr Russell Spock has done it again.
FITZ:	Talking of deserting, you ever thought about going back to work?
VICKY:	Many times. Why do you ask?
FITZ:	Just a thought. I mean if Russell decides to work for himself at home, it'll be a while before he starts earning. You might need a regular wage packet coming in.

VICKY:	Well, yes. But who would look after Emma? Russell doesn't believe in nannies. He thinks handing a child over to a professional stranger is a crime.
	RUSSELL COMES IN HOLDING A DIRTY NAPPY AT ARM'S LENGTH. HE TAKES IT OVER TO A LARGE LIDDED POLYTHENE BUCKET, REMOVES LID, DROPS NAPPY IN, AND REPLACES LID.
FITZ:	Well, what's the verdict then, Russ?
RUSSELL:	Nappy rash.
FITZ:	I'm talking about your future.
VICKY:	The bitter truth.
FITZ:	She's done it again. Vicky, joking can damage your health.
RUSSELL:	Well, if I do go solo, what are we supposed to live on until I start rolling out the barrel?
VICKY:	I could go back to work.
RUSSELL:	Force yourself, would you? And who would look after Emma?
FITZ:	Can I say a word?
RUSSELL:	No. This is family business.
FITZ:	Look, my opinion, for what it's worth, is that you, Russ, could easy look after the kid yourself, seeing you'll be hanging around the house all day taking the rise out of your yeast.
RUSSELL:	Leave off!
FITZ:	No, let's face it, what's motherhood? Three feeds a day if it's peckish. Three changes of nappy if it's wet and windy. A bit of burping, and a quick run round the block. What's that? A couple of hours a day?

VICKY:	Oh! So that's all there is to it?
FITZ:	Well, that and a bit of cleaning, I suppose. But that's not work. I mean this idea that housework is a full-time job is Women's Lib propaganda.
RUSSELL:	No, be fair, Fitz. A woman's work is never done, is it, Vicky?
VICKY:	(NOT FALLING FOR RUSSELL'S CUNNING) It can be, if you organise yourself.
RUSSEL	But I'm not cut out to look after a baby.
VICKY:	You already do more with Emma than I do.
FITZ:	She's right. I mean, who just changed the baby's nappy?
RUSSELL:	Only because crappy nappies make Vicky queasy. But it stands to reason that when it comes to bringing up kids, a woman must have at least a couple of natural advantages.
VICKY:	Not now Emma's on the bottle. And you're better at emptying bottles than anyone I know.
FITZ:	Except his Dad.
RUSSELL:	Can you imagine me pegging out the babygrows? What would the neighbours think?
VICKY:	If you were at all bothered what the neighbours thought of you you wouldn't have touched up Mrs Fotheringham at the Jubilee street party.
RUSSELL:	That was Royalist fervour.
VICKY:	That was indecent assault. You're lucky she didn't press charges.
FITZ:	He told me she pressed everything else.

Shooting the Pilot

RUSSELL: Look, it must be nearly three in the morning, I think we should sleep on it.

FITZ: On what? Mrs Fotheringham?

RUSSELL: (LOSING PATIENCE) Goodnight Fitz. I'm sorry you've got to push off.

FITZ: Go?

RUSSELL: Yes, go.

FITZ: Only I thought I might kip on your sofa.

RUSSELL: We've pawned the sofa.

FITZ: Oh, well, it's back to that mouldy doss-house, with no heating and rising damp, and hot and cold running mice chasing the bedbugs. It's like a miniature White City in my room.

VICKY: There's a sleeping bag in the hall cupboard.

FITZ: (HOPEFULLY) I can stay, then?

RUSSELL: No, you can take it home with you.

VICKY: Goodnight Fitz.

FITZ COLLECTS HIS GEAR AND LEAVES BY INTERNAL DOOR. WE HEAR A DOOR CLOSE. VICKY AND RUSSELL LOOK AT EACH OTHER, THEN FOLLOW THE PATH FITZ HAS JUST TAKEN INTO HALL. VICKY OPENS UP HALL CUPBOARD, AND WE SEE FITZ CURLED UP IN A SLEEPING BAG UNDER THE STAIRS.

DISSOLVE.

RESOLVE ON VICKY'S HAND STUBBING OUT CIGARETTE IN A FULL ASHTRAY. IT IS GETTING LIGHT OUTSIDE. THEY BOTH LOOK VERY TIRED, AND RUSSELL LOOKS STUBBLY-CHINNED.

VICKY: So, what about a nanny?

RUSSELL: (SLEEPY, BUT ADAMANT) Victoria, for the last time...

VICKY: But we could afford a good one when I get my old rank back.

RUSSELL: Do I have to keep telling you what I think about farming out children?

VICKY: But Russell, we can afford a nanny...

RUSSELL: No....

VICKY: Shushhh a second. So that means we can afford to pay someone to help you with the beer.

RUSSELL: (NODDING OFF UNTIL VICKY PRODS HIM IN THE RIBS) What?

VICKY: (FIERCELY) Look, don't go to sleep, I might not be here when you wake up.

DISSOLVE.

RESOLVE ON THEM STILL SITTING AROUND THE TABLE. THE TABLETOP IS NOW COVERED IN SHEETS OF PAPER WITH SUMS ON THEM. BOTH RUSSELL AND VICKY HOLD A FELT-TIPPED PEN. RUSSELL IS SCRIBBLING AIMLESSLY ON A PIECE OF PAPER.

RUSSELL: What's twelve times a hundred?

VICKY: Twelve hundred.

RUSSELL: Oh, I'll have to get myself a calculator.

VICKY: Russell, we've already reckoned out how much money the beer will bring in during the first few months.

RUSSELL: (YAWNS AND TRIES TO KEEP HIS EYES OPEN) How much?

VICKY: Oh, for God's sake, Russell! You worked it out.

RUSSELL: Oh yes. Let's see? (SEARCHES FOR RELEVANT PIECE OF PAPER) Oh, here it is.

VICKY: And if I go back to work and we employ someone part-time for the brewery, how much do we end up with?

RUSSELL: (LOOKS FOR ANOTHER PIECE OF PAPER) I make it... seventy seven and a half pence more if I take promotion and we go to Workington.

VICKY: So is it really worth moving 400 miles for, what, fifteen and six?

RUSSELL: (PUTS HIS PEN DOWN) When I was a boy, you could have a seat at the Gaumont, a drink on a stick, a slap-up meal at Lyons, and a Red Rover, and still have enough change left for five Woodbines if you could get a grown-up to buy them for you.

VICKY: (TERSELY) That's not what I asked you.

RUSSELL: Well, fifteen and six went a long way in those days.

VICKY: You're evading the issue.

RUSSELL: I know. And do you know why? Because I'm nervous.

VICKY: About becoming your own boss?

RUSSELL: About looking after Emma.

VICKY: (PUTS HER ARM AROUND HIM) Every new mother's nervous. I was nervous. Just because I'm a woman, it doesn't mean I knew everything about babies by instinct. I worked at it. In a way it's harder for a woman. Everyone thinks we should all be natural mothers... whatever those are.

RUSSELL: I suppose so.

VICKY: But all that matters is that we both love Emma and we both care. And as long as we do, to hell with the neighbours. Think of it as a team effort, it doesn't really matter who does what.

RUSSELL: So we're just swapping positions? I'm going in goal and you're moving up into the attack.

VICKY: Right.

RUSSELL: (WRITES SOMETHING ON A PIECE OF PAPER. WORKING OUT AN EQUATION) Right then, if I'm going in goal, I'll need the green jersey, won't I?

HE GOES OVER AND MAKES AS THOUGH HE'S ABOUT TO PULL HER JERSEY OFF. SHE PUTS UP A MINOR STRUGGLE.

VICKY: Russell, please, not at this time of the night.

RUSSELL: Actually, it's this time of the _morning_. (STILL FIGHTING) Oh, come on.

VICKY: Russell!

RUSSELL: I need something for my night starvation.

AS THEY ARE LARKING ABOUT, THE BABY STARTS CRYING. THEY STOP WHAT THEY'RE DOING INSTANTLY, AND SIMULTANEOUSLY AND INDEPENDENTLY MOVE TOWARDS THE DOOR AND EMMA.

FREEZE FRAME OF THEM BOTH AT DOOR.

<u>ENDS</u>

2
Shine On Harvey Moon

LAURENCE WRITES: *One summer's day in the mid-1970s I was wandering along Camden Passage, a maze of little antique shops in Islington. There was a stall selling old magazines, and the cover of a* Picture Post *from 1945 caught my eye.*

"How much?" I asked.

The dealer said that the magazine was one of a bundle, and he wasn't prepared to split it. I'd have to buy the lot for, "What shall we say? Thirty-five pence?"

Even 45 years ago that wasn't a great deal of money.

The black-and-white photograph that so enthralled me showed a British soldier coming home from the war. His wife, daughter and little boy wait outside their flag-draped prefab, arms outstretched, joy on their faces. I loved that photograph. It made me smile and it made me wonder. What happened after the man of the prefab returned to Blighty? Did he manage to put his terrifying experiences behind him? Were they happy? Did they prosper?

Then my comedy writer's instinct kicked in. While most returning soldiers were hailed as heroes, I couldn't help wondering, "What if this housewife was hoping her old man had been tortured at the hands of the Japanese?" The thought compelled me to add a line of my own at the bottom of that iconic photo. I've still got that old Picture Post. *My caption reads, "Oh shit, he survived!"*

My caption didn't come out of nowhere. The woman in the photograph had put me immediately in mind of my Auntie Miri, a spirited woman from an impoverished background who found the war intoxicatingly liberating. It allowed her to leave her restrictive family home, get work in a Piccadilly bar serving Allied soldiers, to go dancing, have fun, and sleep in the Underground if she didn't have a better offer from an American, Canadian or Free Polish airman. Not that I was imagining that Auntie Miri harboured murderous thoughts, she was far too kind-hearted; but all the family knew that the day Miri's husband returned from the war was the day her life turned from Technicolor back into black and white.

We tell this story because all too often we're asked if we base our characters on real people. Usually the answer is – not really. Most characters are formed partly out of bits of people we know and partly out of bits of ourselves. Shine On Harvey Moon *was different. It was our tribute to Auntie Miri.*

We discussed our new, untitled project for months. Who would people this comedy? What was the setting, the story? Clearly the photograph offered us four central characters: a man who returns to two children who love him, and a wife who doesn't. Unlike our first TV series, *Holding the Fort*, this new show would have to be bittersweet – a comedy with tears. However, we really can't remember when we chose to call the show *Shine On Harvey Moon*, inspired, of course, by 'Shine On Harvest Moon', one of those sentimental ballads that were always being played on the BBC Light Programme when we were growing up. Perhaps it was on the wireless one day and it got jammed in one or other of our brains, suggesting a character called Harvey Moon who would shine on through our series.

But who was Harvey Moon? Well, if he was going to do the shining, it seemed obvious that he should be the boy in the picture, a ten-year-old who had survived the bombs and doodlebugs and had his whole life ahead of him. His father, who we decided to call Stanley, would do everything to make sure little Harvey had a shinier life than he'd had in the 1920s. We were excited at the thought of writing about a child making his way through post-war Britain. If he was eleven in 1945, he'd be twenty-one in 1955, just the right age to become a Teddy boy in season ten! Completing the family photograph were mum Rita, and big sister, Maggie. Now we could get on with creating their world.

We were both born a good few years after the war ended but we can just about remember rationing, which on some items, especially sweets, continued into the Fifties. Indeed the aftermath of the war lasted well into our childhood. There were numerous bombsites to turn into unofficial adventure playgrounds, and "pigbins" on the street, where household food waste – not that there was much – could be left to help feed the nation's livestock. We remember horse troughs too, where the milkman's horse stopped to quench its thirst. In many ways the world in which we grew up still shivered in the grey shadow of the war.

As adults we remained fascinated by the post-war history of Britain, and the widespread hope that a fairer society would rise from the ruins. We felt that our homecoming soldier should personify the optimism that Clem Attlee's reforming Labour government was going to change everything for the better. Yes, Stanley Moon was working class, but hadn't all the class barriers been destroyed by the war he had just fought and won?

As we plotted and planned, we became aware of the superficial similarities between the late 1940s and the early 1980s. Life for ordinary people in post-war Britain was tough, but Britain in the early Eighties was no picnic either. The country had endured a decade of high inflation, frequent strikes and rising unemployment. But whereas 1945 saw a reforming Labour government voted in with a landslide majority, the 1979 General Election had sent the busted flush of a Labour government packing, to be replaced by a tough Tory party determined to crush the trade unions and privatise everything in sight.

However, we were convinced that for most of our contemporaries the hardship of the early Thatcher years was purely relative. People might be worrying whether they could afford a colour telly *and* one of those new-fangled microwave ovens, but our parents' generation had to cope with food rationing, clothes rationing, a housing crisis, queues everywhere, no luxuries and few necessities. We couldn't begin to imagine how we would manage on eight ounces of bacon, one and tuppence worth of meat, a pound of sugar, and sixteen ounces of sweets per month. Yet we were also aware that the spirit of 1945 was one of hope, whereas the mood of many in 1980 was one of despair. We wanted our new show to be a corrective as well as an entertainment. We were saying to our audience – assuming we sold the idea to a broadcaster – that things today weren't so terrible after all.

Right. So we knew we wanted to tell the story of one working-class London family in 1945, but what would episode one, the all-important pilot script, contain? Clearly, we had to be with Stanley – the "head of the family" – as he returns home; but should we start by replicating that iconic photograph, or should we get to know him first? We decided on the latter course to allow him to share with us his hopes and fears as he makes his way home. But to reveal Stanley's innermost feelings we needed to give him a confidant, so we provided company in the form of Lou Lewis, a young fellow soldier who would become a major character as the series developed, but who was little more than a spivvy sidekick when we first met him.

Once Lou has peeled off to rejoin his own huge family, who he claimed were throwing him a fantastic welcome-home party (a pathetic lie as it turned out – Lou was an orphan), we accompany Stanley all the way back to his home in Hackney, East London. Except for some reason we thought it would be funny if he finds his house is little more than a bombed-out ruin and assumes his family have been obliterated by a V2 rocket. When we mentioned this to the man who commissioned the script, he said, "Are you sure this is a comedy?" We couldn't have been surer.

Eventually Stanley learns his family have survived and are now living in a prefab in Tottenham. He dashes there, imagining the welcome he's going to receive, only to find his wife Rita in a state of depression because her American boyfriend hasn't taken her back to the States as he promised. And now here's her old man back from the war, to make a bad day worse. Thankfully Maggie and Harvey are thrilled to have their father home, especially the irrepressible Harvey, who, to Stanley's delight and relief, hero-worships his dad.

The "man who commissioned the script", mentioned above, was Tony Charles, who worked for a new company, Witzend Productions. Witzend was founded by our heroes Dick Clement and Ian La Frenais, creators of *The Likely Lads* and *Porridge*. It was a privilege and an education to work with Dick and Ian on the pilot script. They taught us how to always end a scene on a laugh or a tear, how to make one scene glide into another, and how to ensure the audience always want to know what is going to happen next – especially important at "end of part one" if the show was going to be on commercial TV, with a break half way through for adverts.

Most importantly, without Ian La Frenais there wouldn't have been a Nan. At our very first meeting Ian said he liked what we'd written, but we didn't have a Nan, and back in the olden days, "Everybody had a Nan." Ian was right, so on the spot we invented a mum for Stanley, a grandmother for Harvey, and an enemy for Rita, Stanley's fiery wife.

By the time we sat down at our electric typewriter to write the first draft the characters and their predicaments were so clear to us that it's barely an exaggeration to say that the script wrote itself. That can happen when you've spent so much time thinking about your characters that they seem to dictate their dialogue. Sometimes you can't shut them up. It's an extraordinary feeling. The downside is you overwrite, which we did in shovel-loads in the early drafts of *Harvey Moon*. Clement and La Frenais had the wisdom and experience to encourage us to "kill our babies" – the melodramatic term writers use when they have to cut their favourite lines. If a speech or a scene slowed the storytelling, or if a joke was out of character, then it had to go. It didn't matter if the joke was funny; if it was blocking the traffic it was out.

Eventually our ninth draft was deemed good enough to be shot, with cameras and real live actors. Immediately Tony Charles set about gathering a cast, and the man he wanted to play the lead was Adam Faith. This was a thrilling suggestion. Adam was a star. He'd had number-one records and a hit TV series, and we were going to meet him!

At this juncture, allow us to resolve the confusion if you're wondering whether we've mixed up the names of father and son, Harvey and Stanley? Has there been some sort of problem at the printers? The answer is simple. Adam Faith liked our script. Indeed he loved the script. But there was one thing he didn't understand: "If the show's called *Shine On Harvey Moon*, then why am I called Stanley?"

Adam's point was blindingly obvious as soon as he made it. We swapped Harvey's and Stanley's names and looked forward to working with Adam. Indeed Tony cast Lee Whitlock and Linda Robson to play the kids partly because they shared Adam's colouring. Ironically a few weeks before the pilot was to start shooting, Adam, in his own words, "lost his bottle" and had to be replaced by the magnetic Ken Cranham.

Tony's other casting coups included Maggie Steed as Rita and Elizabeth Spriggs as Nan. We have chosen not to dwell on casting in this book, because the emphasis of these introductory essays is on the craft of pilot writing. We're making an exception for *Harvey Moon* because the interaction of the script and the cast was so profound. The first cast readthrough was an extraordinary experience for us. Though it sounds like a cliché, the actors really did bring the script to life. Maggie Steed's interpretation of Rita was key. Rita had developed during the writing of the script into a very different character from Laurence's Auntie Miri. Rita was waspish, impetuous, funny, fiercely protective of her children yet happy to stay out all night if there was a lock-in or a party to go to. Above all, she was promiscuous, or at least that is how it seemed to Nan, who had less than no time for her slutty daughter-in-law.

"If you'd have listened to me you wouldn't have married her in the first place, miserable cow!"

"I had to do the decent thing, Mum. I got her in trouble."

"No, Harvey, you got her up the stick, then she got you into trouble. Anyway, for the last six years she's been the toast of the less choosy members of the Allied Forces."

"Toast? What do you mean toast?"

"As in done both sides."

By the end of the readthrough everyone involved in the script felt we had a hit on our hands. So did the Controller of Programmes at ATV, who viewed the tape of the pilot show and immediately commissioned a series. Was it all because of the hard work everyone had put into that pilot script? We would like to think so.

We weren't given long to write the remaining five scripts. We splashed some of our advance on a primitive computer. Nobody else in television seemed to have one, and producers who had never heard the term "cut and paste" couldn't understand how we could turn rewrites around so quickly.

The series was to be shot that summer. Luckily, during the writing and rewriting of the pilot we had generated a raft of ideas and had a healthy balance in the story bank. Could Harvey possibly return to his pre-war job as a professional footballer for Leyton Orient reserves? If not, where would he work? If a factory, would he join the union and become politically active? Would Stanley remain convinced that the job of "stores clerk" was just his dad's cover and Harvey was really a spy? Would Maggie Moon fall for "wide boy" Lou Lewis? Would Harvey fall for Stanley's new schoolteacher?

The pilot, now episode one of a new comedy series, was transmitted on a winter's night in January 1982. In comedy, timing is everything. *Shine On Harvey Moon* reached Britain's television screens during a blizzard that locked in the nation. Their options were BBC1, BBC2 or ITV, and almost eighteen million of them tuned into our show. Maybe television audiences were wearying of feeling depressed and were thirsting for light-hearted patriotic reassurance. Perhaps they were cheered by the knowledge that a previous generation had been far worse off. Whatever the reason, they stayed loyal to Harvey and the Moons for four seasons.

Finally, we must acknowledge that *Shine On Harvey Moon* supercharged our careers in many ways. Because the classically trained cast were uncomfortable at the thought of performing in front of a live audience, the show was recorded without a "laughter track" and was acclaimed as a comedy drama as much as a sitcom. Our fascination with the Second World War and the fun we had writing about ordinary working-class Londoners led us to write *Birds of a Feather* and *Goodnight Sweetheart*, and even the political content of *Harvey Moon* was a precursor of *The New Statesman*. Would we have written any of those series if Laurence hadn't spotted that *Picture Post* magazine at the bottom of a blue plastic tray in an Islington junk shop?

SHINE ON, HARVEY MOON

CHARACTERS IN ORDER OF APPEARANCE.

STAN MOON.

LOU LEWIS. An RAF clerk, about 24 years old. Stan's best mate.

SAILOR.

COPPER. A police constable, probably in his late 40s.

NAN MOON. A 63 year old, short-sighted, warm hearted, commonsense Cockney matriarch.

MAGGIE MOON. A 17 year old, buxom, personable. Stan's daughter.

CHUCK SANDOWSKI. A good looking, US Q/M Sergeant. About 35 years.

RITA MOON. A fairly attractive, but hard faced, 38 year old.

HARVEY MOON. A 10 year old, street-wise urchin, though a bit of a romantic where his dad is concerned.

August 1980

Shooting the Pilot

SCENE ONE. INT. STUDIO. DAY:

WE OPEN IN A BELOW DECKS CORNER OF A TATTY TROOP SHIP BRINGING THE BOYS HOME FROM THE FAR EAST. STAN AND LOU, IN AIRFORCE UNIFORM, ARE PLAYING POKER WITH A SAILOR. THERE IS A FAIR BIT OF CASH IN THE KITTY.

LOU: (HOLDING HIS CARDS VERY PROFESSIONALLY) Righty ho. Your three quid and up two. (PUTS WHITE FIVER IN THE POT)

STAN: (FOLDING HIS CARDS IN DISGUST) Up yours!

LOU: You throwing in then, Stanley?

STAN: Have to, Lou. Got a hand like a foot.

LOU: So, it's up to you, Jolly Jack Tar?

SAILOR: (LOOKS FROM CARDS TO TEMPTING POT AND BACK TO CARDS AGAIN. WE SEE HE HAS A FULL HOUSE OF JACKS AND EIGHTS BUT IS A BIT SHORT OF READIES) Trust me for a couple of quid, mate?

STAN: Lou don't give credit.

LOU: Well put, Stanley.

SAILOR: (REMOVING HIS WATCH) Here, this must be worth a couple of nicker. It's anti-magnetic.

LOU: Look chum, I don't care if it's anti-semitic, I don't need no more watches. No offence, but I've got dozens of watches lost by hopeful mugs like you.

STAN: He's got time to spare.

LOU: Chuck 'em in, mate. We're nearly home anyway.

SAILOR: I should coco, with a hand like this. (TAKES TWO MEDALS FROM POCKET) How about me medals? Sweated blood for these.

STAN:	What are they?
SAILOR:	Burma Star and Distinguished Flying Cross.
LOU:	Oh, yeah. And how does a sailor win them sort of medals?
SAILOR:	In a cardschool in Port Said.
STAN:	Look, I'll give you a couple of quid for them.
SAILOR:	Done. (MONEY AND MEDALS CHANGE HANDS)
LOU:	You have been.
STAN:	No. Something to show my nipper, innit? I mean now the war's over, my Harvey wants to be able to look up to his dad.
SAILOR:	(PUTS HIS MONEY IN POT) All right, sunshine, I'll see you.
LOU:	(COCKY) Two pairs.
SAILOR:	(EXULTANT) Full house. (SHOWS CARDS AND REACHES FOR KITTY)
LOU:	Just a second. A pair of fives.... and another pair of fives. (SHOWS AND GATHERS POT)
SAILOR:	You.... (FILTHY INVECTIVE BLOTTED OUT BY VERY FORTUITOUS BLAST OF FOGHORN)
STAN:	(RISING) I've known you for five years, Lou Lewis, and I still don't know how you do it. Coming upstairs? Must be nearly there.
SAILOR:	(SURLY) It's not 'upstairs', it's 'on deck'.
	<u>CUT TO:</u>

Shooting the Pilot

SCENE TWO. EXT. (FILM) DAY:

STAN ON DECK. IT'S VERY VERY FOGGY AND HE CAN'T REALLY SEE BEYOND THE RAIL. THE SAILOR HAS COME ON DECK WITH HIM.

STAN: It's bleedin' amazing. You know, there were times out in India when I never thought I'd see England again.

SAILOR: Well you can't see it, can you? You can hardly see the funnel.

STAN: Don't signify. I still know that we're in home waters, that we'll soon be heaving to in Southampton.... Funny, the weather was just like this when we left.

CUT TO:

SCENE THREE. EXT. (FILM) DAY:

THE MIDDLE OF A GREY AFTERNOON IN LONDON. OCTOBER 1945. STAN AND LOU ARE WAITING FOR A BUS OUTSIDE A SMALL EAST LONDON B.R. STATION.

STAN: So this is London in the heady aftermath of Victory? Bit of an anti-climax, ain't it?

LOU: Well at least we made it back.

STAN: That's another thing. I volunteered to see a bit of action.... heaven knows, the last time I saw any with my Rita was the night of the Abdication broadcast. That's why I joined the RAF.

LOU: Well you didn't expect to become one of The Few, did you? All handlebar moustache and private income?

STAN:	Well I expected better than being made a clerk and sent to India by boat. Don't think I saw a bleedin' aeroplane more than twice.
LOU:	Still, Stan, look at the opportunities that face us.
STAN:	What opportunities? Remember, I'm too old for football now. Anyway, I never wanted to be a Clapton Orient reserve. I wanted to captain England.
LOU:	Well, your Harvey will have to do that instead.
STAN:	That's right, he will. Did I ever tell you about the plans I've got for that kid?
LOU:	Yeah, you told me.... several times. He's going to play football for England. Cricket for Essex. Go to university. Get into Parliament. Become Prime Minister....
STAN:	Well why not? I mean Labour's in power now. I might have to make do with a Government training course in centre lathe turning, but that don't mean Harvey's going to be fobbed off with second best.
LOU:	(LOOKS AT HIS WATCH) I see the buses ain't got no better. I've got a party tonight.
STAN:	What party?
LOU:	Oh, they're throwing a surprise welcome home party for me. My family's gathering in strength. I'd invite you along, but then they'd know I'd got wind of it, wouldn't they?
STAN:	Yeah. of course.

Shooting the Pilot

LOU: Still, Stan. I want to say that we got to stay mates. We've been through a lot together. So don't be a stranger. My home is your home.

STAN: That's a very nice sentiment, Lou.

SOUND OF BUS FROM AROUND CORNER.

LOU: You know you're home, don't you, when you hear the cough of a red London double-decker. (ROLLS UP SLEEVE TO EXPOSE AN ARMFUL OF WATCHES) Before I forget, Stan.... (TAKES ONE WATCH OFF AND GIVES IT TO STAN) This one's yours, innit? (STAN NODS AND TAKES IT) Do us a favour, Stan, and give up Poker.

BUS HOVES INTO VIEW. IT IS NOT A RED LONDON DOUBLE-DECKER. IT IS AN ORANGE/BLUE/LILAC BUS AS LTE BORROWED BUSES FROM MANY REGIONAL AUTHORITIES DURING THE WAR. THEREFORE, WE WILL SEE A LOGO SUCH AS "BOURNEMOUTH & BOSCOMBE BUS COMPANY LTD", HALF COVERED BY A SIGN "ON LOAN TO LONDON TRANSPORT".

LOU GETS ON THE BUS. STAN DOESN'T.

LOU: (FROM PLATFORM OF BUS) Come on, then.

STAN: No, I'm not riding on a foreign bus first day home. I'll wait for a red 'un.

LOU: (AS BUS PULLS OUT) Well make sure you stay in touch, mate.

STAN: (TO HIMSELF) He's a good lad that Lou. All heart.... Hold on, how can I stay in touch? The rotten sod never told me where he lived.

<u>CUT TO:</u>

SCENE FOUR. EXT. (FILM) DAY:

WE SEE STAN GETTING OFF A PROPER RED BUS AND WALKING DOWN HIS OLD STREET TOWARDS HIS OLD HOUSE. LIMP BUNTING HANGS FROM LAMP POSTS. FADED UNION JACKS FLAP FROM WINDOWS. VARIOUS "WELCOME HOME" MESSAGES PAINTED ON OLD SHEETS FLOP OUTSIDE HOUSES.... BUT NONE OF THEM ARE FOR STAN. SOME OF THE HOUSES AND SHOPS HAVE SUFFERED DIRECT HITS.

STAN ARRIVES AT HIS OLD FRONT DOOR. HE AND WE SEE ONLY THE DOOR AND SURROUNDING BRICKWORK. STAN, HALF IN REVERIE, UNLOCKS THE DOOR WITH HIS KEY AND STUMBLES THROUGH TO DEVASTATION. WE NOW SEE THAT ALL THAT IS LEFT OF HIS HOUSE IS THE PART OF THE FRONT ELEVATION AT GROUND FLOOR LEVEL THAT CONTAINS THE FRONT DOOR. OTHERWISE, STAN'S HOUSE AND THE SEMI TO WHICH IT WAS CONNECTED, NEXT DOOR, HAS MORE OR LESS CEASED TO EXIST. STAN'S HOME IS RUBBLE. HE STEPS OUT OF FRONT DOOR, CHECKS IT IS INDEED HIS HOME – HE CAN TELL BY THE NUMBER. HE SITS, STUNNED, ON THE LOO, WHICH IS THE ONLY AVAILABLE SEAT, HAVING FALLEN INTACT FROM THE FLOOR ABOVE. HE DOES NOT NOTICE A PILE OF NEWSPAPERS ON THE RUBBLE WHERE THE HALL CARPET SHOULD BE. HE HOLDS HIS HEAD IN DESPAIR. WE HEAR WHISTLING AND THEN THE EVENING PAPER POPS THROUGH THE LETTER BOX TO JOIN THOSE ALREADY THERE. THIS ENRAGES STAN, WHO PICKS UP THE LOO AS IF TO HURL IT THROUGH THE DOOR, BUT A PASSING P.C. HAS SPOTTED HIM. STAN NOTICES THE POLICEMAN AND PUTS LOO DOWN AS COPPER APPROACHES.

COPPER: You all right, son?

STAN: All right? I'm ecstatic. Bloody rich ain't it? I spend the war safe and sound in India, while my family catches the lot. Well, I tell you, if there's a god....

COPPER: You live here, then?

STAN: Yeah, that's right. I like plenty of fresh air....

COPPER: What you need, sir, is a cup of strong, sweet tea.

STAN: Right, I'll put the kettle on. One lump or two.

COPPER: Look, you've had a shock. Don't you have nowhere else you can go?

CUT TO:

SCENE FIVE. INT. (STUDIO) DAY:

STAN IS STANDING OUTSIDE THE FRONT DOOR OF HIS MOTHER'S FLAT IN A VICTORIAN PEABODY DWELLINGS TYPE TENEMENT IN CLAPTON. KNOCKS ON KNOCKER. THE DOOR IS OPENED BY NAN.

STAN: Hello, mum.

NAN: Stanley? Blimey, you're a stranger.

STAN: There has been a war on, you know.

NAN: We had heard. Well come in then... if you ain't the tally man. (USHERS HIM THROUGH)

STAN: I've just seen the house.

NAN: What house?

STAN: Where I used to live. What a bloody shambles. I supposed they died instantly?

NAN: What you talking about, Stan?

STAN: My family. What was it? Messerschmidt? Heinkel? Doodlebug?

NAN: Oh, I'm with you. No, no-one's dead. That silly cow of a wife of yours went out one morning and left the gas on.

STAN: So they're all right? What about Harvey? And Maggie?

NATI: They're all right considering Rita's taken them to live in a prefab over Tottenham way.

STAV: Thank God.

NAN: Why? Tottenham's nothing to write home about. Here, Stan, you sit down and I'll make you a nice cup of tea. Dr Hill on the wireless says it's just the thing for shock.... or was it piles?

STAN: I see Rita managed to blow up next door an' all? I bet they weren't pleased.

NAN: No they weren't. They'd only just redecorated.

CUT TO:

SCENE SIX. EXT. (FILM) DAY.

AN ESTABLISHING SHOT OF GROUP OF PREFABS, ONE OF WHICH HAS BLACKOUTS IN PLACE.

SCENE SIX A. INT. (STUDIO) DAY.

INSIDE RITA MOON'S PREFAB'S FRONT ROOM. IT IS A SMALL ROOM, OVER FURNISHED, SOME UTILITY FURNITURE AND SOME QUITE GOOD STUFF BOUGHT SECOND HAND. THE ONLY LIGHT COMES FROM A DIM BULB IN THE STANDARD LAMP, THE BLACKOUTS BEING DRAWN. ON THE SOFA YOUNG MAGGIE MOON AND CHUCK SANDOWSKI, A 35 YEAR OLD AMERICAN Q/M SERGEANT, SNOG. SOUND OF RITA'S KEY IN DOOR. THEY JUMP UP AND STRAIGHTEN THEMSELVES AS RITA ENTERS WITH SHOPPING BAG.

RITA:	Bloody queues! Oh, hello, Chuck. Bit early for you, ain't it? And hello Maggie, an' all. And what do you think you're doing home at half past three?
MAGGIE:	Had a migraine.
RITA:	(OPENING BLACKOUTS) That must account for why you've got the blackouts drawn three months after the end of the war.
MAGGIE:	Er... cup of tea, mum?
RITA:	Yes, and I'll make it. You can go and pick Harvey up from school.... assuming the little monkey isn't playing truant again. (TO CHUCK) He needs a man around to steady him.
MAGGIE:	It's a bit early, mum.
RITA:	Well me and your Uncle Chuck want to be alone, don't we, Chuck?
CHUCK:	Do we?
RITA:	Yes, we do! (HOLDS FRONT DOOR OPEN UNTIL MAGGIE EXITS) So where were you last night?
CHUCK:	I came round here at eight like we agreed.
RITA:	We agreed eight outside the Cafe de Paris. I waited ages.
CHUCK:	Well so did I. Maggie made me very comfortable.
RITA:	I bet she did. The little minx! Well it better not happen again, Chuck, I'm warning you.
CHUCK:	Look, Rita, let's not quarrel.... I've had some news.
RITA:	About going back to the States?
CHUCK:	That's right.
RITA:	It's about time an' all. Well?

CHUCK: We embark Thursday.

RITA: Thursday? Don't give me much time, does it? How am I supposed to get all packed and sort out passports....

CHUCK: I can't take you with me, Rita.

RITA: And I got to give notice down the pub, I'm working a week in hand....

CHUCK: I'm sorry, Rita. I can't take you with me.

RITA: (STUNNED) What are you talking about?

CHUCK: Rita, look, I've got a wife and two children in Des Moines, Iowa.

RITA: You bastard. You never mentioned them before. Slipped your mind, did they? Three of the best years of my life you've had and....

CHUCK: You never told me you're still married either.

RITA: What do you mean?

CHUCK: You told me your husband died in combat.

RITA: Well, he might have done. I haven't heard from him for ages. The war's well over and....

CHUCK: Come on, Rita. You know the troop ships take months to get back from India.

RITA: India? Who's been telling you.... Maggie!? I'll break her flaming neck when she gets back. You promised to take us with you. We'd grow wheat, you said. Eat steak and butter. You'd teach me to drive. (STARTS CRYING QUITE CONVINCINGLY) You rotten liar.

CHUCK: What can I say, Rita?

RITA: Say you'll take me with you.

CHUCK:	I can't. I told you I've got kids in the US.
RITA:	It's only because I've been taking precautions that you ain't got kids in the UK. You can't just go off and leave me in this sodding prefab.
CHUCK:	I'm sorry, Rita. (TAKES OUT WALLET) Look, you've been a lot of laughs, but it's got to finish. I've cleared out my savings account over here. £79/10/-.
RITA:	You think you can buy me off? You think I want your stinking money?
CHUCK:	Come off it, Rita. You liked the smell of my bankroll well enough when I was keeping you in nylons and scent and Hershey Bars from the PX. Look, can't we part as friends? (PUTS MONEY IN HER HAND)
	RITA THROWS THE MONEY IN HIS FACE. HE SHRUGS. EXITS. SHE STOPS CRYING AND GATHERS UP MONEY AND GOES TO FRONT DOOR AND SHOUTS OUT AFTER HIM.
RITA:	I hope your bloody ship sinks.

SCENE SEVEN. INT. (STUDIO) DAY:

STAN IS SITTING WITH A CUP OF TEA AND A BUN, LOOKING AT A NEWSPAPER IN A RATHER SHABBY CAFF IN TOTTENHAM.

MAGGIE ENTERS. SHE HAS TIME TO KILL. SHE GOES TO COUNTER AND ORDERS CUP OF TEA. TAKES IT TO SIT DOWN. SEES STAN. RECOGNISES HIM. SITS OPPOSITE HIM. HE DOESN'T LOOK UP.

MAGGIE:	Is this seat taken.... erm.... Dad?
STAN:	(LOOKS UP) Blimey!! Maggie. (JUMPS UP. GOES AROUND TABLE AND HUGS HER) You've grown into a big girl.

	I can see rationing's done you no harm. How's Harvey?
MAGGIE:	He's fine. N'arf missed you.
STAN:	It's mutual.... I missed you and all, Maggie.
MAGGIE:	Did you, Dad?
STAN:	How's your mum?
MAGGIE:	Oh, she's not too bad. Mind you, she won't be pleased to see you.
STAN:	That's what your nan said.
MAGGIE:	Well, she rather thought you were dead. She was looking forward to the Widows Pension.
STAN:	Oh, that's nice. Talk about "Hail The Conquering Hero Comes". Why am I supposed to be dead?
MAGGIE:	Well, you never wrote. Don't they have ink in India?
STAN:	I stopped writing to your mum cos she never replied.
MAGGIE:	Well, she lost your address.
STAN:	I wrote to your Nan... when I could. Didn't she pass the letters on?
MAGGIE:	Mum and Nan don't really see eye to eye. Mind you, Harvey always knew you'd be coming back.
STAN:	Tell us about Harvey. How is he? Where is he? Is he really all right?
MAGGIE:	You can ask him yourself in a little while. I've got to collect him from school.... assuming he bothered to go in today.

STAN: Isn't he much cop at school, then? He's a bright nipper... ain't he?

MAGGIE: Bright, but undisciplined... according to his teacher. He's good at sport.

STAN: Is that all?

MAGGIE: And plasticine work. But he ain't really had much schooling. We've had a war too, you know. Harvey's turned into a right little urchin.

STAN: How d'you mean?

MAGGIE: Well, when he was five, she had him evacuated down to Dorset somewhere. He hitch-hiked back to London. Then he started his gang and got into trouble with the police for nickin' things out of bombed out houses....

STAN: What did your mother say about that?

MAGGIE: She gave him a good hiding. But he's tough. He took no notice. I must say he's built up a great collection of shrapnel and used johnnies.

STAN: Margaret Cynthia Moon!!

MAGGIE: Come off it, dad. I'm seventeen. I work for me living.

STAN: So?

MAGGIE: Down the rubber factory. Quality control.

STAN: Well I just hope you don't bring your work home with you.

MAGGIE: Dad, I'm grown up. I thought you'd noticed. You know, you can get around.... without leaving town.

STAN:	Oh, woman of the world, are we? And to think that when I joined up you were wearing navy blue knickers and ankle socks.
MAGGIE:	I still do.... for one of my boyfriends. He likes that sort of thing.
STAN:	I hope I'm not a grandfather before my time?
MAGGIE:	Don't be silly... I get a staff discount.
STAN:	Look, I know I've been away six years, but I am your father...
MAGGIE:	(S/V) At least that's what mum says......
STAN:	And now that I'm home there'll be some discipline in the household. You're not too big to feel the back of my hand.
MAGGIE:	Look, dad, things have changed a lot while you've been away. You just can't expect to pick up where you left off. I mean it's been a long time for mum. She is a woman, dad.
STAN:	That's one thing that has changed, then.
MAGGIE:	She's worked most of the war in a pub up Leicester Square where a lot of Yanks go. She's made a lot of new friends.... soldiers and that.
STAN:	I made friends in the Forces, too.
MAGGIE:	I mean _close_ friends, dad. The sort me and Harvey are supposed to call uncle.
STAN:	No wonder she wished the Japs had got me. Well the war's over now. It's time for new starts and I'm not having my Harvey tainted by that sort of loose living....
MAGGIE:	Save it for your wife, dad. Come on, school should be out by now.

Shooting the Pilot

CUT TO:

SCENE EIGHT. EXT. (FILM) DAY:

STAN AND MAGGIE APPROACH VICTORIAN SCHOOL BUILDING. STOP AT RAILINGS TO WATCH A GROUP OF KIDS PLAYING FOOTBALL WITH A SMALL RUBBER BALL AND COATS AS GOALPOSTS.

MAGGIE: Oh. So he did go to school today for a change? They must have had rice pudding for afters.

STAN: (WATCHING INTENTLY) I've been away over half of his lifetime, you know. Can't credit it. I can't even recognise my own kid.

ONE OF THE KIDS IS CLEARLY THE BEST FOOTBALLER.

NAGGIE: (POINTING) That's Harvey. The one with the maroon pullover and the body swerve.

STAN: Blimey, he's shot up.

MAGGIE: What did you expect?

HARVEY JINKS PAST TWO KIDS AND SCORES A LOVELY GOAL.

STAN: (SHOUTS) Good goal, Harvey!

HARVEY HALF TURNS.

STAN: Harvey.... over here, son.

HARVEY: (TURNS FULLY. SEES STAN IN UNIFORM) Dad! Dad! (HE SPRINTS TO THE SCHOOL GATE AS STAN ENTERS PLAYGROUND AND STARTS TOWARDS HARVEY. THEY NEAR EACH OTHER. WHEN THEY ARE JUST A FOOT APART....

FREEZE FRAME:

END OF PART ONE:

PART TWO

SCENE NINE. INT. (STUDIO) DAY:

WE'RE IN RITA'S PREFAB. RITA HAS DRAWN THE BLACKOUTS AND SITS WITH THE STANDARD LAMP ON AND A BOTTLE OF GIN BEFORE HER. SHE HAS POURED HERSELF A LARGE ONE. MAGGIE ENTERS TENTATIVELY. RITA LOOKS UP HOPEFULLY FOR A MOMENT AND IS DISAPPOINTED THAT IT IS NOT CHUCK COMING BACK.

RITA: Oh, it's you. (BECOMING AGGRESSIVE) I'm surprised you've got the gall to come back in here after what you....

MAGGIE: (GLANCING TOWARDS BEDROOM) Has Chuck gone?

RITA: Course he's bloody gone. You did a good job of frightening him off, didn't you?

MAGGIE: Look, mum, dad's....

RITA: Yeah, you had to tell him all about your dad.

MAGGIE: No. I mean dad's almost....

RITA: Listen, I don't give a monkey's about your dad. Don't care if he's alive or dead, you didn't have to tell Chuck about him. But you were jealous, weren't you? Couldn't bear to see me having a good time, could you? Not content with flaunting yourself before half the men in London, no, you had to steal my....

MAGGIE: Mum, shut up a second. What I'm trying to tell you....

BEFORE MAGGIE CAN TELL RITA, THE DOOR OPENS AND STAN AND HARVEY, HAND-IN-HAND, ENTER. RITA IS SHOCKED.

STAN: Hello, Rita. I'm back.

Shooting the Pilot

RITA: I'm back, he says. You'd think he's just popped out for ten Woodbines. You could have warned me, Maggie.

MAGGIE LOOKS LONG SUFFERINGLY HEAVENWARDS. STAN CROSSES AND PECKS RITA ON THE CHEEK.

STAN: How are you, Rita?

RITA: I'm.... (MAKES AN EFFORT) I'm glad you're all right. I thought you might be...

STAN: Dead? You knew I wasn't in a combat zone.

RITA: Oh, weren't you. Must have slipped my mind.

HARVEY: Dad was a secret agent. That's why he couldn't write much.

RITA: He couldn't write much because he's a lazy sod. (TO STAN) Did you tell him you were a spy?

HARVEY: He couldn't tell me, could he? It's a secret. I worked it out for meself.

RITA: (TO STAN) But you didn't tell him you weren't a spy?

STAN: I got to say you're all looking well.

MAGGIE: Anyone for a game of Unhappy Families?

RITA: Well, it was nice seeing, you, Stan. Let us know when you get somewhere to live.

STAN: Look, I'm sorry, Rita. I should have sent you a telegram.

RITA: Oh, a telegram would have made all the difference in the world.

STAN: Oh, come on, Rita, it can't be that bad.

RITA: Look, Stan, I've had a terrible day and since you walked through the door it hasn't got any better.

MAGGIE: Shall I make a cup of tea? (ESCAPES TO KITCHEN)

THERE IS A PAINFUL PREGNANT PAUSE, THEN STAN REMEMBERS MEDALS. TAKES THEM FROM POCKET AND GIVES THEM TO HARVEY.

STAN: Here you are, son.

HARVEY: Cor, smashing. Did Mr Mountbatten give you these?

STAN TOUCHES HIS NOSE, CONFIDENTIALLY.

RITA: Probably won them playing cards. Oh, I forgot, you're not a winner, are you?

STAN: Look, shall I go out and come in again?

RITA: No, go out and don't come in again.

HARVEY: How can you talk like that to my dad? He's an 'ero.

RITA: Gawd help us.

STAN: I brought you an ivory statuette for your mantlepiece, Rita. (SEARCHES KITBAG FOR IT) Some goddess with lots of arms. (PULLS IT OUT OF BAG, IT'S BROKEN) Oh, dear. Perhaps it wasn't ivory after all. Still, they say it's the thought that counts, don't they?

RITA: They do, and I thought you were dead. Does that count?

HARVEY: D'you kill a lot of Japs, dad?

RITA: (BITTER LAUGH) Japs? Harvey, your father was a clerk, that's all. All he killed was time.

HARVEY: You don't understand, mum. That was just dad's cover. Like Superman pretends to be Clark Kent in them comics Uncle Chuck brings me.

Shooting the Pilot

STAN: Uncle? I didn't know you had a brother called Chuck, Rita?

HARVEY: He's one of mum's American friends. He's all right. He brings me comics and sweets, and he gives mum....

STAN: I can guess what he gives mum. He'll have to go, Rita.

RITA: He already has. The pig's going back to the States without me. And he promised.... If Maggie hadn't shot her mouth off about you still being around...

STAN: That's my girl.

RITA: Yes. You keep telling yourself that, Stan.

HARVEY: What does mum mean, dad?

STAN: Fancy some fish and chips, son?

HARVEY: Not 'arf!

STAN: Here you are, Harvey. (GIVES HIM A TEN BOB NOTE)

HARVEY: Blimey! Ten bob! (RUSHES FOR DOOR)

STAN: Lots of vinegar on your mum's.

HARVEY EXITS.

STAN: (ATTEMPTING TO PLAY THE FORGIVING, YET AUTHORITATIVE HUSBAND) Rita, come and sit down. (SHE DOES SO WITH ILL GRACE) Now I know our marriage has had its ups and downs....

RITA: You'll have to jog my memory about the ups...

STAN: And I want you to know that I understand. After all, I've been away a long time and you've had to bring up the kids and you've had to work, and I know things must have been hard. Now I appreciate that you might have needed a certain amount of

Shine On Harvey Moon

	masculine attention, and if you made one or two friends....
RITA:	One or two.
STAN:	.... I don't mind, but I want you to put them behind you now. It's peacetime and we've got to pull together to build a warm, happy home for our family. I'm prepared to let bygones be bygones and resume my rightful place as head of the household.... and my rightful place in your bed.
RITA:	Really?
STAN:	Naturally.
RITA:	Because if you think you're staying here the night you've got another think coming.
STAN:	(STUNNED) But this is my home.
RITA:	No it ain't. It's *my* home and I've got a rentbook to prove it.
STAN:	All right, what about the small matter of that pleasant house in Walthamstow what you blew up, saving the Luftwaffe the petrol. That was *my* house.
RITA:	Wrong. That was Clapton Orient's house and they wrote me in '43 saying they'd want it back after the war.... for a <u>first team</u> player.
STAN:	Oh, this is choice. What am I supposed to do? Pitch a tent in the park?
RITA:	You can't do that. They've ploughed the parks up to grow vegetables.
STAN:	(DESPERATE NOW) But Rita I'm still your husband.
RITA:	Look, Stan, face facts. You're a failure. The only thing you've ever been any good at is failure. I

	only married you because Maggie was on the way and there was a fair chance she was yours.
STAN:	Oh, I see, only a fair chance? I thought I was your one and only, and now you tell me I was simply favourite in a large field.
RITA:	Field? As I recall it was a bus shelter.
STAN:	(WORRIED) Harvey's mine, though. Ain't he?
RITA:	(ILLOGICALLY) Course he is. What sort of woman do you take me for?
STAN:	I'm beginning to wonder.
RITA:	So really as an husband, a father, a footballer, even as a member of His Majesty's Forces you've been pretty much of a dead loss.
STAN:	Rita....
RITA:	Let me have my say, Stan. I've taken some hard knocks in this war... none harder than today.... but I've had some laughs as well and I've met men who haven't all been losers. There's no way I'm having you back. There's nothing between you and me, Stan. There never was really, so you'd be doin' yourself a favour if you took the hint and pushed off.
STAN:	And what about my Harvey?
RITA:	He's done without you for six years, Stan, do you really think he needs you?
STAN:	But I've got his future all mapped out.
RITA:	Poor little basket.
STAN:	I'm not giving him up, Rita.

RITA:	Well before you start sorting out his life, I suggest you get yours in order. For a start, you ain't got nowhere to sleep tonight, have you?
STAN:	You throwin' me out? What about me fish 'n' chips?
RITA:	It's better you're not here when the kid gets back. I don't want him unsettled.
MAGGIE:	It's you that's unsettled him, mum, with your....
RITA:	You watch your lip, young lady.
STAN:	It's all right, Maggie. I'll go. I don't want Harvey to see us fighting.... again. (GETS HIS STUFF TOGETHER AND LEAVES)
MAGGIE:	How could you kick him out like that? Where's he gonna go?
RITA:	I don't know and I don't really care. There's always the Sally Army.... or the Secret Agents' Rest Home, perhaps. I wish that kid would get back with my supper. I'm starving.
MAGGIE:	How can you think of food after you've just thrown your husband out onto the street?
RITA:	I'm hungry. I've had a trying day and believe me, we don't need. him. He's a loser, Maggie.
MAGGIE:	No, mum. You're the loser. You've lost two blokes in one day. Dad and Chuck.
RITA:	Chuck? Whose fault was that , young lady?
MAGGIE:	He wasn't going to take us with him, mum. He played you along.
RITA:	Maybe. Anyway, where's my fish and chips?
MAGGIE:	Dad's fish and chips.... and I ain't got any appetite.

Shooting the Pilot

RITA: Well I'll eat yours an' all.

THERE IS A KNOCK ON THE DOOR. MAGGIE LETS IN HARVEY WHO IS CARRYING FOUR PARCELS WRAPPED IN NEWSPAPER.

RITA: About time too.

HARVEY: Where's dad?

RITA: Bulldog Drummond? He's gone.

HARVEY: What, gone out without no supper?

MAGGIE: Not gone out. Gone. Mum don't want him here no more.

HARVEY: She's fibbing, ain't she, mum?

RITA: (PUTTING FOOD ON PLATES) Eat your rock salmon before it gets cold.

HARVEY: I don't want rock salmon, I want my dad. Where is he?

RITA: He's gone down the Secret Agents' club.

HARVEY: Where's that?

MAGGIE: (GENTLY) We don't know where he's gone exactly, Harvey, but I'm sure he'll get in touch soon.

HARVEY: Why's he gone? Why isn't he staying with us?

MAGGIE: Cos mum don't want him around. There's still one or two Uncles she's got high hopes of....

RITA: Margaret you can go to your room.

MAGGIE: (GETTING UP AND GETTING HER COAT FROM THE BACK OF THE DOOR) No thanks mum. I think I'd rather go out. I might go for a walk along the canal to the sewage plant. The air's sweeter than it is here. (EXITS)

HARVEY:	Mum, if you don't like dad.... why can't he stay here and you can go away?
RITA:	(CUFFING HIM AROUND THE EAR) That's lovely, innit, from my own flesh and blood, after all the sacrifices I've had to make. Right, you're going to bed without no supper.
HARVEY:	I don't wannoo!

RITA TAKES HARVEY BY THE COLLAR. FROGMARCHES HIM TO HIS ROOM. COMES BACK. SITS DOWN. PILES ALL THE FISH AND CHIPS ONTO ONE PLATE. SHE TAKES A MOUTHFUL AND WE SEE THAT SHE HAS SUDDENLY LOST HER APPETITE.

<u>CUT TO:</u>

<u>SCENE TEN. INT. (STUDIO) NIGHT:</u>

INSIDE THE PRINCE OF WALES PUBLIC HOUSE. A LARGE EDWARDIAN PUB IN WALTHAMSTOW. STAN, STILL IN UNIFORM, SITS ALONE AT CORNER TABLE NURSING A PINT. THE PUB IS FULL OF MEN IN DEMOB SUITS. STAN SPOTS LOU NEAR THE BAR.

STAN:	(SHOUTS AND WAVES) Oy! Lou! Over here! (LOU SEES HIM. SMILES. WAVES AND COMES OVER.) Lou, oh am I pleased to see you here. I come in expecting to see a few of the old regulars, someone prepared to pretend he's glad you're back, but I don't recognise anyone. The Landlord's forgotten me. Everything's changed.... 'Cept that pie in the glass cabinet. That's been there since the old Queen died.
LOU:	Yeah, you got better beer in Bombay. So what d'you make of Civvy Street, then?
STAN:	Well I must admit that the first four hours have not been undiluted pleasure.

Shooting the Pilot

LOU:	Something wrong, mate? Where's your Rita, then? I'd have thought you'd have plenty saved up for her first night home. I can tell you, my wallet's bulging.
STAN:	Rita's thrown me out.
LOU:	Blimey, that was short and sweet.
STAN:	I don't know about sweet. What you doing here, anyway? Having your party in the upstairs room?
LOU:	Not exactly.
STAN:	Oh, so you've just popped in for more supplies?
LOU:	There ain't no party, Stanley.
STAN:	No party? Your family'll be disappointed. All them aunts, uncles and cousins who were coming down special.
LOU:	There ain't no aunts, uncles or cousins.
STAN:	Lou, I'm so sorry. What happened? This bloody war?
LOU:	No. There never was any family. I made them up.
STAN:	You're pulling my leg. What about your brother what was going to take you into his business? (LOU SHAKES HIS HEAD) What about your Joan, who used to let you take all those racy photos?
LOU:	Don't know who she is. I won those photos off a merchant seaman who picked 'em up in Cairo.
STAN:	Well, I never. You must have a mum and dad?
LOU:	Who knows? I was abandoned in the Black and White Milk Bar in Finsbury Park. I was in a Childrens Home until the war started and I joined up.

STAN: (SHAKES HIS HEAD IN AMAZEMENT) Blimey! And to think how I envied you, with all your family and your mates and all your post-war prospects.

LOU: I've still got prospects, Stanley. I've still got all these ideas. I know I'm going to amount to something, one way or another. What I don't know is where I'm gonna kip tonight.

STAN: Join the club, mate. (THEY SHAKE HANDS) And to think, when you didn't give me your address I thought it was because I weren't good enough for your family. I didn't think you was an homeless orphan.

LOU: Well, I hear they do a very nice bench down the Embankment.

STAN: Yeah, complete with running water.... the Thames. Fancy another drink?

CUT TO:

SCENE ELEVEN. INT. (STUDIO) NIGHT:

OUTSIDE NAN'S FRONT DOOR. SOUND OF FEET ON STONE STEPS, ONE PAIR VERY UNSTEADY. STAN AND LOU'S VOICES COMING UP THE STAIRS.

STAN: Come on, Lou, old mate. Just one more flight.

LOU: That's what they always say in the Air Force.

THEY APPEAR OUTSIDE NAN'S FRONT DOOR AND KNOCK ON IT. WE HEAR HER VOICE FROM WITHIN. STAN SUPPORTS LOU.

NAN: Who is it?

STAN: It's me, mum.

NAN: Who?

Shooting the Pilot

STAN: It's me. Stan. How many sons you got?

NAN: Stanley? (SHE OPENS THE DOOR. SHE'S IN HER DRESSING GOWN AND WITHOUT HER GLASSES. SHE USHERS THEM IN) Oh, blimey, O'Reilly. (MIXING THE TWO MEN UP) He's been wounded. (TO LOU) Speak to me, son.

STAN: I'm Stanley, mum. Where's your bins?

NAN: (GETS SPECS OUT OF DRESSING GOWN POCKET AND PUTS THEM ON) Oh, hello, Stanley. Rita thrown you out then? Who's this?

STAN: This is my friend, Lou.

NAN: Is he wounded?

STAN: No, just a bit drunk. He's been celebrating a bit too much.... though God only knows what he's got to celebrate.

LOU: I'm ever so tired, Stanley.

STAN: Can we put him up for a night or two, Nan?

NAN: It won't be the first time, will it? You'll have to share a bed, though.

STAN HELPS LOU THROUGH TO SPARE BEDROOM AND LEAVES HIM THERE. HE REJOINS NAN IN LOUNGE, WHERE SHE'S POURING TEA. THE LOUNGE IS UNTIDY, CLUTTERED, WARM AND HOMELY... LIKE NAN. IN THE CORNER IS A VIRGIN TELEVISION, BOUGHT BY STAN THE DAY BEFORE THE BBC CLOSED DOWN FOR THE DURATION OF THE WAR. THERE IS A CABINET FULL OF SOUVENIRS OF STAN'S PLAYING DAYS, MOST OF THEM ATTEST TO UNFULFILLED SCHOOLBOY POTENTIAL. A COAL FIRE BURNS.

NAN: Nice cup of tea, Stan? I've just brewed fresh.

STAN:	Just what the doctor ordered. You must have been expecting me?
NAN:	I know Rita. I'll grant her this, she doesn't waste time, does she?
STAN:	Don't you start, mum.
NAN:	If you'd have listened to me you wouldn't have married her in the first place, miserable cow!
STAN:	I had to do the decent thing, mum. I got her into trouble.
NAN:	No, Stan, you got her up the stick, then she got you into trouble. Anyway, for the last six years she's been the toast of the less choosy members of the Allied Forces.
STAN:	Toast? What do you mean toast?
NAN:	As in done both sides. Yeah, she should have got the George Cross for services to morale. Mind you, she's never short of a pair of nylons. Yeah, when they wrote "The Yanks Are Coming" they had your Rita in mind.
STAN:	Mum!
NAN:	Just cos I'm 63 don't mean I don't know what makes the world go round. I was in service for 12 years. Some of the things I saw at them country parties...
STAN:	Still, Harvey's turned out a great little nipper, ain't he?
NAN:	No thanks to your Rita.
STAN:	I think we've established she ain't my Rita any more.... if she ever was. Still, Harvey's gonna have a proper future if I've got anything to do with it.

NAN: Well, don't go blabbing your plans in Rita's direction. She'll block 'em just for spite.

STAN: Do you reckon she can keep Harvey away from me, then?

NAN: That depends on him, don't it?

STAN: I tell you something for nothing, mum, Harvey ain't going to be no reserve for Clapton Orient.

NAN: Nothing wrong with Clapton Orient. You, your dad and your Uncle Archie, you all got a decent living from Orient reserves.

STAN: I know that, mum. But there's got to be more to life for Harvey. I've seen his body swerve. I mean, I didn't face the Yellow Peril....

NAN: I know. You were a clerk.

STAN: Let me finish, mum. I didn't, metaphorically speaking, face the Yellow Peril so that Harvey could grow up to face Gillingham reserves in front of 350 people. There's got to be more in life for Harvey even if there weren't for me.

NAN: In the meantime, how are you going to earn your living?

STAN: I'll get a job all right. Mr Attlee says we've got a country to rebuild. Jobs and homes and security for us what have done our bit. I mean, there's got to be a great future ahead. Mind you, I'd be grateful if I could stay here a bit.

NAN: You shouldn't have to ask, Stan. (KISSES HIM) I'm glad you're back, son.

STAN: Really?

NAN:	(GOING TO SOUVENIR CABINET, SHE REMOVES A SCRAPBOOK) Come over here, Stan. (STAN JOINS HER) Here. (GIVES BOOK TO STAN).
STAN:	(FLICKS THROUGH BOOK AND FINDS SOME NEW ENTRIES) Here, you've kept it up to date.
NAN:	Harvey and me kept it up to date. He keeps it round here out of Rita's way.
STAN:	(SURPRISED BY A PARTICULAR CUTTING) How did he get this one?
NAN:	(LOOKING) I suppose he must have swapped some shrapnel for a bundle of newspapers.
STAN:	(READING) "This is my dad, Stanley Moon, scoring for the RAF in 1941 against a Bombay Select XI. The Indian goalie must have been wounded 'cos his head's all bandaged up. Dad must have got leave from his secret work to play in this game."
NAN:	You know that kid thinks the sun shines out of your football boots.
STAN:	I feel the same about him. I won't let him down. The thing is I got to find a way to keep him with me.
NAN:	If he wants to be with you, Harvey'll find a way.

CUT TO:

SCENE TWELVE. INT. (STUDIO) NIGHT:

STAN, WHO HAS FALLEN ASLEEP IN CHAIR, SCRAPBOOK OPEN ON LAP. THE FIRE HAS GONE OUT.

THERE IS A KNOCK ON THE FRONT DOOR WHICH WAKES STAN. HE LOOKS AT CLOCK, NEARLY MIDNIGHT.

HE OPENS THE FRONT DOOR. THERE STANDS HARVEY, WITH A LITTLE SUITCASE IN HIS HAND AND SCHOOL

SATCHEL. HE HAS HIS FOOTBALL BOOTS AROUND HIS NECK.

STAN: (VERY SURPRISED) Harvey!

HARVEY: (ENTERING) Sorry I'm late, dad. Mum didn't go to sleep until she finished her gin.

STAN: How did you know I'd be here, son?

HARVEY: (TAPS HIS NOSE, CONFIDENTIALLY) This is where I'd come.... if I wanted to lie low for a bit. Here's your five bob, dad.

STAN: What's this in aid of?

HARVEY: Change from the fish and chips.

STAN: Well you better keep it, son.

HARVEY: Five bob! Blimey! (HUGS HIS DAD) It's really great to have you back, dad. You ain't going away on any more secret spying missions, are you, dad?

STAN: I shouldn't think so, son.

HARVEY: Great. Can we go to the football tomorrow?

STAN: Course we can.

HARVEY: Smashing. Clapton reserves are at home.

STAN: No, Harvey. I'm taking you up the Arsenal. There'll be no more reserve football for you, old son. I got plans.

THE END:

3
The New Statesman

THE NEW STATESMAN was our first bespoke comedy pilot. By "bespoke" we mean that the script was written for the star, rather than offered to the star. It happened by accident; we bumped into the luminescent Rik Mayall and the rest is hysteria.

Rik was *the* brightest light in the new wave alternative comedy universe. Rik had created and co-written *The Young Ones* and so we knew we presented ourselves with a challenge: writing for a writer. It shouldn't have vexed us. Rik was full of weird and wacky ideas, and he proved to be an inspired piece of casting because it brought us a young "right-on" audience, which our previous shows may not have reached.

In the beginning God created Rik. We met him at a comedy symposium, where he challenged us to create for him a funny, new, grown-up character, the polar opposite of the spotty, beret-wearing, right-on student "Wrick" he had created for himself in *The Young Ones*. We agreed to meet again, over lunch. What struck us immediately was: a) how good he looked in a suit; and, b) just how handsome he was. He'd never looked handsome in *The Young Ones*.

We asked him what sort of character he wanted to play. He explained that he enjoyed roles that let him express the dark side of his personality. "I like to cheat and lie. I don't mind the occasional murder. I'd be good at murder. Greed is good. Stealing. Arson… Oh, and lots of sex." Rik continued describing such an abhorrent individual that we feared that it would be a difficult sell, until after a mouthful of peach Melba one of us said, "So you want to play a Conservative member of parliament." He laughed hysterically. We had connected.

It wasn't entirely coincidental that *The New Statesman* was conceived in 1987. Margaret Thatcher and her gang of Conservative brothers (there were no sisters) had just celebrated their third crushing General Election victory and looked so secure it seemed as if Britain was becoming a one-party state. Ghastly self-centred MPs like Alan B'Stard were starting to multiply. It was clearly time to turn the spotlight on greedy, selfish, uncaring Conservatism and try to counter its power with laughter.

The New Statesman was actually a default title. We originally wanted to call it *The Bastard File*, after one of the coarsest of workman's tools. ITV prohibited the use of the word "Bastard" so we came up with three alternative titles: *The B'Stard File*, *Maggie's Wet Member*, and *The New Statesman*. One day during a break in rehearsals, we wrote the three titles on three separate sheets of paper, folded them and put them in a bag. We wandered along the Goldhawk Road, west London, until a young woman came towards us, pushing a baby in a buggy. Her eyes popped when she realised one of us was none other than Rik Mayall. We asked her if she wouldn't mind pulling one of the names from the bag and told her whichever name she chose would be the title of our next television comedy. She was excited, put her hand in the bag and removed… well, *The New Statesman*, of course.

Looking back at notes made at the time, we find it almost inconceivable that Rik had so little serious interest in British politics. We had been fooled by his on-screen persona. We thought that he must be such a committed left-wing radical that he'd be affronted to be asked to portray a Thatcherite toy boy. But politics didn't bother Rik. His primary concern was *laughter*. He demanded lots of it – the best and funniest scenes ever seen on television. Now there was a challenge.

At one point during the writing of the pilot script, Rik said, "There's only eleven laughs on this page." We retorted that was ten more than in most other TV half hours. Rik acknowledged this, but eleven was not enough. "I can get you five more without saying anything…" And he could: with the wiggle of an eyebrow, folding his ear inside out, or an evil smirk. Every week. Rik had supreme confidence in his own talent, in his ability to work the audience. Rik lived for laughter and the love of an audience, which is perhaps why he always did bits of impromptu physical comedy between studio takes to keep his audience simmering. Once he had captured that first laugh, he would sail forever onwards.

Therefore, it was vital that Alan B'Stard MP gave Rik his first laugh early on page one. The laughter relaxed him and he could then go forth and knock his audience dead. Once the studio audience became hysterical, it was like blood to a shark. Rik wanted to make them sick with laughter. He simply wouldn't let up. He was relentless and that is, in part, what made *The New Statesman* so successful.

However, Rik's demands were very taxing. Indeed, *The New Statesman* was the most exhausting show we have ever written. Having finished one series we didn't have the energy to imagine ever embarking upon another one. Our solution was to kill off Alan B'Stard. If we could leave him dead in the last shot of the last scene of the last episode, we could breathe a sigh of relief. But Yorkshire Television always had other ideas. They would make us revive him, even bring B'Stard back from the dead. *The New Statesman* became an instant hit and Yorkshire Television couldn't get enough of it… or the awards that came with it. And yes, it was also the most rewarding series we ever wrote.

To return to the pilot script. As we have said, we created the character before we had written a page of dialogue. We actually sold the idea to Yorkshire Television by sending them little more than Alan B'Stard's grotesque *Who's Who* entry, in which he informed the reader that his recreations were: "Making money, dining at exclusive restaurants at other people's expense, *droit de seigneur* and grinding the faces of the poor." Had there, we wondered, ever been a more noxious television character than B'Stard? We hoped not.

Once the pilot was commissioned, we decided to take the reins off and work toward laughter above all else (which is a good rule in a television comedy), but we still wanted to structure our episode with precision to tell a satisfying chapter in the corrupt and immoral life of Alan B'Stard. Rik's lust for outrage encouraged us to create the most bizarre adventures.

Shooting the Pilot

We decided that much of the action should take place in Alan's office in the House of Commons, where we tried to evoke what we imagined a study would be like in a sleazy public school. Alan had to have a "fag", in the hapless shape of the unworldly and frankly dim-witted Piers Fletcher-Dervish MP, who was so frightened of Alan's sadistic outbursts that he would do anything for him. Also sharing the office was Tory old-timer Sir Stephen Baxter, a sort of ineffective old housemaster character.

With our characters in place we were almost ready to start writing. But though the writer must use his/her imagination in creating a fictional world, we wanted to know how the bubble that is the House of Commons actually worked. We needed informants.

We were lucky that Michael Portillo was MP for Laurence's constituency, so was almost duty-bound to help us. He was generous with his time, even though he was a Tory boy himself. We also had the advice of Renée Short, former left-wing Labour member for Wolverhampton North East. We delighted in her telling off the extras who were playing backbench MPs for behaving too well. Thanks to Michael and Renée we not only became familiar with the topography of the Commons, but also its workings and its members' mischiefs inside the ancient walls. Of course, Rik wasn't at all interested in the law, privileges and proceedings of Parliament, he was only interested in making an audience wet themselves with laughter.

Having completed exhaustive research we started to work out the pilot episode. We thought it would make good sense to begin with Alan B'Stard elected to parliament. Perhaps, left to our own devices, we might have had him squeeze in with a small majority, but nothing Rik ever did was *small*. Alan had to have the biggest majority in the House of Commons. Everything about Alan B'Stard had to be the biggest or the quickest. After all, he was the man who perfected the seven-second orgasm! So to ensure that B'Stard was returned with a majority of over 30,000, we had him assassinate his Labour and Liberal Democrat opponents in the first scene.

We were only on page three when we realised we were writing a sort of real-life cartoon. Everything that happened had to be larger than life. All events had to happen quickly and, if possible, violently. Nobody appeared *normal*. We are not sure this was our intention when we put pen to paper, but we are pretty certain it was Rik's, and between us we created a pilot of well-structured hysteria. Alan's fragrant wife, Sarah, was having a sapphic affair with his political agent, Beatrice. Alan's accountant Norman was going through gender reassignment to escape the clutches of the Inland Revenue. Sidney Bliss, the former public hangman, was bribing Alan to bring back capital punishment. Malachi Jellicoe, the insane Chief Constable of Yorkshire, was blackmailing Alan over the suspicious demise of his political opponents. And there was more. Much more. And all this in a mere twenty-three and a half minutes. It was sitcom on speed. If you didn't like it you could turn over to BBC and watch *Terry and June*.

It took an age to pull it all together. Looking back, we realise there were too many characters, too many subplots, too many scenes – but God it was funny. Rik threw himself into the project enthusiastically and sometimes literally. Our producers at Yorkshire TV never once censored us though they did wonder what drugs we were taking. Could this lunacy really come from the pens of the writers of *Shine On Harvey Moon*?

Before the pilot was even transmitted, the show was controversial, with two Rentaquote Tory MPs, Geoffrey Dickens and Harry Greenaway, claiming they had seen the episode and that it was disgusting and disrespectful to the blessed Margaret Thatcher. The fact that they *hadn't* seen it didn't seem to matter to them. They could lie with the best of the Tory party.

The pilot was recorded in front of a wildly enthusiastic audience, driven into hysteria by Rik's inter-scene mugging. We chose to sit in the audience rather than in the director's box, to experience the full effect of Rik working a crowd. Once the show went into series, we wrote what we thought wilder and wackier episodes, except that our stories started to come true. When a Tory MP called Robert Hicks moved his mistress into his family house, the *Daily Mirror* front page headline screamed "WHAT A B'STARD!" The story continued: "The row comes as an embarrassment to the Tories at a time when the country is laughing at the TV antics of sex-mad politician Alan B'Stard." As they say, you couldn't buy publicity like that. Although perhaps Alan B'Stard would know the right people.

It looked as though low life was imitating low art. Another episode in season one hit the headlines when Alan B'Stard buried a consignment of nuclear waste under a primary school in Grimsby. A few weeks later the tabloid press ran the story of a Tory MP hiding nuclear waste under a school in Hull. Friends and journalists were convinced that we were being tipped off by some "Deep Throat" inside Parliament, but it seemed to be the other way around. What we wrote one day, a Tory MP was doing the next. The more this happened, the more *The New Statesman* was the "must watch" show at 10pm on Sunday nights, a slot it shared with *Spitting Image*. How interesting is it to consider that the two comedies that took on the Tories were both on ITV.

So what was our endgame? We always said we wanted B'Stard to be around after Thatcher had gone. On November 22, 1990, our wish came true.

THE NEW STATESMAN

Episode One: HAPPINESS IS A WARM GUN

Written by Laurence Marks & Maurice Gran

Spring 1988

1 - EXT. HALTEMPRICE, YORKSHIRE. DAY.

WE OPEN ON A SUNLIT MORNING IN THE YORKSHIRE TOWN OF HALTEMPRICE ON ELECTION DAY 1987.

WE MOVE AROUND THE STREETS UNTIL WE SEE A YELLOW CAR, WITH YELLOW BALLOONS EVERYWHERE. THERE'S A LOUDSPEAKER ATTACHED TO ITS ROOF FROM WHICH COMES AN AMPLIFIED VOICE.

MARTIN ROPER: (V/O) ... SDP, SDP. Vote for me, Martin Roper, your SDP candidate, because (There's a pause)... Why should they vote for me?

SDP DRIVER: (V/O) Because you're decisive.

MARTIN ROPER: (V/O) Right. Vote for me because I am more decisive. (To his driver) Shall I turn left or right at the bottom of the road?

CUT TO:

2 - MOMENTS LATER. HALTEMPRICE STREETS.

ANOTHER HILLY STREET. OVER THE BROW OF THE HILL COMES A RED CAR. AGAIN, IT HAS MANY RED BALLOONS FLYING IN THE WIND AND FLOATING OUT OF ITS WINDOWS. A LOUDSPEAKER IS DISPLAYED ON ITS ROOF.

WILLIAM HASLON: (V/O) Vote Labour, Vote Labour. This is William Haslon, your Labour candidate... Vote for me... Please!

	THE TWO CARS ARE COMING DOWN DIFFERENT HILLS. THEN WE CAN SEE THAT THEY ARE HEADING TOWARD ONE ANOTHER.
WILLIAM HASLON:	(V/O) Can you slow down, please.
LABOUR DRIVER:	(V/O) There's something wrong with the brakes, I can't seem to...
	WE SEE THE DRIVER'S FOOT BANGING DOWN ON THE CAR'S BRAKES BUT NOTHING SEEMS TO HAPPEN. THE CAR IS BUILDING UP SPEED AS IT RUNS DOWN THE HILL.
	DOWN THE OTHER HILL WE SEE THE YELLOW CAR DESPERATELY TRYING TO STEER, BUT IT'S GOING OUT OF CONTROL NO MATTER WHAT THE DRIVER TRIES. THE TWO CARS ARE HEADING TOWARD ONE ANOTHER AT HIGH SPEED.
	THERE IS A TERRIBLE HIGH SPEED HEAD-ON CRASH. DEVASTATION.
	THE LOUDSPEAKERS FALL OFF EACH CAR. BALLOONS BURST. THIS IS SURELY FATAL FOR THE OCCUPANTS OF BOTH CARS.
	<u>CUT TO:</u>
	<u>3 - EXT. NIGHT. THE BALCONY OF HALTEMPRICE TOWN HALL.</u>
	WE ARE AT THE HALTEMPRICE COUNT ON ELECTION NIGHT. THE RETURNING OFFICER, WEARING HIS CHAINS OF OFFICE IS READING THE RESULT OF THIS ELECTION.
RET. OFFICER:	Haslon, William Richard...
TV VOICE OVER:	Labour. Intensive care.

RET. OFFICER:	Three thousand, two hundred and thirty seven. Roper, Martin Cyril...
TV VOICE OVER:	SDP. Critical.
RET. OFFICER:	One thousand, two hundred and sixty five. Sutch, Screaming Lord, five thousand and nineteen.
SCREAMING LORD SUTCH:	(Raises his top hat) Up the Loonies.
RET. OFFICER:	B'stard, Alan Beresford...
TV VOICE OVER:	Conservative.
RET. OFFICER:	Thirty one thousand, seven hundred and fifty-six.

THERE IS HEARTY CHEERING FROM THE CROWD BELOW. A DELIGHTED ALAN KISSES HIS ATTRACTIVE WIFE, SARAH, THEN HE SHAKES HANDS WITH THE RETURNING OFFICER AND LORD SUTCH. THE OTHER TWO CANDIDATES ARE IN HOSPITAL. THERE'S MORE CHEERING.

RET. OFFICER: And I therefore declare Alan Beresford B'Stard is returned as Member of Parliament for the constituency of Haltemprice. Congratulations.

B'STARD GIVES A SMUG GRIN, AS IF HE KNEW HE COULD NEVER LOSE. BUT THEN HE DID KNOW, DIDN'T HE? HE SHAKES HANDS WITH OTHERS ON THE BALCONY. WHAT A POLITE YOUNG MAN. HE MOVES TO THE MICROPHONE.

ALAN B'STARD: Thank you. Thank you, thank you. I should like to begin by thanking my loving wife, Sarah. My political agent, Beatrice Protheroe... and in particular...

THE UNIFORMED CHIEF CONSTABLE JOINS ALAN ON THE BALCONY.

Shooting the Pilot

ALAN B'STARD: The Chief Constable of East Yorkshire, Sir Malachi Jellicoe, who has ensured that this election has been conducted within the boundaries of the law. (A sad pause) However, my great victory has been marred by tragedy. A very profound tragedy that has befallen two of my... worthy opponents. I would therefore ask you all now to stand in silence with me for one minute.

AFTER A FEW SECONDS WE CLOSE UP ON ALAN, WHO CAN'T PREVENT HIMSELF SMIRKING.

SLOWLY AND VERY MEASURED, MALACHI JELLICOE SIDLES UP AND WHISPERS.

SIR MALACHI: I know why those cars crashed, B'Stard. And I know you know why they crashed.

ALAN B'STARD: How much do you want? Ten thousand? Twenty thousand pounds?

SIR MALACHI: Why do you assume I'm angling for a bribe?

ALAN B'STARD: But you can't arrest me here, now, it's the greatest day of my life. Please.

SIR MALACHI: I'm not going to arrest you. You're far more use to me in parliament than in prison. There's a law... I want passing.

CUT TO:

4 - EXT. DAY. WESTMINSTER BRIDGE.

A DARK BLUE BENTLEY IS CROSSING THE BRIDGE TOWARDS THE HOUSES OF PARLIAMENT. ALAN B'STARD IS AT THE WHEEL, DARK BESPOKE SUITED, GOLD WATCH. A TRUE THATCHERITE TOY BOY.

CUT TO:

5 - INT. DAY. THE LOBBY OF THE HOUSE OF COMMONS.

AS AN OVERWHELMED B'STARD GOES INTO THE CHAMBER HE IS STOPPED BY A HOUSE OF COMMONS OFFICIAL.

OFFICIAL: Sorry sir, members only.

ALAN B'STARD: I am a member. I've got the largest majority in the House.

OFFICIAL: Name?

ALAN B'STARD: B'stard!

OFFICIAL: I'm only doing my job.

ALAN WALKS INTO THE HOUSE OF COMMONS CHAMBER.

CUT TO:

6 - INT. MOMENTS LATER. HOUSE OF COMMONS CHAMBER.

ALAN FAMILIARISES HIMSELF WITH THE EMPTY CHAMBER. HE PICKS UP THE CEREMONIAL MACE, TRYING IT FOR SIZE. HE LOOKS AROUND AT THE ROWS OF GREEN SEATS WHERE MANY GREAT AND FAMOUS PEOPLE HAVE SAT BEFORE HIM. THEN HE GOES OVER TO THE SPEAKER'S CHAIR AND DROPS HIMSELF INTO IT. HE LIKES THE FEEL OF THIS PLACE, THAT MUCH IS OBVIOUS.

CUT TO:

7 - INT. DAY. ALAN'S OFFICE IN THE HOUSE OF COMMONS.

ALAN B'STARD: (Reading from notes)... We claim we are full and enthusiastic members of the European Community and yet we are the only member state whose police don't carry guns. How then can the English

	policeman be expected to respond when heavily armed French bank robbers come swarming through the Channel Tunnel?
PIERS FLETCHER DERVISH:	I say Alan, that's awfully good.
ALAN B'STARD:	You like it?
PIERS:	It's wonderful.
ALAN B'STARD:	It must be rubbish then. (Screws up the speech and throws it across the room to join his many other screwed up efforts) Damn! Damn, damn, damn, damn!
PIERS:	You're having a bit of trouble with that speech, aren't you Alan?
ALAN B'STARD:	I really don't know why you're not in the Cabinet, Piers, with a razor sharp brain like that. How did you ever get to be an MP anyway? Oh, but then of course your constituency is south of Watford, isn't it, where they'd elect a hat stand if it had a blue rosette on it.
	ALAN'S PHONE RINGS.
ALAN B'STARD:	Hello, Alan B'Stard. Biggest majority in the House of Commons. Oh, Sir Malachi. Yes. (Alan pushes Piers out of his way) Yes, Chief Constable, they're voting on it this afternoon so with any luck you should be shooting suspects by teatime. Now, about that little car crash I had nothing to do with...
	IN ENTERS ALAN'S OTHER ROOM-MATE, SIR STEPHEN BAXTER, AN OLD SCHOOL, ONE NATION TORY.
SIR STEPHEN:	Ah ha! Big day for you B'Stard. Third reading of your Private Members Bill.

ALAN B'STARD: Oh, is it today? Oh well thank you for reminding me, Sir Stephen. I was going to pop off at half past two and visit a massage parlour.

PIERS FINDS THIS VERY FUNNY.

SIR STEPHEN: Ah, very good. I know a joke when I hear one and I think I may just have heard one then.

ALAN B'STARD: Look, I'm trying to write a speech. Go away.

SIR STEPHEN: I'm very sorry old boy. I won't say another word.

ALAN B'STARD: Good.

SIR STEPHEN GOES TO HIS DESK. NOW ALAN, PIERS AND SIR STEPHEN ARE AT THEIR DESKS LIKE SCHOOLBOYS TAKING AN EXAM, IN THIS CRAMPED OFFICE.

SIR STEPHEN: (To Piers) Extraordinary really, B'Stard's only been in the House three months and he's on the verge of arming the police.

PIERS TIPTOES OVER TO SIR STEPHEN'S DESK AND WHISPERS...

PIERS: Alan's got writer's block.

SIR STEPHEN: Oh, have you? Well, look, may I give you a preview of my intended oration. It might help you stimulate your creative juices.

ALAN B'STARD: No thank you.

NEVERTHELESS, SIR STEPHEN READS FROM HIS WRITTEN SPEECH. HE CLEARS HIS THROAT

SIR STEPHEN: For a century and a half, the British Bobby has patrolled his beat on his trusty bicycle, armed only with his sturdy truncheon, his whistle and his considerable courage...

PIERS: Hear, hear.

Shooting the Pilot

ALAN B'STARD: (Disregarding) Old hat.

SIR STEPHEN: Oh, do you really think so? Oh, all right. (He gets out his pen) "Armed only with his whistle, his considerable courage... and his old hat."

CUT TO:

<u>8 - INT. AFTERNOON. HOUSE OF COMMONS CHAMBER.</u>

IT IS PRETTY FULL AND SOUNDS LIKE THE ZOO AT FEEDING TIME.

THE SPEAKER: Order, order! Mr B'Stard.

ALAN, SITTING IN HIS PLACE ON THE BACK BENCH - RIGHT AT THE BACK - STANDS, PULLS HIS NOTES FROM HIS POCKET.

ALAN B'STARD: For a century and a half the British Bobby has patrolled his beat on his trusty bicycle, armed only with his sturdy truncheon, his considerable courage and his old hat.

OTHER MEMBERS CHEER OR GROAN OR LAUGH.

CUT TO:

<u>9 - INT. MOMENTS LATER. ALAN'S OFFICE IN THE HOUSE OF COMMONS.</u>

SIR STEPHEN IS ALONE IN THE OFFICE, SCRAMBLING AROUND HIS DESK LOOKING FOR SOMETHING. HIS SPEECH, PERHAPS?

SIR STEPHEN: I thought I left my notes on the desk.

CUT TO:

<u>10 - INT. MOMENTS LATER. THE CHAMBER OF THE HOUSE OF COMMONS.</u>

B'STARD IS STILL ON HIS FEET.

ALAN B'STARD: ...As Wordsworth put it, 'Who is this happy warrior, who is he that every man in arms should wish to be...' (Checks his notes) Should wish to be. But enough of poetry. (He puts his notes in his inside pocket) In my opinion arming the police is simply common sense.

LOTS OF 'HEAR, HEARS' FROM THE TORY SIDE OF THE CHAMBER.

ALAN B'STARD: And so, in the immortal words of Hill Street Blues, "let's do it to them before they do it to us".

THE TORY BENCHES ARE VERY IMPRESSED WITH ALAN. NOT SO THE LABOUR BENCHES.

THE SPEAKER: Order, order! Mr Robert Crippen.

UP STANDS A TYPICAL LABOURITE, OLD TWEED JACKET, RED TIE, BRISTLING ATTITUDE.

BOB CRIPPEN: Thank you very much, Mr Speaker. I speak against this Bill. As a man who on demonstration, picket line and sit-in, has very often been on the receiving end of the brave Bobby's sturdy truncheon. I now realise, of course, a bullet in the brain would have put less strain on the National Health Service.

ALAN STANDS TO 'HEAR, HEAR'.

BOB CRIPPEN: The very idea, Mr Speaker, that arming the sort of thug we have seen in recent disputes fills me with absolute horror. Have we already forgotten...

AS CRIPPEN GOES ON, SIR STEPHEN SUDDENLY APPEARS AND SITS ALONGSIDE ALAN AND PIERS.

SIR STEPHEN: (To Alan) I can't find my speech...

ALAN B'STARD: Really? Perhaps it's in your pocket.

Shooting the Pilot

	AS SIR STEPHEN STARTS SCRAMBLING THROUGH HIS POCKETS, ALAN REMOVES SIR STEPHEN'S SPEECH FROM HIS OWN POCKET AND PUTS IT ON SIR STEPHEN'S SEAT. ALAN POINTS IT OUT TO PIERS.
PIERS:	(To Sir Stephen) Oh, here it is. Just sitting there.
BOB CRIPPEN:	... And if this Bill becomes law this Thatcherite toy boy will have a heavily armed force at his disposal, thus taking us one step further toward a right-wing Tory police state.
	MUCH CHEERING AND CHANTING FROM THE LABOUR BENCHES.
ALAN B'STARD:	(Jumping to his feet) Exactly the point of my Bill, Mr Speaker.
PIERS:	(Jumping to his feet) Exactly the point of Alan's Bill, Mr Speaker.
THE SPEAKER:	Sir Stephen Baxter.
SIR STEPHEN:	(Rises. He has been in the House for a long, long time. He knows the ropes) I'm obliged, Mr Speaker. (Reads from his notes) For a century and a half the British Bobby has patrolled his beat on his trusty bicycle, armed only with his stout truncheon...
	THERE ARE JEERS FROM THE OPPOSITE BENCH. HAVEN'T THEY HEARD THIS ONCE BEFORE ALREADY? BUT SIR STEPHEN GOES ON...
SIR STEPHEN:	... his whistle and his considerable courage...
	LOTS OF 'SIT DOWN YOU OLD FOOL' FROM AROUND THE CHAMBER.
THE SPEAKER:	Order, order!
SIR STEPHEN:	And his old hat.

CUT TO:

11 - INT. AN HOUR LATER. ALAN'S OFFICE.

PIERS IS POURING A GLASS OF CHAMPAGNE INTO A DISTRAUGHT SIR STEPHEN'S GLASS. ALAN IS ON THE PHONE TO SARAH.

ALAN B'STARD: ... Yes, it's through darling. It's wonderful, isn't it. Tomorrow Downing Street, eh. (Laughs) Yes, it got an enormous majority.

PIERS FILLS ALAN'S GLASS WITH CHAMPAGNE. THIS IS CAUSE FOR CELEBRATION.

ALAN B'STARD: ... Well... eleven. It would have been twelve but Piers got so excited during the debate that he spent the entire division in the loo...

PIERS: Sorry Alan.

ALAN THROWS HIS CHAMPAGNE IN PIERS' FACE.

CUT TO:

12 - INT. MOMENTS LATER. ALAN AND SARAH'S BEDROOM.

SARAH LIES ON THE BED IN A SKIMPY NIGHTDRESS, HER LEGS KICKED UP AND A PHONE IN ONE HAND.

SARAH B'STARD: Oh darling I do miss you. I wish you were here with me now.

INTERCUT WITH:

13 - INT. DAY. ALAN'S OFFICE.

ALAN B'STARD: Well that's politics, fluffy bottom. By the way, have you seen Beatrice Protheroe?

14 - INT. ALAN AND SARAH'S BEDROOM.

SARAH B'STARD: No, why?

15 - INT. ALAN'S OFFICE.

ALAN B'STARD: Well, she doesn't seem to be in London at the moment and I need her to organise saturation media coverage for my magnificent victory.

16 - INT. ALAN AND SARAH'S BEDROOM.

SARAH B'STARD: Oh, well if I see her I'll tell her. Listen, must dash, bath's running.

MIX TO:

17 - INT. ALAN'S OFFICE.

ALAN B'STARD: Oh, all right darling. (Insincere) Yearn for you... longingly.

18 - INT. ALAN AND SARAH'S BEDROOM.

SARAH B'STARD: Darling that's lovely. I'm your little rabbit...

19 - INT. ALAN'S OFFICE.

ALAN B'STARD: And I'm a rabbit too. (Crinkles his nose)

ALAN HANGS UP. PIERS AND SIR STEPHEN ARE STARING AT HIM.

ALAN B'STARD: Right, I'm off down Stringfellow's to commit adultery.

PIERS: Can I come, Alan?

ALAN B'STARD: I've no idea, Piers.

ALAN EXITS FOR SOME FUN. POOR OLD PIERS STANDS AND LOOKS ON, WONDERING WHAT HE IS MISSING.

CUT TO:

20 - MOMENTS LATER. ALAN AND SARAH'S BEDROOM.

SARAH GETS BETWEEN THE SILK SHEETS, JUST AS BEATRICE PROTHEROE COMES FROM THE EN SUITE, BRUSHING HER HAIR.

BEATRICE: Who was that on the telephone?

SARAH B'STARD: Alan. His Bill's through. He wants you to arrange saturation media coverage. The conceited little prat.

BEATRICE: Will it keep until morning?

SARAH B'STARD: That will. (She pulls back the bed covers) I won't.

BEATRICE CLIMBS INTO BED WITH SARAH, WHO TURNS OUT THE LIGHT.

END OF PART ONE.

PART TWO.

20 - EXT. DAY. HALTEMPRICE CATHDRAL.

A SUNNY MORNING. WE SEE THE EXTERIOR OF THIS MAGNIFICENT PLACE OF WORSHIP.

BISHOP: (V.O.) I believe that this country will not be better placed...

MIX TO:

21 - INT. MOMENTS LATER. HALTEMPRICE CATHEDRAL.

WE MIX INTO THE BISHOP OF HALTEMPRICE, IN HIS PULPIT DELIVERING HIS SERMON.

BISHOP: ... when every Bobby on the beat is, to use, I believe, a contemporary expression, tooled-up.

WE SEE ALAN AND SARAH SITTING IN THE FRONT PEW. SITTING NEXT TO ALAN IS SIR MALACHI.

BISHOP: If Mr B'Stard passes through the Commons with his Bill. But I pledge myself to muster opposition to this Bill in the Lords, where with God's help we will throw this foul Bill out. Let us pray.

ALAN CHECKS HIS WATCH. HE HASN'T TIME FOR ALL THIS RELIGIOUS MUMBO-JUMBO. HE IS NUDGED BY SARAH AND THE PAIR OF THEM FALL TO THEIR KNEES, AS DOES SIR MALACHI.

ALAN B'STARD: Stupid old duffer ought to be put out to grass.

SARAH B'STARD: I thought that's why he was in the House of Lords.

ALAN B'STARD: This isn't a laughing matter, Sarah. You heard what he said, he's going to vote against my Bill. What if it doesn't get through?

SARAH B'STARD: Actually darling, I won't be that upset if your stupid Bill doesn't get through. I've been thinking about it. I don't want some butch traffic warden with a sixshooter bearing down on me every time I double park outside Harrods.

ALAN B'STARD: Oh how very loyal! (Looks up at the pulpit) Amen. (Angrily, to Sarah) I don't know why I married you...

SARAH B'STARD: You married me, my darling, because you're nouveau riche, and I can trace my family tree back to Edward the Second... Amen.

ALAN B'STARD: Amen.

SARAH B'STARD: And my father's chairman of the local Conservative Association, and he has your parliamentary seat in his gift.

ALAN B'STARD: Yes, well it was a rhetorical question, wasn't it. And anyway, Edward the Second was a poof.

WE HEAR SIR MALACHI'S PERSONAL RADIO CRACKLE. HE ANSWERS IT.

SIR MALACHI: I'm on my way. (To B'Stard) Suspected witchcraft in Pontefract.

ALAN B'STARD: But what about my dossier?

SIR MALACHI: The Bill's not law yet. You heard the Bishop. (Shouts up at the pulpit) There's God's work to be done outside this place! (He walks out the cathedral)

ALAN B'STARD: (Still on his knees, he looks to the heavens) Please God, don't let the Bishop knacker my Bill.

THERE ARE AMENS ALL THROUGH THE CATHEDRAL.

ALAN B'STARD: Amen.

WE MIX INTO:

22 - MONTAGE

WE SEE A SPINNING SELECTION OF FRONT PAGES OF NATIONAL DAILY PAPERS.

THE DAILY MAIL HEADLINE READS "GUN LAW SHOOTS THROUGH LORDS".

THE SUN READS "HANDS UP".

THEN THERE'S THE GUARDIAN, WHOSE HEADLINE READS "HUNTIN', FISHIN' AND ESPECIALLY SHOOTING."

THE STAR'S BANNER HEADLINE IS "LORDS GIVE LICENCE TO BANG".

CUT TO:

23 - EXT. AFTERNOON. A DERELICT RAILWAY SIDINGS.

ALAN'S BENTLEY GLIDES THROUGH THIS OVERGROWN WASTELAND. IT STOPS. ALAN GETS OUT, AND WALKS ACROSS ABANDONED TRACKS TOWARDS A BROKEN DOWN GOODS WAGON.

ALAN B'STARD: Hello. Hello?

ALAN BANGS ON THE DOOR, NO REPLY. HE WALKS AROUND THE FRONT.

ALAN B'STARD: (Tentatively) Hello?

HE WALKS AROUND THE OTHER SIDE AND SEES AN OPEN DOOR. HE SMIRKS DANGEROUSLY, CLIMBS INSIDE, AND BANGS VICIOUSLY ON A LOCKED INTERIOR DOOR.

ALAN B'STARD: All right Norman, we know you're in there.

MIX TO:

24 - INT. CONTINUOUS. INSIDE THE GOODS WAGON.

AN EFFEMINATE LOOKING MAN IS URGENTLY BURNING A STACK OF FILES.

ALAN B'STARD: (V.O.) The game's up. We've got the full scam on the Chernobyl timeshare scandal.

ALAN PUSHES THE DOOR OPEN TO CONFRONT A TERRIFIED NORMAN BORMANN.

ALAN B'STARD: April Fool. (Laughs) What a ghastly place you got here, Norman.

IT REALLY IS GHASTLY. EVERYTHING SEEMS TO BE CRACKING AND PEELING AND BROKEN.

NORMAN POURS LIGHTER FLUID ON HIS BONFIRE, WHICH FLARES UP.

ALAN B'STARD: It's a bit of a comedown for my business consultant, isn't it? What happened to the plush offices in Cavendish Square?

NORMAN: They finally caught up with me. Inland Revenue. The VAT Gestapo. The Fraud Squad. A man makes fifty or sixty accounting errors, they call him a thief.

ALAN B'STARD: Well does it affect me?

NORMAN: No.

ALAN B'STARD: It's not important then, is it Norman. Right, that's enough small talk. What am I doing here?

ALAN GRABS THE HANDKERCHIEF IN NORMAN'S TOP POCKET TO WIPE THE FILTHY CHAIR CLEAN SO HE CAN SIT DOWN. AS HE TURNS BACK TO FACE NORMAN, HE PULLS A GUN ON ALAN. ALAN LOOKS TERRIFIED.

NORMAN: I have found you... as asked... a supplier of perfect copies of Smith and Wesson, point 38,

	standard seven-shot police revolvers. (He hands Alan the gun)
ALAN B'STARD:	(Relieved) Splendid. Quanto mucho, as we are all saying in Westminster these days since the visit of King Juan Carlos.
NORMAN:	As many as you like for ten pounds a piece.
ALAN B'STARD:	(Spinning the gun on his finger) They're a little light, aren't they Norman?
NORMAN:	That's because they're made out of recycled frying pans. Probably blow up if fired.
ALAN B'STARD:	Oh. Well, not to worry, eh. As I was saying the other day in the House of Commons, they're not for firing, they're for deterring. So, if you can give me the name and address of the supplier, Norman…
NORMAN:	Ah ha! Now that information will cost you.
ALAN B'STARD:	(Suspicious) How much?
NORMAN:	An Archer.
ALAN B'STARD:	A whole Jeffrey! That's two thousand pounds!
NORMAN:	(Sweating) I need the money, Alan, and you'll make fifty times that selling these guns to the police.
ALAN B'STARD:	All right.
	ALAN TAKES A BUNDLE OF READIES FROM HIS JACKET POCKET AND RELUCTANTLY HANDS THEM OVER TO NORMAN, WHO GRABS THEM. BUT ALAN HOLDS ONTO THE NOTES.
ALAN B'STARD:	Ah ah!
	NORMAN HANDS OVER THE INFORMATION. ALAN READS IT.

The New Statesman

ALAN B'STARD: Mohammed Iqbal Shah, International Armaments Limited.

NORMAN IS BUSY CHECKING THE NOTES. HE KNOWS ALAN'S LITTLE GAMES.

ALAN B'STARD: Is this a Third World set-up?

NORMAN: Yeah, they're in Accrington.

ALAN GETS UP TO LEAVE THIS FLEAPIT.

ALAN B'STARD: Well done, Norman. Good luck. (Pauses) Just a minute. What are you doing with all that money? You fleeing the country?

NORMAN: No. That's what they expect me to do. No, I've decided to kill myself off...

ALAN B'STARD: Oh. Well, you don't need two grand to do that. (Goes to grab his money back) Jump off something...

NORMAN: (Pulls the money away from Alan) No, I'm not committing suicide. No, Norman Bormann is simply going to cease to exist.

ALAN B'STARD: How do you mean... exactly?

NORMAN: I'm going to become a... woman.

ALAN B'STARD: (Thinks about this for a moment) Oh...

CUT TO:

25 - EXT. NIGHT. REMOTE PUB.

A VERY REMOTE PUB STANDING ALONE ON THE MOORS. ALAN'S BENTLEY PULLS UP OUTSIDE, BEHIND A LARGE BLACK DAIMLER. WE PAN UP TO THE PUB SIGN. IT IS CALLED 'THE HANGMAN'S KNOT INN', WITH APPROPRIATE ILLUSTRATION.

MIX TO:

26 - INT. NIGHT. INSIDE THIS COSY COUNTRY PUB.

THE BARMAN IS EXCITEDLY READING THE LOCAL PAPER. THE BAR IS CROWDED. IN SWAGGERS ALAN.

ALAN B'STARD: Good evening Sidney.

SIDNEY BLISS: (Puts his newspaper down and is very pleased to see Alan) Oh good evening, sir. A great day for you, sir. You've struck a blow for law and order.

ALAN B'STARD: Yes, I have had a pretty good day, Sidney. How about yourself?

SIDNEY BLISS: Oh me, sir, I haven't had a good day since they abolished hanging. (Urgently) You did promise to bring back the rope.

ALAN B'STARD: Yes, I know Sidney. But it's a long haul to the short drop.

SIDNEY BLISS: Well, I haven't lost my knack, sir. (Sidney pulls a pint as if pulling the lever that opens the trap door.) There we are, sir. On the house.

ALAN B'STARD: Thank you Sidney, but if it's all the same I'd rather have a large brandy... on the house.

SIDNEY GOES TO POUR THIS LARGE BRANDY. ALAN PLAYS WITH A NOOSE THAT HANGS OVER THE BAR.

ALAN B'STARD: The police won't dare breathalyse me tonight. Where's Sir Malachi? Is he in tonight? What's he drinking?

SIDNEY BLISS: Dandelion and Burdock, sir, and a pint of bitter for his friend.

ALAN B'STARD: His friend? He's supposed to be alone.

ALAN TAKES THE PINT OF BITTER OVER TO THE SNUG, IN WHICH SITS SIR MALACHI, IN FULL UNIFORM, TALKING TO AN EMPTY CHAIR.

SIR MALACHI: Ah, there's not much doubt about this one, is there? Really? Charlton to win at Liverpool? No, no, if you say so.

ALAN STANDS AND WATCHES SIR MALACHI APPARENTLY TALKING TO HIMSELF. THEN GENTLY WALKS INTO THE SNUG.

ALAN B'STARD: Evening Chief Constable.

SIR MALACHI: Ah, B'Stard. Here's to you. You struck a blow for justice and Jesus today...

ALAN IS JUST ABOUT TO SIT IN THE EMPTY CHAIR.

SIR MALACHI: (Sharply) Don't sit there! It's somebody's seat.

SIR MALACHI POINTS TO THE OTHER EMPTY CHAIR. ALAN SITS.

ALAN B'STARD: Did you bring it with you?

SIR MALACHI: Bring what?

ALAN B'STARD: My dossier...

SIR MALACHI: Oh that. (He bends down for his briefcase) Oh, by the way, what do you think of this...

HE PULLS A FRIGHTENING LOOKING COLT 45 FRONTIERSMAN FROM HIS CASE.

ALAN B'STARD: Very pretty.

SIR MALACHI: I wasn't talking to you. (He turns to the empty chair) It's a Colt 45 Frontiersman. It'd blow the balls off one of those flying pickets at fifty yards, eh?

ALAN LOOKS IN AMAZEMENT AT SIR MALACHI TALKING TO THE EMPTY CHAIR. IS HE MAD? ALAN IS A LITTLE FRIGHTENED.

Shooting the Pilot

SIR MALACHI: (Listening to the empty chair's reply) Yes, they certainly would be airborne. (Pointing to the chair and sharing the joke with B'Stard) Airborne.

SIR MALACHI POINT THIS LARGE WEAPON AT ALAN.

ALAN B'STARD: Yes, isn't it pretty. Shall we put it back in its little house now. Bye bye.

SIR MALACHI PUTS THIS GUN BACK INTO HIS LEATHER BRIEFCASE.

ALAN B'STARD: (Urgently) Listen, you promised me that I could have that dossier the moment...

SIR MALACHI: Oh you mean the dossier that proves you were responsible for that tragic car crash on the eve of the general election...

ALAN B'STARD: Shhhhh!

SIR MALACHI: It's all right, He knows. Mmm? (He "listens" to the empty chair) What? Yes, yes... (To Alan) No, the Almighty thinks we would be very silly not to keep this very useful hold over you while there's still so much of His work to be done.

ALAN REALISES HE'S DEALING WITH A MADMAN. AS POLITELY AS HE POSSIBLY CAN, HE TURNS TO THE EMPTY CHAIR.

ALAN B'STARD: Er... Almighty... Perhaps if I built you a church...?

SIR MALACHI: The Lord of Hosts doesn't need any more churches, he needs you to work for him in Parliament. For example, how about a Bill to criminalise atheism?

ALAN B'STARD: Yes. It's a good idea. It's a great idea. But you've both got to realise that the chances against a backbencher getting a Bill through parliament are a thousand to one. I was very, very lucky last

	time to do so well in the ballot for a Private Members Bill.
SIR MALACHI:	(Turning to empty chair) He thinks it was luck.
ALAN B'STARD:	(Humouring Sir Malachi) You mean it was a miracle? In that case who am I to cavil or demur?
SIR MALACHI:	Now that's the spirit, B'Stard. Have a pork scratching sayeth the Lord.
ALAN B'STARD:	(Takes one) Thank you Lord. (To Sir Malachi) There may be one... small... problem though.
SIR MALACHI:	Oh, what's that?
ALAN B'STARD:	Well, even with heavenly help, Bills take time to get through parliament. We would be giving the forces of darkness time to build up their strength.
SIR MALACHI:	You mean... Lucifer?
ALAN B'STARD:	No, I mean the Bishop of Haltemprice.
SIR MALACHI:	Oh that old fool. He doesn't bother us (Turning to the empty chair) does he?
ALAN B'STARD:	Well he should do. Don't you remember his sermon? I respect atheists, idolaters, and... cannibals, he said. And he opposed the gun law, which we all know was God's will. And, last Christmas, while you were away on pilgrimage duty, he preached that not only was Mary not a virgin, she was also technically a surrogate mother.
SIR MALACHI:	(Fuming) He never did!
ALAN B'STARD:	Cross my heart. In fact, not only is the Bishop of Haltemprice almost certainly an unbeliever, I suspect he is the secret leader of all who oppose the will of God.

Shooting the Pilot

SIR MALACHI: You don't mean...

ALAN B'STARD: (Whispers) The anti-Christ.

SIR MALACHI: Yes, of course. It all adds up. (Turns to the empty chair) What do you think? (Turns back to Alan) The Almighty says you're right (Back to chair) Yes.

SIR MALACHI OPENS HIS CASE. ALAN PUTS HIS HANDS UP, FEARING HE'S ABOUT TO BE SHOT. BUT SIR MALACHI GIVES HIM A FOLDER.

SIR MALACHI: Your dossier. He says it's the least we can do. Right, I'm on my way. Thy will be done.

SIR MALACHI STRIDES THROUGH THE PUB AND EXITS. ALAN GETS OUT HIS MOBILE PHONE AND CALLS...

ALAN B'STARD: Can I speak to deputy Chief Constable Ginsburg, please.

CUT TO:

27 - EXT. LATER. HALTEMPRICE CATHEDRAL.

SIR MALACHI'S DAIMLER PULLS UP OUTSIDE THE MAIN DOOR TO THE CATHEDRAL. HE GETS OUT OF HIS CAR AS A CLAP OF THUNDER IS HEARD. SIR MALACHI GIVES THE HEAVENS A NOD AND THEN GOES INSIDE.

MIX TO:

28 - INT. CONTINUOUS. HALTEMPRICE CATHEDRAL.

THE DOORS OPEN, LETTING IN SHAFTS OF LIGHT. IN COMES SIR MALACHI.

SIR MALACHI: Get thee behind me, Bishop! The game's up!

SIR MALACHI SLOWLY MARCHES UP THE LONG AISLE. HE PASSES THE CHOIR UNTIL HE REACHES THE DOZING BISHOP, IN HIS GRAND THRONE. SUDDENLY

	THE BISHOP LOOKS UP. SIR MALACHI IS ALMOST IN THE BISHOP'S FACE.
BISHOP:	Sir Malachi. How agreeable.
SIR MALACHI:	Come on Beelzebub. (He pushes his Colt 45 into the Bishop's face) Make my day!
	BEFORE HE CAN SHOOT THE BISHOP, THE CHORISTERS SUDDENLY PUT ON POLICEMEN'S HELMETS AND OVERWHELM SIR MALACHI. THEY DRAG HIM AWAY. IN THE MELEE SIR MALACHI'S GUN GOES OFF AND BRINGS DOWN A PLASTER ANGEL.
	OUT OF THE SHADOWS STEPS DEPUTY CHIEF CONSTABLE GINSBURG, A VERY JEWISH CHAP.
D.C.C. GINSBURG:	He should never have passed his probationary period, he was hearing voices ten years before the introduction of personal radios. You did the Force a good turn, sir, grassing on that meshugener.
	ALAN APPEARS OUT OF SOME OTHER SHADOWS.
ALAN B'STARD:	I was only doing my public duty... Chief Constable Ginsburg.
D.C.C. GINSBURG:	(Likes the sound of that) Chief Constable. That's right. Now I'm the Ganze macher. So, if there's any little favour I could do for you...
ALAN B'STARD:	Well... Has your force placed an order for handguns yet? Because I can get them for you, you know, wholesale.
	<u>CUT TO:</u>
	<u>29 – INT. DAY. ALAN'S BENTLEY/EXT. COUNTRY ROADS</u>
	ALAN DRIVES ALONG HAPPILY. DIRE STRAITS' 'MONEY FOR NOTHING' PLAYS ON THE CASSETTE DECK.

ON THE PASSENGER SEAT IS A NEWSPAPER WITH THE HEADLINE: "SIR MALACHI JELLICOE ENTERS MONASTERY".

ALAN PUTS HIS FOOT DOWN, SPEEDING THROUGH THE B-ROADS. HE ADMIRES HIMSELF IN THE REAR VIEW MIRROR.

THE BENTLEY SPEEDS PAST A POLICE TRAFFIC CAR.

CUT TO:

30 - INT. DAY. INSIDE THE TRAFFIC CAR.

TWO UNIFORMED TRAFFIC POLICEMEN WATCH THE BENTLEY WHIZZ PAST THEM.

POLICEMAN ONE: Blimey, who's that? Dennis Waterman? What's it say on the radar?

POLICEMAN TWO: Made in Taiwan.

POLICEMAN ONE: How fast?

POLICEMAN TWO: Let's say one hundred and ten.

POLICEMAN ONE: Let's get him, rich sod!

THE COPS PUT ON THEIR CAPS, TURN ON THEIR BLUE LIGHTS AND BEGIN THE CHASE, BUT THEY ARE NEVER GOING TO CATCH THE BENTLEY. ALAN PICKS UP HIS CAR PHONE...

31 - INT. MOMENTS LATER. ALAN'S BENTLEY

ALAN B'STARD: ... So Hertfordshire police have bought five hundred guns. Fantastic! Well done, Norman. Or is it Norma?

ALAN CAN SEE IN HIS REAR VIEW MIRROR THAT THE POLICE ARE GETTING CLOSER. THEY FLASH THEIR HEADLIGHTS BUT ALAN IGNORES THEM.

MIX TO:

32 – EXT. MOMENTS LATER. A COUNTRY VILLAGE.

BOTH CARS TAKE A CORNER AT EXTREMELY HIGH SPEED... AND STILL THE POLICE CAN'T CATCH ALAN.

MIX TO:

33 – INT. DAY. INSIDE THE POLICE CAR.

POLICEMAN ONE: He's not slowing down!

POLICEMAN TWO: (Taking his gun out) Shall I have a pop at his tyres, like they do on the telly?

POLICEMAN ONE: Yeah, go for it.

CUT TO:

34 – EXT. DAY. OUTSIDE THE POLICE CAR.

TRAFFIC POLICEMAN PUTS HIS ARM OUT OF THE WINDOW TO SHOOT OUT ALAN'S TYRES. BUT WHEN HE FIRES THE GUN EXPLODES IN HIS HAND. THE DRIVER LOSES CONTROL AND THE POLICE CAR CRASHES.

MIX TO:

35 – INT. DAY. INSIDE ALAN'S BENTLEY.

ALAN GRINS IN DELIGHT. OBVIOUSLY THE GUN WAS MADE OF RECYCLED FRYING PANS, AND ALAN HAS WON THE DAY.

THE END.

4
Birds of a Feather

IN EARLY 1989 WE HELPED invent the bright and brassy species that became known as Essex Girls. It was an accident, honest. All we were trying to do was find somewhere for Tracey Stubbs to live.

Let us try to recall the moment. Yes, it was the previous Christmas we laid the egg that hatched out into *Birds of a Feather*, one of the biggest comedy hits of the Nineties. Like many successful TV shows, the set-up was so simple: two working-class sisters have to cope when their bank-robbing husbands get sent to prison.

The moment we had the idea, we knew Linda Robson and Pauline Quirke had to play the sisters – let's call them Sharon and Tracey, because we did. Linda and Pauline had known each other since primary school and their rapport on and off screen was instinctive. We'd worked with them on *Shine On Harvey Moon*, where they had played lifelong friends. We knew their strengths and how to tailor their dialogue. In short, they were perfect.

We took Linda and Pauline out for a beer and told them about our new idea. We explained how one of the sisters lives in a sort of *Dynasty*-style mansion, somewhere in Essex, while the other sister inhabits a two-bedroom council flat, on the eighteenth floor, where the lifts are always out of order. Pauline Quirke turned to us and said, "I wonder which one I'm going to play?"

Now we had to construct the pilot script and lay foundations deep enough to support a high-rise series. We never imagined there would be well over a hundred episodes, although Maurice did say, "This is going to be a massive hit," because when we sat down in front of that blank computer screen, the characters started speaking to us, and all we had to do was write down what they said.

One of the first secrets Sharon and Tracey told us was that neither of them knew their husbands were career criminals. We agreed. It would be almost impossible to retain audience sympathy for women who wave their husbands off to work knowing they've got sawn-off shotguns in their sports bags. Since the sisters had no notion they're gangsters' molls, they are aghast when their husbands are arrested, tried and sentenced to twelve years' imprisonment. (We gave them very long sentences just in case *Birds* became a very long-running series.) In simple terms, that was the first chunk of the pilot story taken care of.

Then what happens? Simple. Sharon and Tracey realise that their lives can be so much better without their controlling worse halves telling them what to do and how to do it. Their men may be locked up, but the girls are free to let their hair down and flash their husbands' cash. There's a twist of course: the jealous spouses hire another villain to keep an eye on the girls and make sure they behave themselves.

We were pleased with our efforts. We had our pilot, setting up a series featuring two sparky young women with a zest for life, trying to out-manoeuvre their minder every week. Our sense of well-being lasted for a whole weekend. Then clouds of doubt started to block out the sunshine of enthusiasm. Did our idea have the legs to sustain a series? What prevented each episode from being more or less the same as the one before? Did we have enough to drive the series forward, week after week?

Light dawned and pennies dropped. We'd been talking about Sharon and Tracey as if they were a single composite character rather than two distinct personalities. We were using that forbidden four-letter word, "they". It's a beginner's error and we shouldn't have made it. In drama, as in real life, no two people are ever in complete accord. Characters have to disagree, bicker, argue, fight. Drama demands conflict to fuel its engine, and comedy is simply another form of drama, one which some people – comedy writers – say is by far the hardest to write.

We didn't study creative writing at university, primarily because such courses hadn't been invented, but we did study, and love, the classic comedies we grew up with. Not for us *On The Buses*, set in a garage full of leering beta males, or *Mind Your Language*, which featured an English classroom full of "funny foreigners". We wanted to write comedies like *Steptoe and Son*, one of the enduring classics of the genre.

The setting of *Steptoe* was a brilliantly reproduced scrapyard full of amusing junk, but what drove the series was the conflict between the two protagonists. Harold, the younger Steptoe, wants to better himself but he hasn't the guts to break away from his wily father Albert. Albert in his turn is so terrified of abandonment he'll do anything to manipulate Harold into staying. The pilot episode is as tragic as it's funny, and influenced a generation of writers, including us.

We returned to first principles. Two sisters are married to career criminals who get sent to prison. How do they react? We agreed that if one wife is devastated, the other must be relieved, even joyous. This we illustrated in the courtroom scene where Darryl and Chris have just been sentenced to twelve years. As the two men are led away…

TRACEY: I love you, Darryl!

DARRYL: Wait for me Tracey!

CHRIS: Wait for me an' all Sharon!

SHARON: What? You must be bloody joking! I've waited long enough!

Those four lines were among the first we wrote and we kept them in mind as we constructed the backstories. We decided that Tracey and Darryl had fallen in love at school and married very young. Darryl became a successful building contractor and they had a son, Garth, on whom they dote. When we first meet them, they've just moved into their luxurious suburban palace, complete with indoor heated swimming pool. We can see Darryl spoils Tracey something rotten, and that Tracey knows Darryl's the best thing that ever happened to her.

As we have implied, Sharon wasn't so lucky. At school she was brighter than Tracey, but insolent as well as indolent. A good-time girl, she ended up with Chris, a good-time guy who seemed like fun until Sharon found out he was even lazier than she was. Now she's lumbered with a semi-employed minicab driver who wastes all his money, and most of hers, betting on three-legged horses. While Tracey revels in suburban splendour, Sharon founders on the upper floors of a sleazy council high-rise where the lift always stinks of urine.

We knew that at the end of the pilot Sharon moves in with Tracey; where might that be? We always like to specify real locations for our shows, places we know well, that add their own character and texture. How about the Stockbroker Belt? Then a police detective friend happened to remark that more houses were bought for cash in Chigwell, Essex, than anywhere else in the country. He asked us why we thought that was.

"Because bank robbers don't need mortgages?" we ventured.

He tapped the side of his nose conspiratorially.

We were intrigued, so we took a drive out east and liked what we saw: a leafy, affluent town with some very expensive cars parked outside some very expensive shops being visited by some very expensive-looking women. It seemed like the ideal place for a successful bank robber to invest his undeclared income. Subsequently we were berated by sundry Chigwellians, some who accused us of depressing house prices, and some who accused us of inflating them.

Now we'd grounded our sisters in their respective worlds, it was easy to work out the rest of the plot. The husbands get arrested; Tracey's world falls apart; Sharon inveigles herself into her sister's house, ostensibly to take care of her, but really because she envies Tracey's lifestyle.

The last lines of the pilot were also amongst the earliest we jotted down.

Sharon offers to move in…

TRACEY: You don't want to stay with me, you got your own life to lead, ain't you?

SHARON: True, but I'd rather lead yours.

So far, so good. But as we knew the fortnightly prison visit would be the highlight of Tracey's existence (and the bane of Sharon's), we wanted to know more of the real lives of prisoners' wives, to be able to give *Birds of a Feather* a documentary-like edge. We consulted Tony Hoare, a brilliant writer who had worked on *The Sweeney*, one of TV's grittiest crime series. (Scriptwriting wasn't Tony's first choice of career; previously he'd been an armed robber, but during a long stretch in prison he discovered he was better at creative writing than at handbrake turns. He sent a speculative script to the producers of the long-running cop show *Softly Softly*. They liked it enough to invite him in for a meeting. Unfortunately, he couldn't get the day off.)

Tony introduced us to his ex-wife, Pauline, who had set up a prisoners' wives charity while Tony was doing time. She was generous with her advice, detailing the indignities loaded onto prisoners' wives. We heard how the police would keep "popping round" to try to catch the girls living off the proceeds of crime. We learned how mentally and physically exhausting it is just to get to see your man in prison, and how prisoners are suspicious of any change in the outside world, so that if Tracey alters her hairstyle, Darryl will instantly assume she's screwing around.

We now had some meaty source material, but there was a risk that any broadcaster we offered the show to might say, "But is it funny?" In truth, they always ask this question (see next chapter). We needed another character, a third bird, who could lighten the tone when required. We decided on a next-door neighbour who could enter "carrying the sub-plot", as one of our writing team so succinctly put it. Our neighbour needed to come from a very different background to Sharon and Tracey, and be preloaded with attitudes, quirks and a bucketload of comedy potential. As Chigwell has a significant Jewish population, we figured that Tracey's neighbours would be Jewish too, and so was born Dorien Green and her seldom-seen, oft-cuckolded, workaholic husband Marcus.

Dorien is the perfect foil for Tracey's naivety and Sharon's slobbishness. She's an educated, nosy, oversexed, spoilt, childless woman ("I had to choose between children and white fitted carpets. I chose carpets"), who somehow becomes the sisters' best friend. But in our pilot she crashes into their lives and stampedes Tracey into agreeing to host a sex aids party. Tracey is aghast, Sharon is tickled, and it's clear that Dorien is going to broaden their horizons in all sorts of unimagined ways.

We decided that Lesley Joseph, whom we'd recently seen and enjoyed in the theatre, had the sass and the hair for the part. We gave her the nails. Now we had a balanced trio of characters, all female. We knew how they would behave, what they would say and how they would say it. What was more, we had created three classic Essex Girl types and hadn't even noticed.

Once the show reached its audience people began asking if we found writing for women a challenge. We didn't. We'd grown up among strong women, and half the people we knew were women. It still seems strange to us that male writers are expected to be more comfortable writing about monsters and aliens and figures drawn from the depths of history than they are writing about people like their mothers, sisters and wives.

As we say in the introduction, scripts can change a lot between the page and the studio floor, but the pilot script of *Birds of a Feather* in this book found its way almost unchanged onto the screen and, dare we say, into millions of hearts. We wanted to create something that was honest as well as funny, and with the help of a brilliant cast and a terrific production team we succeeded.

"BIRDS OF A FEATHER"

by Laurence Marks & Maurice Gran

EPISODE ONE: "NICKED!"

May 1988

1. EXT. CAMELOT HOUSE. DAY:

ONE OF THOSE SYSTEMS-BUILT MID-60s TOWER BLOCKS THAT EVERYONE NOW ADMITS WERE A MISTAKE, BUT PEOPLE STILL HAVE TO LIVE IN THEM. THE LIFTS NEVER WORK BECAUSE THE URINE DEPOSITED THEREIN BY KIDS AND DRUNKS – AND SOMETIMES BY DRUNKEN KIDS – HAS CORRODED THE ELECTRIC CIRCUITS. WE PAN UP THE SIDE OF THE BUILDING UNTIL WE REACH THE 9th FLOOR. WE ZOOM IN ON THE OPEN WALKWAY, THEN PAN ALONG TO SEE THE LIFT DOORS WITH THE "OUT OF ORDER" SIGN. ALONGSIDE THE LIFT IS THE STONE STAIRWELL.

TOILING UP THE STAIRS, PANTING AND BLOWING, COMES SHARON THEODOPOULOPODOUS, IN A CHEAP PINK VELOUR TRACKSUIT, DRAGGING A LARGE SHOPPING TROLLEY FULL OF WASHING. SHE MAKES IT TO THE TOP OF THE STAIRS, AND LEANS PANTING AGAINST A WALL FOR SEVERAL SECONDS. A YOUNG MUM – LET'S CALL HER LISA – WITH PEROXIDE HAIR, MINI SKIRT, BARE LEGS, WHITE STILLETOES, AND WITH THREE KIDS SCRAPPING ROUND HER, IS COMING TOWARDS SHARON.

LISA: Still out of order is it?

SHARON: Do you need to ask? Bloody flats! I'd go on rent strike if we weren't seven months in arrears!

LISA: Is that all? (LAUGHS AND HEADS OFF DOWN THE STAIRS)

Birds of a Feather

SHARON SETS OFF DOWN THE WALKWAY TO HER FRONT DOOR, AND LETS HERSELF IN.

2. INT. SHARON'S LIVING ROOM. DAY:

WE FADE UP ON A WEDDING PHOTOGRAPH OF SHARON AND HER HUSBAND, CHRIS. SHE WEARS WHITE, HE WEARS A LOUNGE SUIT COVERED IN BANK NOTES WHICH HAVE BEEN PINNED TO HIM (A GREEK TRADITION). WE THEN PULL BACK TO REVEAL A NASTY ROOM, WITH A NASTY SWIRLY CARPET, A NASTY CHEAP THREE-PIECE SUITE IN PALE TAN PVC LEATHERETTE, CONTAINING FOAM WHICH, IF IGNITED, WILL ASPHYXIATE THE VICTIM FAR QUICKER THAN THE GAS CHAMBER AT PARCHMAN STATE PRISON, MISSISSIPPI. THERE'S A WALL-MOUNTED ELECTRIC HEATER, A CLASSIC FEATURE OF THE EARLY 1960s COUNCIL FLAT, AND SOME VERY DODGY WALLPAPER. THERE'S A MIDI-SOUND SYSTEM WITH THE RADIO ON, TUNED TO CYPRIOT PIRATE RADIO STATION. THERE'S A BIG TV AND A VIDEO - THE TV IS ON TOO, OF COURSE. THERE'S ALSO A WELL STOCKED COCKTAIL CABINET OF 1950s VINTAGE. LYING ON ONE OF THE CHAIRS OF THE AFOREMENTIONED THREE PIECE SUITE, IS CHRIS THEODOPOULOPODOUS, SHARON'S HUSBAND.

CHRIS WEARS CHINOS, A BLACK SLEEVELESS MICHAEL JACKSON "BAD" TEE-SHIRT, A HEAVY GOLD CHAIN AND CRUCIFIX, AND A SMALLER CRUCIFIX DANGLES FROM ONE EAR. CHRIS IS WATCHING A DAYTIME GAME SHOW, WHILE SINGING ALONG WITH THE RADIO, SMOKING A ROTHMAN'S, EATING A BACON SANDWICH AND DRINKING A MUG OF NESCAFE. SHARON STAGGERS IN WITH THE SHOPPING TROLLEY. SHE'S STILL OUT OF BREATH.

SHARON: I see you tidied up then?

CHRIS: I been waiting for my shirt. (SHARON TIPS THE CONTENTS OF THE WASHING ON TO THE SOFA. CHRIS EXTRACTS A CREASED DAMP SHIRT AND PUTS IT ON)

Shooting the Pilot

                You took your time, didn't you? (HE PICKS UP HIS WALLET FROM THE COFFEE TABLE AND POCKETS IT)

SHARON: I could hardly drag myself away, it was so romantic watching your jeans wrapping themselves around my knickers. Took me right back to when a quick tumble meant more than twenty pee's worth of hot air!

CHRIS: Hot air? You can talk about hot air! Next time Richard Branson feels like crossing the Atlantic in that giant Virgin Johnny of his, he can come round here and you can talk him up. Now, you want a lift round your sister's or you gonna stay here nagging the wallpaper off the wall?

SHARON: Hang on, I'll just do me face.

CHRIS: I can't wait that long, my tax disc expires in October. Come on...

        CHRIS PICKS UP HER HANDBAG AND THROWS IT TO HER. SHE CATCHES IT, AND AUTOMATICALLY TAKES OUT HER PURSE AND CHECKS ITS CONTENTS.

SHARON: There was thirty quid in here when I went to the launderette!

CHRIS: No!? Some thieving Turk must have had it away while you was adding the fabric conditioner.

SHARON: I didn't take my purse up the launderette, you lying merchant! (TRIES TO GET AT HIS WALLET AND HE PUSHES HER OFF) That's my shopping money! I worked bleedin' hard for that, you thieving ponce! (PUNCHES HIM) Do you know how many customers I had to short change to scrape that thirty quid together? Going to put it on one of your three-legged horses, were you?!

CHRIS: (PUSHES HER AWAY AND SHE SUBSIDES ONTO THE SOFA) What I do with my money is down to me!

SHARON:	Your money?! You parasite! You're supposed to be the bread winner, instead you nick the crumbs off my plate! What sort of husband are you?
CHRIS:	Don't start all that, at least I didn't marry you under false pretences.
SHARON:	Meaning what?
CHRIS:	You know...
SHARON:	Say it.
CHRIS:	What's the point?!
SHARON:	Say it!
CHRIS:	All right. If I'd known you couldn't have kids...
SHARON:	You bastard!!
CHRIS:	You told me to say it! You're bloody mental! (STORMS OUT OF THE ROOM)
SHARON:	What about my lift?! (SHE HURRIES AFTER HIM)

3. EXT. CAMELOT HOUSE. DAY:

CHRIS AND SHARON, THE LATTER WELL OUT OF BREATH, COME OUT OF THE BLOCK. CHRIS CROSSES TO A PINK CAPRI WITH LEOPARDSKIN UPHOLSTERY AND LOTS OF AERIALS AND HEADLAMPS. HE UNLOCKS IT WITH PRIDE.

SHARON:	What happened to the B.M.W?
CHRIS:	Swapped it.
SHARON:	Through what? Exchange and Prat?!

SHARON GETS IN AND BELTS UP. CHRIS GETS IN TOO, DOESN'T PUT HIS SEAT BELT ON, STARTS THE CAR AT THE FOURTH ATTEMPT, AND SQUEALS OFF.

Shooting the Pilot

4. INT. CAPRI. DAY:

THE CAR IS DRIVING THROUGH NONDESCRIPT NORTH-EAST LONDON. THE RADIO IS TUNED TO THE GREEK STATION. CHRIS IS SINGING ALONG, OBVIOUSLY IN LOVE WITH THE CAR. SHARON IS DISGUSTED WITH THE INTERIOR, WHICH HASN'T BEEN CLEANED FOR YEARS.

SHARON: ...look at the state of this! There's more dogs on this floor than down Battersea! I know I'm a bit untidy...

CHRIS: Like the Atlantic Ocean's a bit wide...

SHARON: (OPENS GLOVE COMPARTMENT AND FINDS A PAIR OF KNICKERS IN IT) Eugh!

CHRIS: (TRYING TO JOKE) Last time I get you a romantic little surprise.

SHARON: You've had a bird in here, ain't you?!

CHRIS: Leave it out. I only picked it up yesterday (SHARON GLARES AT HIM) ...the car I mean!

SHARON: You got to be doing it with someone, cos we ain't had it since Christmas! And then you kept calling me Sonia, you were so pissed!

CHRIS: I had to be pissed to do it! (LIGHTS A FAG FROM THE CIGAR LIGHTER)

SHARON: But then why should I expect any different? You're a lousy provider, why should you be any better in bed?!

CHRIS: I might be if you lost a couple of stone – you could make a start by cutting your tongue out.

SHARON: If only I'd married someone like Darryl! My sister wants for nothing. Half a million that new house cost! Indoor pool...her swimming costume cost more than my entire wardrobe.

CHRIS:	And your swimming costume is bigger than her entire wardrobe! (HEARS AN 11.30 TIME CHECK ON THE RADIO) Blimey, they're off in five minutes! (ACCELERATES)
SHARON:	Red light!
CHRIS:	What..? Where?!

5. EXT. CROSSROADS. DAY:

A BUSY CROSSROADS, CONTROLLED BY TRAFFIC LIGHTS. CHRIS SPEEDS THROUGH A RED LIGHT. A MOTORCYCLIST COMING THE OTHER WAY IS FORCED TO SWERVE, AND COMES OFF THE BIKE, WHICH SKIDS ON ITS SIDE INTO AN ONCOMING VAN. THE VAN DRIVER LEAPS OUT OF HIS CAB AS THE BIKER PICKS HIMSELF OFF THE GROUND. THEY TURN TO SEE CHRIS'S CAR DISAPPEARING UP THE ROAD. AN EAGER SCHOOLBOY IS AMONG THE PASSERS BY WHO HURRY OVER TO THE SCENE OF THE CRASH.

SCHOOLBOY:	It's all right, I got his number...

6. INT. CAPRI. DAY:

INSIDE THE SPEEDING CAR, CONTINUOUS, SHARON AND CHRIS ARE DISCUSSING THE ACCIDENT.

SHARON:	You bleedin' nutter!!
CHRIS:	It's okay, no-one's hurt, I can see in the mirror...
SHARON:	You got to go back and give them your insurance company...
CHRIS:	What insurance company?

SHARON ROLLS HER EYES. CHRIS SCREECHES TO A HALT OUTSIDE A BETTING OFFICE AND DASHES IN.

7. INT. INDOOR POOL. DAY:

IN UTTER CONTRAST, WE NOW FIND OURSELVES IN THE LUXURIOUS POOL AREA OF TRACEY AND DARRYL STUBBS' NEW CHIGWELL HOME. IT'S A BIG POOL, IN A SWEDISH STYLE PINE LINED ROOM, WITH ONE WALL OF SLIDING GLASS DOORS THAT LOOK OUT ONTO BIG GARDENS. TRACEY LIES BACK IN AN EXPENSIVE SUN LOUNGER, WEARING A BATHING COSTUME UNDER A SHORT TOWELLING WRAP. SHE IS PAINTING HER TOE NAILS, PUTTING TISSUE BETWEEN HER TOES AS SHE GOES. THERE ARE PILES OF HOLIDAY BROCHURES ON THE TABLE THAT MATCHES THE LOUNGER, AND SHE'S LOOKING THROUGH THEM, WHILE KEEPING HALF AN EYE ON THE TINY COLOUR PORTABLE TV ON WHICH PLAYS THE SAME GAME SHOW CHRIS WAS WATCHING EARLIER. IN THE POOL, DARRYL IS FINISHING DOING HIS LENGTHS. HE COMES TO THE EDGE OF THE POOL AND HANGS ON TO THE EDGE.

DARRYL: What time is it, Trace?

TRACEY: What's happened to your new gold and platinum Rolex diver's watch as worn by Seve Ballesteros, Frederick Forsyth and Kiri Tekanawa?

DARRYL: It's stopped.

TRACEY: What? That's a five thousand quid watch!!

DARRYL: (A BIT SHAME FACED) No it ain't, it's a fifty quid copy I bought off Chris...

TRACEY: Oh Darryl! you ought to know by now his moody gear is always rubbish!

DARRYL: (GETTING OUT OF POOL) I know, but he was a bit short, and he won't take a hand out, so it was either the watch or a set of genuine porcelain thimbles depicting prehistoric animals.

Birds of a Feather

TRACEY: (STARTS DRYING DARRYL WITH BIG TOWEL WITH A PICTURE OF A BOTTLE OF CHAMPAGNE ON IT – LAURENCE CAN SUPPLY) Sometimes I think Chris is a bit prehistoric... Why my sister stays with him...!

DARRYL: Yeah, well, so what is the time anyway?

TRACEY: Nearly twelve a clock... assuming this watch you got me for me birthday is a real Cartier?

DARRYL: As if I'd ever stint when it comes to you! What?! Look at our palace, the pool, the cars, all for you and Garthy! Why d'you think I work all the hours God sends?

TRACEY: I know, I'm really lucky to have you...

DARRYL: You haven't yet, but I think I can squeeze you in... (DROPS HIS TOWEL AND HUGS HER)

TRACEY: Ooh, you're all cold!

DARRYL: You can always warm me up!

TRACEY: Not here, Darryl!

DARRYL: Why not? No-one can see us, we're detached now... (THEY CUDDLE, DARRYL TRIES TO WRESTLE TRACEY ONTO THE GROUND, SHE RESISTS, IT'S ALL VERY LIGHTHEARTED, BUT THEY KNOCK A LOAD OF BROCHURES ONTO THE FLOOR) I've never seen so many brochures! You found anything yet?

TRACEY: There's one thing I really fancy...

DARRYL: Me too, but I ain't making much progress!

TRACEY: Oh you! I mean this six week Far Eastern Paradise cruise, calling at Bali, Bangkok, Hong Kong, Singapore, Bora Bora and Sydney... (FINDS THE BROCHURE AND SHOWS HIM)

Shooting the Pilot

DARRYL: Don't know, don't really fancy all that Boran Boran nosh!

TRACEY: It's nearly eight grand apiece, though, but that's for the best cabin!

DARRYL: Posh...

TRACEY: I should hope so for that sort of dough!

DARRYL: No, P.O.S.H. – "Port Out Starboard Home", those were the best cabins in the golden age of the great liners...

TRACEY: Why?

DARRYL: I don't know, it's just something I remember from a film about the Titanic.

TRACEY: Oh lovely! You trying to put me off?

DARRYL: Course not. It's a great idea, a cruise. After all, it's months since we went on that safari.

TRACEY: So shall I book it?

DARRYL: Yeah, course...

TRACEY: (THROWS HER ARMS ROUND HIM) I really love you!

DARRYL: (LAYS HIS TOWEL DOWN ON THE ASTROTURF POOLSIDE) Come on then, one for the road...

TRACEY GIGGLES BUT GETS DOWN ON THE TOWEL WITH HIM. THEY KISS. THEN THE DOOR CHIMES SOUND.

DARRYL: Stuff me! The first time your brother-in-law's been on time in his life! (RELUCTANTLY GETS UP)

8. EXT. TRACEY'S HOUSE. DAY:

A DETACHED HOUSE BUILT SINCE THE ACCESSION OF QUEEN MARGARET HILDA 1 (1979 – ?). IT'S BIG, NEO-GEORGIAN, DOUBLE FRONTED. AT LEAST SIX

> BEDROOMS. THERE'S A LARGE FRONT GARDEN AND A DRIVE UP TO THE DOOR. THE TRIPLE GARAGE DOORS ARE HALF OPEN, TO REVEAL DARRYL'S NEW JAGUAR, AND TRACEY'S NEW JAPANESE SPORTS CAR. CHRIS'S CAR IS PARKED IN THE DRIVE, AND SPORTS A NEW DENT IN THE FRONT. CHRIS IS STANDING AT THE FRONT DOOR. SHARON IS STANDING BACK TO GET THE FULL EFFECT.

SHARON: What a gorgeous house!

CHRIS: Bit flash...

SHARON: That's good, coming from the owner of a pink Capri with leopardskin seats and more aerials that the Russian Embassy. (PEERS INSIDE GARAGE) They've changed their cars again, too! Blimey, he mustn't half erect a lot of conservatories! You ought to get him to take you on full time.

CHRIS: I got me own business...!

SHARON: Yeah; self-employed minicab driver and walking bookies' Christmas bonus!

> TRACEY OPENS THE FRONT DOOR HERE. SHE STILL IS IN HER WRAP OVER HER COSSIE.

CHRIS: Get you out of bed?

TRACEY: We was poolside...

CHRIS: Oh, pardon me for breathing...

SHARON: She might. I won't... (CROSSES TO HER SISTER, AND THEY KISS) It's fabulous, it's like something out of Dynasty!

TRACEY: You can come in you know, there's no charge on a weekday...

DARRYL: (EMERGING BRISKLY, IN SMART JEANS, NEW TRAINERS, BRUCE SPRINGSTEEN OFFICIAL ROAD CREW

SWEATSHIRT AND GOLD I.D. BRACELET AND ROLEX) No time for guided tours, we got to be in Newport Pagnell by one... (KISSES TRACEY)

TRACEY: Don't be late home, I got you a fillet steak for tea...

SHARON: You take your time Darryl, I'll make sure your steak goes to a good home.

9. INT. TRACEY'S LOUNGE. DAY:

HALF AN HOUR LATER. THE LOUNGE OF TRACEY'S NEW HOUSE IS LARGE, WITH WIDE BAY WINDOW. IT'S EXPENSIVELY FURNISHED IN FIRST DIVISION FOOTBALLER'S TASTE, SO IS UNLIKELY TO BE FEATURED IN "HOMES AND GARDENS". EVERYTHING IS EXPENSIVE, BUT DOESN'T QUITE MATCH. THE FITTED DEEP PILE CARPET IS SMOKY PINK; THE TWO SOFAS AND TWO WING CHAIRS ARE IN BLACK SUEDE. THE WALLPAPER IS SILK-FINISH, VAGUELY CHINESE, FEATURING LARGE CHRYSANTHEMUMS. THERE ARE SPOTLIGHTS INSET IN THE CEILING, BUT THE WALL LIGHTS ARE NEO LOUIS XIV. THERE'S A COUPLE OF CHINESE STYLE LACQUERED COFFEE TABLES, ONE LONG, ONE SQUARE. THE CURTAINS AND PELMET ARE IN MAROON VELVET, WITH LOTS OF SWAGS AND TAILS. ON THE WALL ARE A NUMBER OF PSEUDO ORIENTAL PICTURES BOUGHT BY MAIL ORDER FROM ATHENA. THERE'S AN INCONGRUOUS G-PLAN GLASS FRONTED CABINET CONTAINING WEDDING PRESENT SILVER AND CROCKERY, AND A FEW CUPS WON BY DARRYL AS AN AMATEUR GOLFER. THERE'S A BIG HIGH TECH TV AND VIDEO, AND ALSO A LARGE MUSIC CENTRE WITH BIG SPEAKERS.

THERE ARE A NUMBER OF FAMILY PICTURES ON COFFEE TABLES AND THE MANTELPIECE OF THE REAL YORKSTONE FIREPLACE WITH FLAME EFFECT GAS FIRE. THERE ARE FASHION MAGAZINES SCATTERED ON

Birds of a Feather

THE COFFEE TABLES, BUT NO BOOKS ANYWHERE. THERE ARE LOTS OF ASHTRAYS AND A NUMBER OF EXPENSIVE TABLE LIGHTERS ON DIFFERENT SURFACES. SOME PACKETS OF DUTY FREE EXTRA LONG LUXURY CIGGIES LIE ABOUT.

AS WE OPEN, THE ROOM IS EMPTY, BUT THEN SHARON AND TRACEY ENTER. TRACEY WEARS AN EXPENSIVE BEIGE ANGORA AND SUEDE SWEATER AND PRESSED JEANS AND HIGH HEELS. SHE WEARS A LOT OF JEWELLERY – CARTIER WATCH AND A GOLD BRACELET ON ONE WRIST. A GOLD CHAIN AT THE NECK, A LARGE TOO BRILLIANT DIAMOND ENGAGEMENT RING, PLUS DIAMOND STUD EAR RINGS. SHE'S MADE UP HER FACE, AND LOOKS ALMOST GOOD ENOUGH FOR A NON-SPEAKING PART IN AN AMERICAN DAYTIME SOAP.

SHARON SINKS LUXURIOUSLY INTO AN ARMCHAIR. TRACEY CROSSES TO THE HI FI AND PUTS ON ONE OF A LARGE COLLECTION OF CDs – SOMETHING LIONEL RITCHIE-ISH. ACOUSTICALLY PERFECT SOFT SOUL FILLS THE ROOM.

SHARON: Blimey, I thought the house in Whipps Cross was big...!

TRACEY: It was all right for a semi, but we was overlooked by the neighbours.

SHARON: Better than being overlooked by the council! We ain't had hot water for three weeks!

TRACEY: Maybe if you paid your rent...

SHARON: Don't you start! You forget what a struggle life is for Chris and me! I mean, Darryl's got a booming business, six erectors and a full time accountant – but what does Chris earn?

TRACEY: I don't know. What does he earn?

SHARON: Search me! Easier to find out the Pope's inside leg measurement! And when he does have money, he spends it on sick animals. Got a fag? (TRACEY PASSES HER SISTER A FAG AND TAKES ONE HERSELF. SHE LIGHTS BOTH WITH A GOLD CARTIER LIGHTER) Ta. If you could get Darryl to take him on full time...

TRACEY: I never interfere in Darryl's business, but I know he don't need no full time driver, only when he goes on long hauls.

SHARON: Oh...

TRACEY: Look, forget about the boys, this is a girls' day out. They got some lovely leather trousers in at Skin of Romford...

SHARON: I can't afford leather trousers! Me purse is plastic! And it's empty, that cowson nicked me spending money!

TRACEY: Again?! (GOES TO HER GUCCI HANDBAG, TAKES OUT HER GUCCI PURSE, REMOVES SOME FOLDING AND PRESSES IT ON SHARON)

SHARON: I can't take your money!

TRACEY: Go on, it's only fifty quid.

SHARON: Well... I don't like to take charity, I got my principles... (BUT SHE PUTS THE MONEY IN HER BAG, GRATEFULLY)

THEN THE DOORBELL CHIMES. TRACEY GETS UP AND EXITS TO OPEN IT.

10. EXT. HOUSE. DAY:

CONTINUOUS. OUTSIDE THE HOUSE IS DORIEN GREEN, A HIGHLY MADE UP AND COIFFED JEWISH HOUSEWIFE OF ABOUT 40. SHE WEARS A CREAM TRACKSUIT WITH BIG SHOULDERS AND SILVER LAME INSERTS, PINK

TRAINERS, RED NAIL VARNISH, LOTS OF JEWELLERY, SUNGLASSES UP IN HER HAIR. AS TRACEY OPENS THE DOOR DORIEN ADOPTS A WORRIED EXPRESSION AND A BREATHLESS TONE.

TRACEY: Oh hello...

DORIEN: Hello, I'm Dorien Green, I live next door, can you help me, I'm in the middle of a terrible crisis!

11. INT. TRACEY'S LOUNGE. DAY:

MOMENTS LATER.

SHARON: (CALLS OUT) All right if I take a fag?

TRACEY: (O.O.V.) 'Course...

SHARON TAKES SEVERAL CIGARETTES AND PUTS ALL BUT ONE IN HER HANDBAG FOR LATER. THE ODD ONE OUT SHE STICKS IN HER GOB AND LIGHTS. TRACEY ENTERS WITH DORIEN.

DORIEN: ... I came back from shopping to find the entire ground floor under three inches of foam!

SHARON: What, you've had the Fire Brigade round?

DORIEN: No, the carpet cleaners came a day early, and the stupid au pair let them in! I told Marcus we shouldn't have a German, but he said live and let live... And I had all the girls coming over for coffee this afternoon, what am I going to do?! I can't make them all sit in the kitchen!

SHARON: Course not, it's hardly bigger than a tennis court.

TRACEY: Why don't you put the kettle on, Shar? (SHARON EXITS)

DORIEN:	I'm not one to interfere, and God knows cleaners are hard to find, but if mine spoke to me like that...
TRACEY:	Sharon's my sister!
DORIEN:	Really?... Oh! (GETS UP AND WALKS ABOUT THE ROOM) You've decorated beautifully...
TRACEY:	Thank you...
DORIEN:	(LOOKS AT FRAMED PHOTO OF 13 YEAR OLD BOY ON WALL) Is this your son?
TRACEY:	Garth. He's away at Fiskes. That's a public school.
DORIEN:	Oh, public school?
TRACEY:	Well, we want them to learn him to talk proper.
DORIEN:	Naturally. So how are you settling in in our exclusive little enclave?
TRACEY:	Your what?
DORIEN:	Bryan Close...
TRACEY:	Oh, you mean round here? It's lovely. A bit quiet, mind...
DORIEN:	Yes, people do keep themselves to themselves... I've just had the most wonderful idea! I was going to have a little get together for a few friends this afternoon – before the disaster with the deep pile... what are you up to this afternoon?
TRACEY:	Well, we was (DORIEN WINCES) going shopping...
SHARON:	(RE-ENTERS) Kettle's on – tea, coffee or pot noodle?
DORIEN:	(IGNORES SHARON) Even better! Because actually my coffee afternoon was going to be in the nature of a product party.

TRACEY: A what?

DORIEN: It's a way of viewing and buying high quality merchandise at wholesale prices in the comfort and privacy of your own home without any high pressure salesmanship! (GRABS HOLD OF TRACEY'S ARM, URGENTLY) Say you'll do it, you'll be saving my life!

TRACEY: I don't know...

SHARON: So it's sort of like a tupperware party?

DORIEN: I like to think it's a tidge up-market from plastic boxes for leftovers, dear.

SHARON: That's me put in my place.

DORIEN: And Tracey, the party hostess gets a 15 per cent commission, and all she has to do is supply the nibbles and the drinkies! You could easily pick up forty or fifty pounds pin money!

TRACEY: (A BIT INSULTED) Thank you Dorien, I don't need pin money!

SHARON: I do! I'll be your hostess!

DORIEN: Thank you dear, but I don't think my friends want to schlap out to a council flat in a tower block where the lift doesn't work and your cabriolet roof gets slashed before you've even parked.

SHARON: (TO TRACEY) You been telling her where I live? (TRACEY SHAKES HER HEAD)

DORIEN: Just a lucky guess.

12. EXT. MOTORWAY SERVICE AREA. DAY:

CHRIS'S PINK CAPRI ROARS INTO THE CAR PARK, SCREECHES ROUND AND INTO A SPACE. CHRIS AND DARRYL GET OUT, TAKE A HOLDALL FROM THE BOOT,

THEN CROSS TO A PARKED JAGUAR WITH TWO LARGE MEN IN THE FRONT SEATS. CHRIS AND DARRYL GET IN THE BACK AND THE JAGUAR DRIVES OFF SEDATELY.

13. INT. KITCHEN. DAY:

A COUPLE OF HOURS LATER. TRACEY, IN A DRESS, IS ARRANGING CRISPS AND NUTS AND TWIGLETS IN LITTLE BOWLS, AND TALKING TO HERSELF.

TRACEY: Why am I doing this? I don't want tupperware, I don't need tupperware, I don't even like tupperware!

AT THIS MOMENT SHARON ENTERS WITH SOMETHING BEHIND HER BACK.

SHARON: It ain't tupperware, Trace!

TRACEY: What?

SHARON: I've just seen that Dorien unpacking her gear, and no way is it tupperware.

TRACEY: Oh, well that's something! What is it, then? Scent? Jewellery?

SHARON: Look... (PRODUCES A PAIR OF NAUGHTY CROTCHLESS KNICKERS FROM BEHIND HER BACK AND HANDS THEM TO TRACEY)

TRACEY: (EXAMINING THEM) Eugh! They ain't got a... you know...

SHARON: A crotch...

TRACEY: They're vile! Who'd wear 'em?!

SHARON: I would if I thought it would make Chris pay attention. But he wouldn't notice me in bed if I had a picture of the Spurs tattooed on my bum!

TRACEY: (UNAMUSED) I just don't want this stuff in my house!

SHARON: These are nothing! Everything else in the front room needs batteries!

TRACEY: (METAPHORICALLY ROLLING UP HER SLEEVES) Where's Dorien?! I'm going to tell her to sling her hook! (SOUND OF FRONT DOOR CHIMES. DORIEN POPS HER HEAD IN) Dorien, what the hell do you..?!

DORIEN: They're here! Action stations! (GOES BEFORE TRACEY CAN SPEAK)

14. INT. TRACEY'S LOUNGE. DAY:

HALF AN HOUR LATER. THE COFFEE TABLES HAVE BEEN MOVED TOGETHER TO MAKE A SORT OF COUNTER, AND ARE COVERED IN NAUGHTY KNICKERS, PEEKABOO BRAS, LEATHER CORSELETTES, PLASTIC MANACLES, LARGE JARS OF DUBIOUS LOOKING UNGUENTS AND SO ON. THERE'S ALSO A LARGE CARDBOARD BOX FULL OF SMALLER BOXES, AND THE SMALLER BOXES CONTAIN VIBRATORS OF VARIOUS SIZES. BUT TO SAVE LORD REES OF MOGG'S BLUSHES, THEY CAN STAY IN THE BOXES. THERE ARE ABOUT HALF A DOZEN WOMEN OF DORIEN'S AGE AND INCOME GROUP HAVING A GOOD TIME, DRINKING COFFEE OR THE FRASCATI THEY BROUGHT WITH THEM, BUT LEAVING THE NIBBLES ALONE BECAUSE THEY'RE ON DIETS. SHARON IS HAVING A FINE OLD TIME, HAVING DRUNK SEVERAL GLASSES OF WINE. SHE'S MODELLING A LEATHER LOOK CORSET OVER HER TRACKSUIT. TRACEY LOOKS FED UP AND EMBARRASSED, AND ISN'T JOINING IN THE LAUGHTER.

SHARON: I'm tempted, just to see his face! (DOES A TWIRL) Yeah, all right, what's the damage?

DORIEN: Damage? These are perfect goods!

Shooting the Pilot

SHARON: I mean how much is it?

DORIEN: Oh... Seventy five pounds.

SHARON: Blimey!

DORIEN: You must have it, it's so you.

SHARON: Nothing what costs seventy five quid is so me!

DORIEN: It's money well spent, darling. It'll put the magic back in your marriage.

SHARON: Paul Daniels couldn't put the magic back in my marriage! (THE GIRLS LAUGH) How about you, Trace, you got the figure for it! Knock your Darryl's socks off if he came home and found you in this!

TRACEY: Our marriage doesn't need artificial aids, thank you very much!

DORIEN: I thought you said you'd been married fourteen years?

SHARON: They have, childhood sweethearts they were, met at Woodberry Down Comprehensive, in detention. She's never even been out with another bloke, let alone slept with one!

TRACEY: Do you mind, mouthy!?

DORIEN: No, it's sweet. I was the same, I met my husband on a kibbutz when I was eighteen, we were engaged for three years, and I was still a virgin when I got married.

TRACEY: Good for you!

DORIEN: (CONSPIRATORIALLY, SHE'S BEEN AT THE FRASCATI TOO) It was only later I started going out with other men.

TRACEY: You mean, you're two-timing...?!

DORIEN:	Certainly not! I'm utterly faithful to Luke!
SHARON:	I thought your old man was called Marcus?
DORIEN:	He is, but Marcus and I haven't had a physical relationship since October 1987. It was the Stock Market crash, you see, it rendered him impotent. And though the FT index has staged a remarkable upturn since then, Marcus hasn't.
SHARON:	So who's this Luke?
TRACEY:	Sharon, nose! (TAPS SNOUT)
DORIEN:	It's all right, all the girls know… (GIRLS GIGGLE) He's gorgeous, only 23, works for Longqvist kitchens. We met when he came round to measure up, and boy, did he measure up…!
TRACEY:	Well I'm sorry Dorien, but I think it's all disgusting! You conned me into having this party, you bring all these horrible smutty gadgets round, and talk about knocking off other fellas…
SHARON:	Tracey, don't be such a prude! Just because you got a perfect marriage and a perfect husband and a perfect house don't mean us poor also-rans shouldn't have a bit of fun!
DORIEN:	Thank you, Sharon… though I rather resent being called an also ran… (TO TRACEY, WOUNDED) I'm sorry if you're offended by my presence, by my attempts to befriend you, to introduce you to my social circle, to ease your way into Chigwell society. But if you're so morally far above us, then I shall pack up my harmless love toys, and vanish from your life as suddenly as I entered it.
	DORIEN HUFFILY MOVES TO DOOR, AND ALL THE GIRLS START TO GET UP TO LEAVE.
SHARON:	Tracey, apologise!

Shooting the Pilot

TRACEY: What for?

DORIEN: It was nice meeting you, Sharon... you might live in a slum but you have a certain grace... (MAKES IT TO THE DOOR, BUT PAUSES DRAMATICALLY)

TRACEY: (FINALLY ACCEPTS THE CUE) No, Dorien I'm sorry, sit down, it's my fault, I'm making a mountain out a molehill...

SHARON: (REFERRING TO DORIEN) She's got a cream that does that.

DORIEN: (RETURNS TO THE SOFA) I accept your apology, dear... (GOES TO HER BIG HOLDALL) Look, you must have something, just to please this incredible husband of yours. (ROOTING THROUGH BAG)... Not one of the battery powered items, obviously... but how about a camisole...?

SHARON: No, he's got an umbrella. (THEY ALL LOOK AT HER) It was a joke, I know what a camisole is, all right?

DORIEN PRODUCES A SURPRISINGLY ATTRACTIVE AND TASTEFUL ITEM IN WHITE SILK, AND GIVES IT TO TRACEY TO EXAMINE.

TRACEY: (SURPRISED) It's gorgeous!

DORIEN: Thank you.

TRACEY: How much?

DORIEN: Have it on me dear.

SHARON: Then you can have it on Darryl.

TRACEY: No, I got to pay...

DORIEN: No, please, it's just a manufacturer's sample...

TRACEY: Well, if you're sure...?

DORIEN:	Of course... (THROW AWAY TONE) so you owe me a favour...
SHARON:	Ain't you going to model it for us then, sis?
TRACEY:	Do you mind?! This is for Darryl's eyes only!
SHARON:	What's his eyes got to do with it?

15. EXT. LONDON STREET. DAY:

LATER THAT AFTERNOON. THE CAPRI DRIVES DOWN A BUSY STREET, WITH DARRYL AND CHRIS INSIDE. CHRIS IS DRIVING A BIT TOO FAST, AS USUAL. THERE'S A ZEBRA CROSSING AHEAD, WITH A PEDESTRIAN ALREADY ON THE CROSSING.

DARRYL:	(V/O) Chris, careful!
CHRIS:	(V/O) Sorry...!

THE CAR SCREECHES TO A HALT TO ALLOW THE PEDESTRIAN TO CROSS. THEN SCREECHES OFF AGAIN. A PANDA CAR IS COMING THE OTHER WAY.

16. INT. PANDA CAR. DAY:

THERE ARE TWO COPS INSIDE THIS CAR.

P.C. 1:	Did you see that pink Capri?
P.C. 2:	Yeah, smart.
P.C. 1:	You are joking, aren't you?
P.C. 2:	(PUZZLED) No.
P.C. 1:	Hold fast, weren't it a pink Capri that failed to stop at an accident in Bowes Park this morning? (REACHES FOR HIS RADIO)

17. INT. TRACEY'S LOUNGE. DAY:

AN HOUR OR SO LATER. THE "GIRLS" ARE ALL GONE, AND SHARON IS HELPING DORIEN TO PACK HER STUFF AWAY, WHILE TRACEY IS PUTTING THE HOOVER ROUND. TRACEY FINISHES HOOVERING, AND STARTS RE-POSITIONING HER COFFEE TABLES. DORIEN SIDLES UP TO HER.

DORIEN: Tracey dear, you remember that favour you said you owed me?

TRACEY: No...

DORIEN: When I gave you that camisole...

SHARON: No, she didn't say she owed you a favour, you said...

DORIEN: Let's not split hairs... the thing is, Luke's got two tickets for Wet Wet Wet at Wembley tonight...

SHARON: You're a bit old for pop concerts, ain't you?

DORIEN: (MIFFED) You're as young as the man you feel, dear.

SHARON: I like that...

DORIEN: Anyway, I need an alibi to tell Marcus tomorrow, so do you mind if I say I went to the ballet with you?

TRACEY: I do mind, as it happens.

SHARON: You can say you went to the ballet with me, if you want.

DORIEN: With respect, Sharon, it has to be a plausible alibi...

THE FRONT DOOR BELL GOES DING DONG. TRACEY GOES TO OPEN THE DOOR...

18. EXT. TRACEY'S HOUSE. DAY:

TWO PLAIN CLOTHES DETECTIVES ARE WAITING OUTSIDE THE DOOR, NEXT TO AN UNMARKED SALOON CAR. THE OLDER, IN A SUIT, IS DETECTIVE INSPECTOR RON TATUM. THE YOUNGER, QUITE GOOD LOOKING, IS DETECTIVE SERGEANT BARRY COLTRANE, WHO WEARS A LEATHER JACKET AND CORDUROY JEANS. TRACEY OPENS THE FRONT DOOR.

TRACEY: Yeah?

TATUM: Tracey Stubbs?

TRACEY: Yeah?

TATUM: (SHOWS WARRANT CARD) CID, can we have a quiet word?

TRACEY: Oh Gawd!

19. INT. TRACEY'S LOUNGE. DAY:

TRACEY ENTERS THE LOUNGE, CLOSELY FOLLOWED BY THE TWO DETECTIVES.

TRACEY: ... (ANGRILY, TO DORIEN) I knew I should never have let you talk me into it!

DORIEN: Me?! What have I done?!

TRACEY: It's only Old Bill, innit?!

DORIEN: Old Bill who?

SHARON: Lilly Law, Dorien!

DORIEN: (LOOKING FROM DETECTIVE TO DETECTIVE) Bill, Lilly, I'm all at sea!

TATUM: (TO TRACEY) What's she talked you into, love?

SHARON: Don't say nothing without a brief...!

Shooting the Pilot

TRACEY: Don't talk to me about sodding briefs! Look, I got nothing to hide! Weren't my idea to have this stupid sex-aids party!

SHARON: Who tipped you off? (TO DORIEN) One of them friends of yours must be a grass!

COLTRANE: (CROSSES TO THE CARDBOARD CARTON OF VIBRATORS, LOOKS INSIDE, AND RAISES AN EYEBROW) There's nothing illegal about things that go bonk in the night, love, but if I were you I'd try marriage guidance first...

TRACEY: Do you mind, I got a perfect marriage!

TATUM: Had...

DORIEN: I think I ought to be getting along...

COLTRANE: Who are you?

DORIEN: Just a neighbour... (PICKS UP AS MUCH AS SHE CAN AND SCARPERS)

TATUM: (TO SHARON) What about you?

SHARON: I'm her sister.

COLTRANE: (CONSULTS NOTEBOOK) What, you're Sharon Theodopo...dopolopo...

SHARON: Yeah, I been married to him for eight years and I still can't pronounce it. Now what do you want?

TRACEY: There ain't been an accident, has there?

TATUM: No, I wouldn't call it an accident, more a stroke of luck from our point of view.

TRACEY: (SUDDENLY VERY WORRIED) What's happened?

COLTRANE: Well, how can I put it? I know; you better stock up on these sex aids, because you won't be having any nookie with your husband again this century.

20. INT. TRACEY'S CAR. DAY:

A COUPLE OF WEEKS LATER. TRACEY'S NEW JAP SPORTS CAR PULLS UP OUTSIDE THE BLOCK OF FLATS, EXCITING THE ATTENTION OF LOCAL KIDS. SHARON IS IN THE PASSENGER SEAT. SHE SIGHS.

SHARON: Oh well, now to run the gauntlet of all them slags...

TRACEY: Oh, it can't be that bad!

SHARON: You try living here!

TRACEY: No thank you!

SHARON: Exactly. I tell you, Trace, I can't take much more of this!

TRACEY: You got to, for the boys! They could be on remand for ages! But once it comes to trial and they get off...

SHARON: Get off? Get off, the law found shooters in the car! There's no way they're going to get off! Oh well, keep smiling. (KISSES HER SISTER, AND GETS OUT OF CAR AND GOES INTO FLATS. TRACEY STARTS CRYING)

21. EXT. CAMELOT HOUSE WALKWAY. DAY:

THE LIFT IS WORKING FOR ONCE, AND THE DOORS OPEN ON SHARON'S FLOOR. SHE IS HOLDING HER NOSE. SHE COMES OUT OF THE LIFT AND WALKS TOWARDS HER FLAT. RABBITING ON THE WALKWAY ARE THREE OF HER NEIGHBOURS – LISA AND TWO OLDER WOMEN, ROSE AND DORA. THEY SEE SHARON APPROACHING, AND START WHISPERING EXCITEDLY. SHARON WALKS STOLIDLY ON. AS SHE NEARS THEM, THE NEIGHBOURS OSTENTATIOUSLY CHANGE THE SUBJECT.

LISA: And you know, they're right, it really does get the wash clean, even at low temperature!

SHARON: All right, ladies, no need to change the subject on my account, I know who you're talking about.

ROSE: Well it ain't every week we get an armed robber on our floor.

SHARON: Yeah, you normally have to make do with drunks and wifebeaters, like your Alf.

DORA: Where's the money from all them raids then, that's what I want to know? You wearing them cheap clothes from the market don't fool us, The Sun reckons you must be sitting on half a million.

SHARON: And if I was do you think I'd still be living in this shit hole?!

LISA: If you ask me it's your fault your Chris turned to crime.

SHARON: You what?!

LISA: He give me a lift the night before he was nicked...

SHARON: That was nice of him...

LISA: Yeah, he'd just got that new Capri, anyway we got talking...

SHARON: Before or after?

LISA: (IN FULL FLOOD)... and he was saying how you couldn't give him babies, and what a disgrace that is for a Greek bloke... He was ever so upset.

SHARON: And you comforted him?

LISA: Yeah, I tried to cheer him up.

SHARON: Well, after you finished cheering him up, you left your knickers in the glove compartment!

MARCHES OFF, LEAVING THE NEIGHBOURS
SPEECHLESS. BUT BY THE TIME SHE GETS TO HER
FRONT DOOR, SHE'S CRYING IN SILENT RAGE.

22. INT. COURTROOM. DAY:

A MONTH LATER. TRACEY AND SHARON ARE IN THE
PUBLIC GALLERY OF A MODERN PROVINCIAL CROWN
COURT. DARRYL AND CHRIS ARE IN THE DOCK WITH 2
UNIFORMED GAOLERS. THE JUDGE IS SUMMING UP.

JUDGE: ... and when stopped could give no satisfactory explanation for the presence of sawn-off shotguns in the boot of the pink Capri owned by Mr Theodopo...dopolodo.... the jury know whom I mean. And finally we have the matter of the large accumulator wager placed by Mr Theo... by Mr Stubbs' co-defendant, a bare half an hour after the security van was raided outside Mothercare, Newport Pagnell. (DARRYL GIVES CHRIS A LOOK OF CONTEMPT) We have heard how bank notes stolen during this evil armed robbery were recovered from the turf accountants' office, and subsequently were found to bear the fingerprints of the afore-mentioned individual of Cypriot extraction. (TAKES A SIP OF WATER) And now, ladies and gentlemen of the jury, as you retire to consider your verdict...

23. INT. OLD BAILEY CANTEEN. DAY:

A SMALL DINGY JOYLESS SUBTERRANEAN CANTEEN,
VERY MUCH LIKE THOSE DOTTED ABOUT TELEVISION
CENTRE. SHARON AND TRACEY ENTER. SHARON PICKS
UP A TRAY.

SHARON: Tea?

TRACEY: Yeah, all right...

SHARON: Anything to eat?

TRACEY: You're joking!

SHARON: I'm not, I'm hungry! I think I'll have a toasted sandwich.

DETECTIVE INSPECTOR TATUM IS SITTING IN THE CANTEEN BEHIND A COPY OF THE DAILY TELEGRAPH. HE LOWERS HIS NEWSPAPER.

TATUM: I'd have an 'am roll if I were you, the jury won't be out long enough to do toast.

TRACEY: Who asked you, you pig?!

TATUM: Just giving you the benefit of my professional experience.

SHARON: You know where you can stick your experience!

TATUM: (RISING) If only I got invited to your sort of party... (EXITS IN HIGH GOOD SPIRITS)

TRACEY: (SCREAMS AFTER HIM) Scumbag!!

SHARON HELPS HERSELF TO A HORRID PRE-WRAPPED SANDWICH FROM THE DISPLAY AND PAYS FOR THIS AND THE TEAS. THE SISTERS SIT DOWN AT A TEA-STAINED TABLE. THERE'S A SAD SILENCE.

TRACEY: I didn't think much to Darryl's barrister, seeing how much he's charging...

SHARON: What I can't get over is Chris doing all these daring armed robberies and I ain't seen nothing of it! At least your Darryl laundered his loot through a legitimate company. Chris laundered his through Ladbroke's, only they lost his laundry.

TRACEY: He should have said the guns weren't even loaded!

SHARON: That don't really signify, does it? Still armed robbery. (BITES INTO ROLL) And this roll is attempted poisoning!

TRACEY: What do you think they'll get?

SHARON: Don't keep asking me that, I don't know...

TRACEY: (TURNS ON SHARON) He'd never be in this mess if your husband wasn't such a bloody awful driver!

SHARON: I know, don't expect me to defend Chris. Two-faced mean little merchant! I'm working my tits off at Tesco's while he's gambling away a hundred thousand a year! When I get him home....

TRACEY: When you get him home!? We're never gonna get them home!

24. INT. COURTROOM. DAY:

BACK IN THE PUBLIC GALLERY, SHARON AND TRACEY WAIT NERVOUSLY AS THE JURY FILE IN AND SIT. THE CLERK OF THE COURT STANDS, AS DOES THE JURY FOREMAN.

CLERK: Have you reached a verdict?

FOREMAN: Yes, sir.

CLERK: Is it the verdict of you all?

FOREMAN: It is, sir.

SHARON: (WHISPERS TO TRACEY) The buggers want to beat the rush hour home, don't they?

CLERK: And what is your verdict?

FOREMAN: We find both the defendants guilty on all charges.

TRACEY: Oh no! (STARTS CRYING)

JUDGE: Darryl Kevin Stubbs and Christopher Theodo.... Theo...

CHRIS: (SHOUTS) It's Theodopoulopodous, you stupid old fart!!

UPROAR AND LAUGHTER IN COURT.

JUDGE: Order! Order! (NOISE SUBSIDES) You are in contempt of court!

CHRIS: Big bleedin' deal, I'm down for a ten stretch anyway, ain't I?!

JUDGE: Wrong. I sentence you both to serve twelve years' imprisonment. Take them down...

IN THE WELL OF THE COURT, TATUM TURNS WITH SATISFACTION TO COLTRANE.

TATUM: (WITH SATISFACTION) A phrase he'll hear often in the predominantly homosexual atmosphere of the average top security prison.

THE GAOLERS PREPARE TO LEAD DARRYL AND CHRIS DOWN TO THE CELLS.

TRACEY: (SHOUTS) I love you, Darryl!

DARRYL: (LOOKING UP) Wait for me, Tracey!

CHRIS: Wait for me an' all, Sharon!

SHARON: What? You must be bloody joking! I've waited long enough!

25. INT. THE CELLS. DAY:

A FEW MINUTES LATER, UNDER THE COURT, IN A BARE BRICK NEON LIT CORIDOR THAT LEADS TO THE HOLDING CELLS. TRACEY AND SHARON ARE CONFRONTING THE CHIEF GAOLER. TRACEY IS WEEPY, SHARON IS ANGRY.

SHARON:	Let her see him, you callous sod!
GAOLER:	(SARCASTICALLY POLITE) I'm sorry, madam, but the transport leaves for funky Brixton in five minutes, and you wouldn't want them to miss their tea, would you? It's spam this afternoon – it's spam most afternoons. Tell you what, though, hang around the tradesman's entrance and maybe you can give them a wave goodbye.

26. EXT. COURT BUILDING. DAY:

MINUTES LATER. TRACEY AND SHARON WAIT OUTSIDE THE HIGH BACK GATES OF THE CROWN COURT CAR PARK. TRACEY GETS OUT HER FAGS, BUT THE PACKET IS EMPTY.

TRACEY:	Got a fag, Shar?

SHARON OFFERS TRACEY A CIGARETTE FROM A PACK OF TEN "NUMBER SIX". SHE TAKES ONE HERSELF, AND THEN TRIES TO LIGHT BOTH CIGARETTES WITH A MATCH, BUT THE WIND BLOWS IT OUT. SHE TRIES ANOTHER MATCH, NO LUCK. TRACEY GETS HER LIGHTER FROM HER BAG AND MANAGES TO LIGHT BOTH CIGARETTES. MEANWHILE, THE GATES HAVE OPENED, AND A SECURED VAN WITH SLIT WINDOWS ROLLS OUT OF THE CAR PARK.

TRACEY:	That's them! Darryl! (SHE WAVES DESPERATELY AS THE VAN SPEEDS OFF) Do you think he saw me?!
SHARON:	I don't know, them windows are just slits...
TRACEY:	I'm sure I saw him waving...
SHARON:	Yeah, course you did... look, let's go, eh, it's perishing.

THE SISTERS LINK ARMS AND WALK AWAY. WE FOLLOW.

TRACEY: What am I gonna do, Shar? I'm gutted! It's like being widowed! He was my whole life. I haven't let myself think about it 'til now, but what's Garth gonna do without a dad? And the house, it'll be so big and empty, and I don't even know how to change a plug...

SHARON: I do...

TRACEY: I'm dreading it, Shar, I'm dreading going home on me own...

SHARON: Look, if you like, I'll come and stay with you for a bit... until you're feeling yourself again... We'll just pop back to the tip and I'll excavate a few clothes, all right...?

TRACEY: (WIPING HER EYES) You don't want to stay with me, you got your own life to lead, ain't you?

SHARON: True... (TAKES FINAL DEEP DRAG ON FAG, DROPS IT AND GRINDS IT OUT WITH SOLE OF FOOT) but I'd rather lead yours. (SUDDENLY GRABS HOLD OF FOOT AND HOPS ABOUT) Oww! Ffff..!

TRACEY: What?!

SHARON: Got a hole in my shoe, ain't I?!

END OF EPISODE ONE.

Holding the Fort (1979): Laurence and Maurice at a commando base, somewhere in Surrey. It was our first time on location. We aren't in disguise; moustaches were big in the Seventies.

A publicity shot of Patricia Hodge, Peter Davison and Matthew Kelly. Patricia and Peter were already TV faces in *All Creatures Great and Small*, and *Rumpole of the Bailey*, but Matthew was only known in the theatre, so our show was his TV breakthrough.

A ticket for the original pilot, which was to be part of LWT's *Comedy Tonight* showcase. The audience was never allowed in because all of ITV was closed down for three months by an all-out strike that started halfway through our dress rehearsal.

LONDON WEEKEND TELEVISION
welcomes you to

"COMEDY TONIGHT"

A new Television Comedy

ON
FRI. 10th AUG. 1979
FROM 7.45 p.m. -9.30 p.m.   N° 069
Doors open 7.15 p.m.- 7.30 p.m.
No admittance after 7.30 p.m.
at SOUTH BANK TELEVISION CENTRE
KENT HOUSE UPPER GROUND LONDON, S.E.1
CHILDREN UNDER 15 ARE NOT ADMITTED

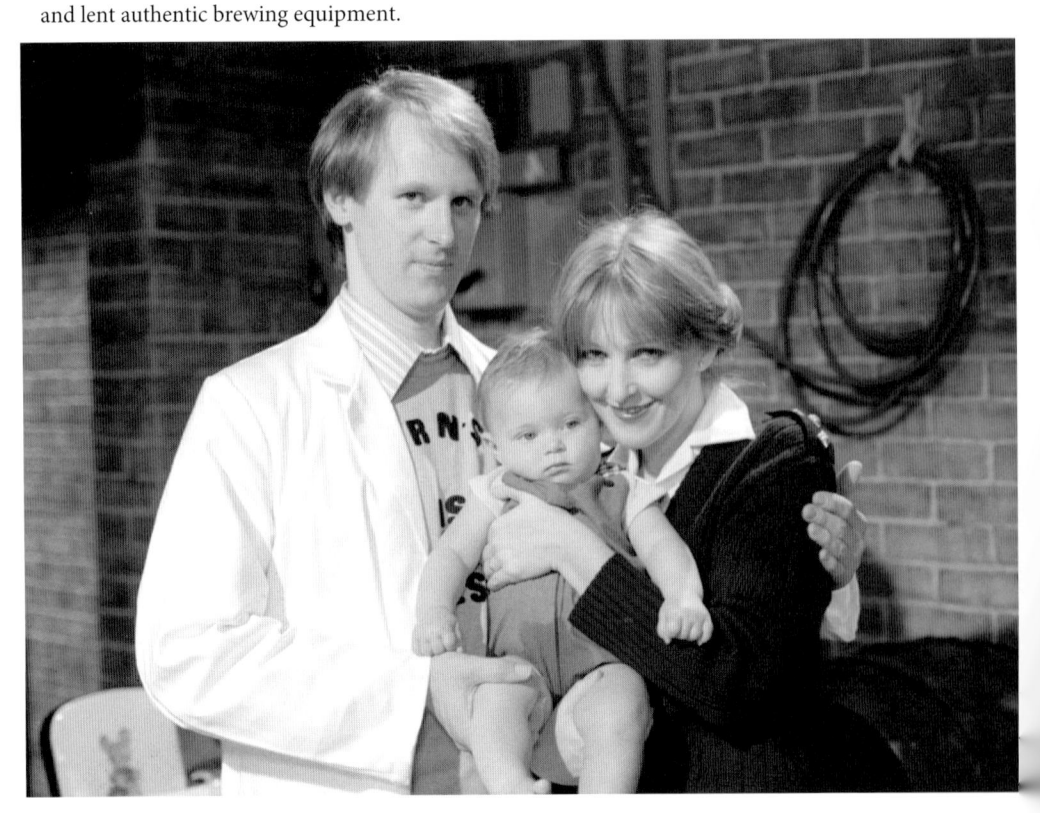

LWT
London Weekend Television

Peter Davison, Patricia Hodge and Victoria Kendall as baby Emma, in costume on the set of Russell's home micro-brewery. We were lucky to have met the founder of the Firkin pub chain, who acted as a consultant and lent authentic brewing equipment.

Shine On Harvey Moon (1981): The all-important photograph from *Picture Post* magazine that inspired the series. It depicts a soldier's joyous return to his family, but we wondered what would happen if the wife had hoped he'd died in combat.

Laurence's Auntie Miri in 1939, when she was 30. Miri had a wonderful war. It allowed her to leave a repressive household, to find work and fun in the West End of London. She is of course the template for the spirited Rita Moon, played so memorably by Maggie Steed.

Maurice on an authentic wartime London bus, on the first day of location shooting in Walthamstow, east London. The coat was also vintage, though not as old as the bus.

The Moon family in Rita's prefab. The brilliant production designer, Stanley Mills, recreated the 1940s with meticulous attention to detail. We particularly loved the valve wireless and the standard lamp.

Harvey Moon (Ken Cranham) and comrade Lou Lewis (Nigel Planer) waiting for the bus Maurice is on. The location in Walthamstow was undergoing slum clearance so stood in perfectly for bomb-blasted London in 1945.

Birds of a Feather (1989): David Cardy and Alun Lewis as Chris and Darryl, the dodgy husbands of Sharon and Tracey. They're about to embark on the armed robbery that will see them put away for twelve years.
(Photo: Fremantle Media/Shutterstock)

Tracey Stubbs and Sharon Theodopolopodous when they were young. Linda and Pauline had been friends since primary school, so their onscreen sisterly chemistry was no surprise.
(Photo: Fremantle Media/Shutterstock)

Leopardskin loving neighbour, Dorien Green. She was intended to be a secondary character, who popped in occasionally to deliver the subplot, but Lesley Joseph exploded onto the screen and soon became an integral part of our Essex trinity.
(Photo: Fremantle Media/Shutterstock)

A publicity still of the five principal characters, taken after David Cardy left the series to be replaced by Peter Polycarpou, who really was Greek. In 'reality' this photograph couldn't exist as the men in it were behind bars. (Photo: Fremantle Media/Shutterstock)

Maurice writing the first episode of *Birds* (Laurence was taking the photograph instead of co-writing) Maurice is hiding behind a state-of-the-art desktop computer, in our office in Laurence's Southgate home. This computer cost nearly £5,000 back in the early 1980s, the same as a brand-new Ford Capri.

The New Statesman (1987/88): The team with the Emmy, won in New York and damaged on its way home to Yorkshire Television. It was hastily repaired, but the wings were stuck on upside down. Maurice, Marsha Fitzalan (Sarah B'Stard), Rik, Michael Troughton (Piers Fletcher Dervish), Laurence; Vernon Lawrence (Controller of Entertainment), Geoff Sax (Director), and David Reynolds (Producer). We think Rik may have drunk a little too much celebratory champagne.

'*Oh dear, oh dear, oh dear!*' was always the prelude to whatever murderous activity Alan was about to inflict on Piers. Eye-gouging and arse-reaming with a giant Black and Decker were Alan's favourites… and what he did to Maggie Thatcher is an official secret.
(Photo: ITV/Shutterstock)

The New Statesman was launched with a nationwide poster campaign, which obviously made a great impression on the young Tony Blair (see above right)

We're sure Tony Blair would deny he was deliberately emulating Alan B'Stard when he adopted this pose. Years later we returned the favour when we wrote a *New Statesman* stage play in which we revealed that B'Stard was in fact the creator of New Labour.

The New Statesman caught the cynical spirit of the age, and Alan B'Stard was soon a favourite with newspaper cartoonists. Young Tory politicians were also taken with him and started adopting his look.

The *Daily Mirror* invoked Alan's name when an equally immoral Tory MP walked out on his wife and set up home with a young secretary. At that moment we realised we had created not only a monster, but also a hit show.

Love Hurts (1992) was the second hit show that we made for our own production company, ALOMO, which we founded with business genius Allan McKeown. Here are the three of us with Jonathan Powell, Controller BBC1, after we signed an exclusive deal to take all our new ideas to the BBC.

A publicity photograph of us as TV bigshots. The cigars are obviously fake, as any true lover of Cuba's finest could tell, but that didn't prevent some people accusing us of forgetting our roots when it appeared in the *Sunday Times*.

A lovely location shot of Zoë Wanamaker and Adam Faith in West Africa, where the pilot episode climaxes. Nancy Banks Smith, considered one of the finest television critics, compared their on-screen rapport to that of Spencer Tracy and Katharine Hepburn.

Zoë and Adam on location again, this time in St Petersburg. Each series of *Love Hurts* took place partly in an exciting and tax-advantageous foreign location. Unfortunately, we were so busy writing the series that we never got to leave north London. (Photo: Fremantle Media/Shutterstock)

Goodnight Sweetheart (1993): Nick Lyndhurst as Gary Sparrow in Duckett's Passage, in 1940. The character rapidly felt more at home in the past than he did in the present. In his briefcase he probably has a few little goodies supposedly from his friend at the US Embassy, but actually from 1993.
(Photo: Fremantle Media/Shutterstock)

Gary at the piano at the Royal Oak, playing 'his' latest composition 'With a Little Help from My Friends'. Posing as a Hollywood songwriter certainly helped him impress the locals and woo Phoebe, the landlord's daughter. (Photo: Fremantle Media/Shutterstock)

Gary's home life in Cricklewood, 1993, was not full of joy. His wife Yvonne (Michelle Holmes) is a go-getter who wants Gary to make more of himself. Of course, she doesn't know that in 1940 he is something of a hero. (Photo: Fremantle Media/Shutterstock)

Gary's flirtation with Phoebe (Dervla Kirwan) rapidly develops into something much more serious. It would not be fair however, to call him a time-travelling adulterer, at least not in series one, although it wasn't for lack of trying. (Photo: Fremantle Media/Shutterstock)

5
Love Hurts

LOVE HURTS, OUR 1991 romantic comedy about "a woman who doesn't want to fall in love again, who meets a man who's never been in love before" became one of the BBC's drama hits of the decade, yet it's hard to remember what provoked us to want to write it. We do recall that in 1988 a producer friend, Guy Slater, had encouraged us to attempt another comedy drama, because he was such a fan of *Shine On Harvey Moon*. We toyed with some thoughts about a middle-aged love affair, then we were distracted by a new assignment, *Birds of a Feather*, which we were commissioned to make for the BBC through our newly formed production company, ALOMO.

The AL was Allan McKeown, an extraordinarily gifted producer, entrepreneur, and all-round force of nature; we were the LOMO. He had set up Witzend Productions with our heroes Clement and La Frenais. Now he had faith enough to create a company for us. We couldn't believe our luck!

To return once more to the question, "Where do your ideas come from?": sometimes they come from other people. On this occasion the other person was an old friend, Alan Field. Alan was (and is) an agent and manager, and he had just taken on a new client, Adam Faith. Adam had been, alongside Cliff Richard, one of the biggest British pop stars of the early Sixties. He became a TV star in the Seventies in the title role of ITV's *Budgie*. He could have been a TV star in the Eighties too – had he played the lead in *Harvey Moon*, but Adam pulled out mere weeks before filming started, due to a sudden lack of confidence. Endearing but unhelpful.

Adam regretted that decision, so when he told Alan Field he fancied getting back in front of the camera, Alan called us and said that if we were prepared to try again, Adam would like to buy us tea at the Savoy Hotel. It should be known that we're not the sort of chaps to bear a grudge when there's a slap-up tea on offer, and the Savoy do provide exceedingly good cakes.

Adam apologised and of course we accepted because he had, after all, provided a soundtrack to our teenage years, and was in sparkling form. "Mr Charisma" we used to call him, for he could illuminate any room. Women all fell for the diminutive guy with the killer cheekbones, and men all wanted to be his mate. And he really wanted to work with us, it seemed. So we, he, and Alan Field sat around a perfectly ironed tablecloth in a very formal setting, with a Palm Court orchestra setting the tone.

"Got any ideas, kids?" he said, fixing us with his pale blue eyes and that smile.

We hadn't really, except for the scrap of a notion about a middle-aged man who falls in love for the first time. Adam reacted with almost excessive enthusiasm. Who was this man? What did he do? What was his name? Could I be him?

We felt it was a bit early to worry about the bloke's name when we didn't even have a story, but Adam was adamant. Names were important, he said, and he liked playing characters whose names reflected their personalities. We came up with Frank Carver, which seemed a perfect name for a man who offers you an honest smile and a firm handshake, then gazumps you behind your back.

As we got stuck into the triple-layered chocolate cake, and Adam ate a slice of toast with marmalade, he had one more question: "Who'll play the bird?"

We suggested Patricia Hodge, a superb actress who had starred in *Holding the Fort*. Adam, always the ladies' man, clearly approved of Patricia. We promised to talk to her and then get back to him.

Tea over, we left the Savoy together. Adam's chauffeur-driven green drophead Bentley pulled up outside the hotel. He could see we were impressed. "You don't have to be a millionaire to live like one," he said, flashing the famous smile. That became one of Frank Carver's catchphrases.

Decades later we learned that after we left, Adam said to Alan, "We'll never hear from them again, will we?"

The thought of writing for Adam – again – appealed to us. He had real on-screen charm, and we knew the camera adored him. Besides, we liked the idea of his being forever in our debt if we relaunched his TV career.

What we didn't know was that he was on the Savoy Hotel's board of directors, so our afternoon tea and several sumptuous lunches and dinners was Adam proving that his millionaire lifestyle was indeed smoke and mirrors.

But the prospect of working with him was so attractive that we found time in the midst of *Birds* to think about how the adventures of Frank Carver might grip an audience. It didn't take us long to realise that while Frank might be our protagonist, we were more intrigued by the "bird", whom we called Tessa. We've always enjoyed creating strong female characters; hers was the journey we'd invite the audience to share – a strong woman, and a complex one.

We wondered about Tessa's backstory. Since there can be no drama without conflict, and no love without obstacles, we knew Tessa definitely didn't want to fall in love again. Why not? What had happened to her? She must have been badly hurt. And there was our title, *Love Hurts*, borrowed with gratitude from the Everly Brothers.

We thought that Tessa should be a high-flying executive in a top London finance company, embroiled in a lengthy affair with her boss. She never married, never had children, and her biological clock was nearing midnight. Her lover always promised he'd leave his wife once the children had grown up, but now that the children *are* grown up and he's still very married, Tessa finally knows that she's wasted the last ten years of her life.

And then she meets Frank, a man from a different world – working class made good through cunning and determination.

We were pleased that Adam liked our ideas, and Patricia was enthusiastic when we told her she was number one on a shortlist of one to play opposite Adam Faith. We decided to introduce them to each other and see if there was any chemistry. Over lunch in a fashionable Covent Garden basement, our "stars" clicked immediately. Not only was there chemistry, there was a glint in Adam's eye that suggested he wouldn't be averse to a little biology either, though we both sensed Patricia was a touch awestruck. But then she probably had Adam's poster on her bedroom wall when she was a teenager in Grimsby.

Encouraged by that lunch, off we went to see Peter Cregeen, the BBC's Head of Drama. He was intrigued by our strapline – "A woman who doesn't want to fall in love again, who meets a man who's never been in love before" – but he wanted to know so much more about the project than we were able to tell him. We couldn't say where Frank and Tessa met, exactly how the relationship would develop, whether he was married – we weren't even sure how Frank made his money. Indeed, it would be fair to say we hardly knew anything at all, but we knew we'd find out once we started writing.

Understandably Peter said, "Why should I commission this?"

According to Laurence's diary, Maurice said, "Because it will be your biggest drama hit of the year." Maurice claims to have no recollection of this act of outrageous chutzpah, but it worked, because Peter commissioned a pilot script there and then.

The moment a commissioner says words to the effect of, "Write me a script, for money," is one of the highlights of the scriptwriter's life. There follow weeks or months of sometimes agonised wrestling with all the elements required to make a pilot script work, and a drama pilot is a much more complex instrument than a comedy. We had to invent a host of compelling characters with stories of their own, able to generate absorbing subplots to contrast with and support the main love story. We also knew that if a series was commissioned, we would need to bring a team of drama writers together to deliver the scripts, so our pilot had to establish a definite style and the characterisations had to be clear enough for other writers to take on, and "run with the ball".

We look back on the characters we devised with some pride. They include the smooth ex-lover whom Tessa sweetly "blackmails" into supporting her new charity work; there's the female Rabbi with whom she went to university, who has employed her at the charity, and whose marriage is slowly falling apart; there's Tessa's slightly pathetic former work colleague, who is still in love with her; and Tessa's parents, an indulgent father and a sardonic yet affectionate mother. Frank's world includes his best mate and chauffeur, Max, who has been with him through thick and thin; and a wild teenage daughter who shares his riverside penthouse. By the time we typed "End of Episode One" we felt and hoped we had created something special.

Then Patricia got in touch. What did we want to hear first, the good news or the bad news? Both were the same: she was pregnant, after years of trying, and couldn't take the risk of signing up for what could be a long-running series. We offered our sincere congratulations, but our hearts sank. She was fifty per cent of the appeal of the show, and we knew that the Controller of BBC 1 was a fervent fan.

Recasting is a fraught business, and everyone at ALOMO had different ideas of who should play Tessa. What was agreed was that Tessa should be striking, sexy, provocative, and have real acting chops. A list of "possibles" was compiled, but none of them really convinced us. Then Laurence saw Arthur Miller's *The Crucible* at the National Theatre and was blown away by Zoë Wanamaker's performance and presence. Although she was a primarily a stage actress, with little exposure on television at the time, Zoë felt right, and worth fighting for, so we did, and the BBC was prepared to back our judgement.

But Zoë's introduction made us reconsider the structure of the pilot. In a romantic comedy it's normal to introduce the two main characters early on, intercutting between their lives, until their first get-together, known in Hollywood as the "meet cute" moment. Instead we decided we had to focus on Tessa for the first third of the pilot, eavesdropping as she dictates a deliciously vicious letter to her lover detailing his duplicity and betrayal, with a copy to the chairman of the company.

We learn quickly that Tessa is not a woman to mess with. We stay with her as she gets drunk and totals her car, lands a new job running an old-fashioned charity – at a fraction of her previous salary – and has to downsize to a modest flat in a dodgy part of London. On her first night in her new home, getting ready for an important fundraising dinner, Tessa discovers that the hot tap in the bathtub won't turn off (a conscious

Shooting the Pilot

harking back to our first TV sitcom, which opened with Patricia Hodge on her back under the sink, wrestling with some errant plumbing).

A plumbing emergency is always maddening. When it happens on the night of your first corporate event, it's a tragedy. In desperation Tessa works her way down the list of plumbers in Yellow Pages, until she finds herself speaking to Frank.

By now the audience has had time to meet and warm to Zoë, and it's Adam's turn to be introduced. Frank Carver is a mere plumber no longer. He's a working-class entrepreneur who's just taken over the builder's merchants where he was once a downtrodden apprentice. Nevertheless when the phone rings he rides to the rescue in a spirit of chivalry and mischief. If we've done our work as writers, the audience should be desperate to see what happens when Tessa lets Frank into her flat. Will she fall for him? Of course not. She is determined never to get hurt by a man again. Any man. Especially one like Frank Carver, a cocky self-made millionaire with a line of cheeky chat guaranteed to outrage Tessa's sensibilities.

But Frank isn't the sort of bloke to give up the chase. He is persistent. And funny. And charming, damn him. Tessa finally allows herself to be cajoled into agreeing a date. *The Guardian*'s Nancy Banks-Smith – the doyenne of TV critics – likened the chemistry of this scene to that generated by Spencer Tracey and Katherine Hepburn. All we could and can say is "wow!"

But Tessa stands Frank up when a work emergency forces her to fly to Africa. Getting no reply from Tessa's front door, he phones her and listens to her "out of office" message; she's had to dash off to the Gambia.

He stares at his mobile in disbelief. "Gambia? I thought we said Langan's!"

We were proud of this line and thought it set the tone for the series, but Guy Slater, who was now producing *Love Hurts*, persuaded us Frank should follow Tessa to the Gambia and we should end the show there. The audience wouldn't expect us actually to film in Africa, so here was our chance to show that this series was different, a British romantic comedy that would go beyond our island borders.

The pilot climaxes when Frank suddenly appears in the Gambia, looking cool and unflappable and dressed for the occasion. Tessa is dumbstruck. There isn't a snappy bon mot, just a wonderful look from the so-expressive Zoë Wanamaker, as Tessa tries to compute why this dangerously charming man has flown halfway around the world. What can he want? It can't be her? Can it?

Before the press show of *Love Hurts*, we stood in the corridor with Adam Faith.

"You coming in to see it?" we asked.

"I've never seen anything I've been in and I'm not going to start now," he replied. "You watch it and tell me what it's like."

As the credits rolled we left the preview theatre and there stood Adam, as if he was waiting for us. "Well?" he asked.

Laurence pronounced, "I think you've got a big hit show on your hands, mate."

"You reckon, kid?"

Maurice was right. It was the BBC's biggest drama hit of the year. It could also have been their biggest flop, because there was a chemistry that was entirely unpredictable. There has to be the right script with the right cast at the right time, and then the stars align. It's what makes writing an unpredictable adventure, and when it all works then it's magical.

LOVE HURTS

by Laurence Marks and Maurice Gran

Episode One: "Crawling From The Wreckage"

1. EXT. SMART WEST END RESTAURANT. DAY.

A CHAUFFEUR waits at the kerb in a Daimler double six, reading the Daily Express. A good looking middle aged man, HUGH MARRINER, hurries out of the restaurant, tight lipped, and gets in to the back of the car. The CHAUFFEUR is slightly taken aback, puts down his paper and drives off.

2. INT. RESTAURANT. DAY.

TESSA alone at a table for two. In front of her an uneaten dessert. In front of the empty chair, an empty dessert dish. An empty wine bottle and a vase with a single rose on the pink tablecloth. TESSA looks awful. She's trying not to cry. Other DINERS are trying not to look as if they're staring at her. A sympathetic WAITER brings a large brandy, which TESSA knocks back. Then she just sits and stares into space.

3. INT. TESSA'S OFFICE. DAY.

An hour later. MIRIAM, TESSA'S secretary, is sitting in her office outside TESSA'S. She taps away on her word processor. TESSA comes in briskly, her face a little flushed. MIRIAM looks up.

MIRIAM: Sian phoned from the Telegraph, she said you promised to show her...

TESSA: (SWEEPS BY) Come and take a letter, Miriam...

TESSA walks straight through to her office. MIRIAM picks up a notebook and goes through to...

4. INT. TESSA'S OFFICE. DAY.

A large stylish office as befits a senior executive. TESSA sits on the sofa. She pats it for MIRIAM to sit next to her.

MIRIAM: No one says "take a letter" any more, Tessa...

TESSA: I know, but it has such a lovely old-fashioned ring to it... It's to Hugh Marriner...

MIRIAM: But you just had lunch with him...

TESSA: I did, it was very informative. We discussed my future...

MIRIAM: Ah...

TESSA: And it's always a good idea to follow up a meeting with a letter, to avoid misunderstandings.

MIRIAM looks a little confused.

TESSA: So where was I?

MIRIAM: You hadn't started...

TESSA: Okay... "Dear Hugh", mmm, yes, "May I be the first to congratulate you on Emma's graduation from St Hilda's? First class honours, quite an achievement. Added to Nick's B.Sc. it just proves what a brainy lot you Marriners are. (Smiles sweetly at MIRIAM). Now that you have seen both your offspring through university and into the real world, may I remind you of a conversation we had on the terrace of the George V in Paris, spring 1984, wasn't it? "Of course I love you, Tess, you're the most fantastic woman I've ever known. But there is no way I could leave Jennifer while the children are still at school, it just wouldn't be fair. I know it's just as unfair for me to ask you to wait, but I am asking you to wait, and I

	promise with all my heart that as soon as Nick and Emily have finished their education, you and I will be together for ever..."
MIRIAM:	(getting really embarrassed) Tessa! You shouldn't be writing this! You shouldn't be dictating it to me, for God's sake!
TESSA:	Why not? Everyone knows I'm the managing director's mistress... was, rather. "Believe me, I remember all your lies."
MIRIAM:	Sorry?
TESSA:	We're back to the letter. "Believe me, Hugh, I remember all your lies. What I can't believe is I fell for them! Six years of prevarication, evasion, snatched suppers, sordid sex, forgotten birthdays, lonely Christmases... and what makes it worse is I hate self pity, and here I am wallowing in it. I should have known, I've seen it happen enough to other people. The long term mistress gets dumped five minutes after the wife, when the "lover" takes up with this year's model. But when I heard you'd left poor old Jennifer for a 23 year old perfume salesgirl from the Giorgio counter at Allder's of Croydon...! At least you could have pulled at Harvey Nix, couldn't you!?"
MIRIAM:	Tessa, I'm so sorry...
TESSA:	(Fighting back the tears) Don't sympathise yet, I'll lose the flow... Where was I?
MIRIAM:	(Reads back embarassed) "At least you could have pulled at Harvey Nix..."
TESSA:	Right... "Under these circumstances, you won't be surprised that I hereby give the requisite three months' notice. If the thought of having me around for thirteen weeks is too embarrassing, you can

Love Hurts

       bribe me to go tomorrow. I'm copying this letter to Marshall Baumblatt in Atlanta, Georgia. I think your boss should know how I feel about my boss. Rot in hell etcetera..."

MIRIAM: You can't!

TESSA: Can't what?

MIRIAM: Copy this to Marshall Baumblatt! He's a born-again Christian.

TESSA: I know... personally I think being born once should be enough for anyone... Well, go on, type it up.

       MIRIAM reluctantly leaves the office. TESSA picks a fat file up and starts methodically shredding the contents.

       5. INT. MALCOLM LITOFF'S OFFICE. DAY.

       The door is half open. On the door it says "Malcolm Litoff, Deputy Director, Personnel and Recruitment." In the office, smaller than TESSA'S, MALCOLM sits behind his desk, with his coffee. On his screen some figures to work on. His phone rings.

MALCOLM: Malcolm Litoff... What?! You are joking!?

       He jumps up and dashes out of the room.

       6. INT. TESSA'S OFFICE. DAY.

       TESSA is still shredding. MIRIAM is on her hands and knees, wading through the shredded paper, trying to jigsaw some of the pieces back together.

MIRIAM: Six months' work!

Shooting the Pilot

MIRIAM gets up and comes round the desk to try to snatch away the unshredded paper. TESSA brandishes a paper knife.

TESSA: Get back!

MALCOLM hurries in.

TESSA: Not now, Malcolm, I'm in conference.

MALCOLM: Jesus, Tess, what is this?!

TESSA: Well, it was the original artwork and campaign strategy for next week's press launch... but now it's ticker tape, and here comes the big parade.

TESSA scoops up an armful of paper and throws it out of the window.

MALCOLM: But your career...!

TESSA: I think that's already out of the window.

7. INT. WINEBAR. NIGHT.

A soulless wine bar somewhere in the City. Not very busy. TESSA is sitting alone with a bottle of wine. MALCOLM comes in, and crosses to her.

MALCOLM: Tessa...

TESSA: Hello Malcolm. I'm glad you could make it, my leaving party was turning into a bit of an anti-climax.

MALCOLM: (Sits) You know how you could have avoided all this unpleasantness, don't you?

TESSA: How?

MALCOLM: You could have had an affair with me instead. I'm single, regular church goer, reasonable tennis player, fair cook, I've always been on the brink of falling in love with you...

Love Hurts

TESSA: I've noticed... but if the chemistry isn't there...

MALCOLM: Yes, you don't fancy me, fair enough. But suppose we skipped the first few sweaty exciting months of the relationship, and went straight on to the comfy boring bits; the theatre trips, going to Tesco's together, walking holidays in the Lake District, early to bed with the Telegraph crossword, hot milk and winceyette jimjams...

TESSA: Sorry, Malcolm, I'm renouncing relationships, it eats into my wine drinking time. Get another bottle will you?

8. EXT. CITY STREETS. NIGHT.

TESSA and MALCOLM come out of the wine bar. MALCOLM hails a taxi.

MALCOLM: We can share...

TESSA: No, it's okay, you take it, I'm going for a long walk...

MALCOLM reluctantly goes off in the taxi. TESSA walks down the street and gets into her own car and drives off.

9. EXT. WEST END BLOCK OF FLATS. NIGHT.

TESSA sits in her car opposite a smart block of flats. She takes an occasional swig from a quarter bottle of brandy. It's nearly empty. After a few moments, a BMW 535i drives up to the flats. HUGH gets out with a young BLONDE. GRAHAM the doorman salutes them and HUGH gives him the keys to the car. HUGH and BLONDE go inside. TESSA gets out of her car and hurries across to the flats. GRAHAM recognises her.

GRAHAM: (EMBARRASSED) Evening, Miss Piggott.

Shooting the Pilot

TESSA: Hello Graham, I've forgotten my key...

GRAHAM: Sorry, Mr Marriner says you can't come in here any more.

TESSA: What?!

GRAHAM: He said to say he'll send your things on. Sorry.

TESSA turns angrily away, and storms across the road to her car, pausing to run a key along the gleaming BMW's paintwork. She gets into her car, and pulls away from the kerb without looking. A taxi, moving along the road at some speed, violently slams into the side of her car.

10. EXT. HOSPITAL. NIGHT.

An ambulance arrives outside the emergency entrance of a grimy Victorian hospital. A stretcher is extracted and rushed inside. Was that TESSA on it?

11. INT. MALCOLM'S BEDROOM. NIGHT.

MALCOLM is asleep in bed. He wears pyjamas. His clothes hang neatly on a trouser press, his change in the little space for change. Everything in its place. The telephone goes. Two red eyes light up - the red eyes of the Mr Froggy novelty phone. MALCOLM wakes - he's the sort of man who wakes instantly and totally. He picks up the phone.

MALCOLM: Yes?... Oh my God...!

12. EXT. MALCOLM'S FLAT. NIGHT.

A vaguely modern block with cars parked in the forecourt. MALCOLM sprints down the front steps. He's put on his suit shirt and tie of earlier, and has shaved hurriedly and has bits of toilet paper adhering to his face. He rushes to his carefully maintained Triumph Stag. He drives off.

13. INT. CASUALTY. NIGHT.

An echoing dirty space scattered with the human detritus of the Thatcherdom. Drunks with cut heads, homeless youngsters with hacking coughs, pinch-faced mothers with sick kids. MALCOLM is at the desk, trying to get information from the RECEPTIONIST.

MALCOLM: You must have some record, she phoned me...

RECEPTIONIST: Then I don't suppose she's at death's door.

Then MALCOLM hears TESSA'S voice echoing down a corridor.

TESSA: Malcolm!

MALCOLM turns and sees her hobbling towards him on a stick. She's cut and bruised and wears a deep foam rubber neck support. MALCOLM rushes over to her, hugs her. She winces.

MALCOLM: Are you all right?!

TESSA: I'll live... The car's a write-off...

MALCOLM: No...!

TESSA: Malcolm, it's only a car... anyway, I was 115 milligrams over the limit, so I won't need a car soon, will I?

MALCOLM: (Affectionately) You stupid cow!

TESSA: I didn't know you cared.

MALCOLM: Yes you did. Come on...

TESSA leans on MALCOLM, they walk towards the exit.

Shooting the Pilot

TESSA: The end of a perfect day...

14. INT. MALCOLM'S CAR. NIGHT.

MALCOLM drives towards his flat. TESSA looks at him from passenger's seat.

TESSA: You're unique, you know...

MALCOLM: Thank you, I think.

TESSA: I mean, who else, answering a plea for help at 2 in the morning, would put on a tie and shave – after a fashion?

TESSA gently removes a piece of toilet paper from his cheek.

MALCOLM: If it makes me seem more human, I forgot to wear socks.

15. INT. MALCOLM'S LIVING ROOM. NIGHT.

A large comfy room, very much the room of an overgrown boy. The bookcase is full of books about classic cars, the War, things scientific. But there are also a lot of books about Marilyn Monroe and "The Joys of Lovemaking". TESSA is sitting in a leather armchair, with a coffee and a large brandy. MALCOLM comes in with some bedding, and starts turning the sofa into a bed.

TESSA: What are you doing?

MALCOLM: I'll sleep in here, you have my bed...

TESSA: Oh don't be so cliched! Why do you think I didn't want to go home?

MALCOLM: (Surprised and embarrassed) What?

TESSA: Don't worry, I'm not calling your bluff. I just want some warmth next to me tonight. Do you mind?

MALCOLM:	Do I mind? Do I mind sleeping with the woman I've fantasised about for five years? No, I don't mind at all.
TESSA:	Fine. Can I borrow a toothbrush?
MALCOLM:	Nothing will happen, I give you my word.
TESSA:	Scout's honour?
MALCOLM:	I know you think I'm an overgrown schoolboy...
TESSA:	I'm sorry, I was teasing... You're a very nice person, Malcolm.
MALCOLM:	I know. Carve it on my gravestone.

16. INT. MALCOLM'S BEDROOM. NIGHT.

TESSA is in bed. She wears a pair of MALCOLM'S pyjamas, and is quizzically looking through a raunchy magazine(!) MALCOLM'S voice comes from off.

MALCOLM:	Are you decent?
TESSA:	Depends who you ask. How about you?
MALCOLM:	(Coming in) Honest decent and truthful... Where did you find that?!
TESSA:	On the bedside table.
MALCOLM:	Oh God! I'm sorry.
TESSA:	It's all right, it's your flat. I just never thought...
MALCOLM:	Thought what?
TESSA:	I don't know...
MALCOLM:	(HOTLY) Look, it's very simple; I'm single, I'm not queer, contrary to some of the office gossip; I

Shooting the Pilot

	haven't had a girlfriend for three years, I don't fancy the idea of going to a prostitute...
TESSA:	It's okay, honestly, you don't have to justify yourself... Only...
MALCOLM:	Please don't give me all that "this exploits women" rubbish, that's all I ask! Men like looking at women without any clothes on, it's normal, I refuse to feel guilty – and I know I'd rather be a porno model than work in Tesco's for £2.25 an hour.
TESSA:	Me too – if that's the only choice.
MALCOLM:	I'm making a complete arse of myself, aren't I? I'll sleep in the other room...
TESSA:	No! Please!
	MALCOLM climbs into bed beside her, and flicks off the bedside lamp. There's a short silence. Then a long sigh from TESSA.
MALCOLM:	Are you all right?
TESSA:	What do you think?
MALCOLM:	Sorry...
	TESSA starts to cry.
TESSA:	Shit Tessa! Stupid!

17. INT. ESTATE AGENT'S OFFICE. DAY.

TESSA sitting opposite a bright young female NEGOTIATOR who is taking down the details of her house.

NEGOTIATOR:	Of course you know the market is somewhat depressed right now...
TESSA:	Not just the market.

Love Hurts

NEGOTIATOR: Houses in your road were fetching three back in '88, but now you'll be lucky to get two five...

TESSA: Then put it on for two...

NEGOTIATOR: Two hundred thousand!? What's wrong with it?!

TESSA: It's haunted.

18. EXT. CLEETHORPES RAILWAY STATION. DAY.

An Intercity train arrives. TESSA gets off with a small suitcase. She looks around, expecting to be met. There's no-one there. She shrugs and joins the queue for the barrier.

19. EXT. RESIDENTIAL STREET. DAY.

A taxi enters a street of solid Edwardian villas. TESSA gets out, pays the fare, and goes up to the front door of a large corner house. (There is a side door too, into TESSA'S FATHER'S surgery and waiting room. A middle aged PATIENT is coming out of this side door. He walks up the side path and into the street.) TESSA takes a key out of her pocket, then puts it back and rings the bell. After a little while, the door is opened by TESSA'S mother, MRS PIGGOTT, a rather faded woman in her mid-sixties. She seems to need a second to remember who TESSA is.

TESSA: Hello mum. I thought you were collecting me from the station?

MRS PIGGOTT: Was I? Sorry, completely forgot. Never mind, there are taxis aren't there?

MRS PIGGOTT disappears into the house. TESSA shrugs – what was she expecting, the red carpet? She enters.

20. INT. TESSA'S PARENTS' HALL. DAY.

There are two large front reception rooms off the hall. To the left is DR PIGGOTT'S surgery. To the right the drawing room. MRS PIGGOTT goes through towards her kitchen.

MRS PIGGOTT: (Over her shoulder) Cup of instant?

TESSA: (Makes a face) Lovely, no sugar... Daddy in?

MRS PIGGOTT: Suppose so...

TESSA taps on the surgery door.

DR PIGGOTT: (From within) Busy!

TESSA: It's me, daddy.

DR PIGGOTT: (From within) Tessa! Plumcake! Come in, come in!

TESSA opens the door and goes into...

21. INT. DR PIGGOTT'S SURGERY. DAY.

TESSA'S FATHER is behind his big desk. Facing him is a middle aged woman, pasty in complexion, dowdy in personality. She doesn't look terribly well.

TESSA: Sorry daddy, I didn't realise...

DR PIGGOTT: (Gets up and goes to TESSA. Huge hugs) You don't mind, do you, Mrs de Groot?

MRS DE GROOT looks as if she does, but is scared to say so.

DR PIGGOTT: Did your mother remember to collect you?

TESSA: She said she had a cold coming on.

DR PIGGOTT: Bloody hypochondriac, that's her trouble...

TESSA: She looks a little run down...

DR PIGGOTT:	And you look splendid, Tess! How's the wonderful world of high finance?
MRS DE GROOT:	Excuse me, Doctor...
DR PIGGOTT:	(All smooth) Mrs De Groot, forgive me... (Scribbles prescription) This is my daughter Tessa...
MRS DE GROOT:	(To TESSA) I know, I was in your year at the Grammar, not the same class of course, you were in Alpha, I was in Beta. (TESSA looks blank) I used to be Deirdre Foster...
TESSA:	Of course! You were school long jump champion! How are you?

Then TESSA realises what a stupid question that is!

22. INT. DINING ROOM. NIGHT.

A solid stolid middle class dining room, with Ercol furniture. Round the table are TESSA, and her PARENTS. They're finishing their Chicken Kievs from Marks and Spencer. DR PIGGOTT is topping up wine glasses with the Marks and Spencer white Rioja.

MRS PIGGOTT:	Is everything all right?
TESSA:	Yes, lovely...
MRS PIGGOTT:	I don't know what I'd do without Marks and Spencer...
DR PIGGOTT:	Anything but cook... only joking. (He isn't though).
TESSA:	It's fine, honestly. I live on M&S food...
DR PIGGOTT:	It's marvellous to see you anyway, you don't come home often enough...

Shooting the Pilot

MRS PIGGOTT: (Sniffily) She leads a very busy lifestyle...

DR PIGGOTT: Absolutely. There was quite a decent piece about you in the Financial Times a couple of months ago...

TESSA: I know... (Drains her glass)

DR PIGGOTT: Why didn't you drive up? Haven't you still got the Alfa?

TESSA: I had a little accident...

DR PIGGOTT: What?!

TESSA: It's all right daddy, nothing dramatic...

MRS PIGGOTT: Had you been drinking?

TESSA: What?

DR PIGGOTT: Marjorie!

MRS PIGGOTT: When you had your accident?

TESSA: No I wasn't!

A few moments silence as they finish eating. DR PIGGOTT finishes first. MRS PIGGOTT starts gathering up the plates.

DR PIGGOTT: And what cook-chilled creation have you defrosted for pudding?

MRS PIGGOTT: I haven't defrosted anything, it's ice cream.

On this small triumph, MRS PIGGOTT takes the plates and exits.

DR PIGGOTT: She does her best I suppose...

TESSA: Why are you always like that with her?!

DR PIGGOTT: Like what?

TESSA gets up suddenly and leaves the room and a puzzled father.

22. INT. KITCHEN. NIGHT.

An unmodernised kitchen. MRS PIGGOTT is affectionately watching her Springer Spaniel wolf down some dog food. On the table an open library book. TESSA enters.

MRS PIGGOTT: Your father's coffee's nearly ready...

TESSA: Need any help?

MRS PIGGOTT: (Crosses to sink) No, I'm fine... (Starts to wash up)

TESSA looks at the cover of her mother's library book. It's "Lives and Loves of a She Devil". TESSA feels she has to make an offering.

TESSA: I was drunk.

MRS PIGGOTT: Any particular reason?

TESSA: I'd just split up with Hugh... well, vice versa really.

MRS PIGGOTT: I never much cared for him.

TESSA: Daddy always liked him.

MRS PIGGOTT: Naturally.

TESSA: Why do you let daddy walk all over you?

MRS PIGGOTT: Why did you let Hugh...?

TESSA: I didn't!

MRS PIGGOTT: You used to scamper around doing his every bidding...

TESSA: I do not scamper!

MRS PIGGOTT: Not as a rule, no.

TESSA:	(Feeling very drained) God...
MRS PIGGOTT:	Come on, let's take Buster for a pee.
TESSA:	What about daddy?
MRS PIGGOTT:	(Deadpan) He can use the toilet.

TESSA looks at her mother with new respect.

23. EXT. FRONT AT CLEETHORPES. NIGHT.

TESSA and her MOTHER and the dog walking into the wind.

MRS PIGGOTT:	So what now? Another job?
TESSA:	Of course...
MRS PIGGOTT:	Doing what? More of the same?
TESSA:	I don't know. I suppose so.
MRS PIGGOTT:	More media relations, more corporate image formation...
TESSA:	It pays very well.
MRS PIGGOTT:	I can see it's made you immensely happy.
TESSA:	What do you think I should do?
MRS PIGGOTT:	You've never asked my advice before.
TESSA:	I have.
MRS PIGGOTT:	Not since you were fourteen. You really want my opinion?
TESSA:	Yes.
MRS PIGGOTT:	All right. I think it's time you did something useful with your life. This world isn't going to get better all by itself.
TESSA:	What are you talking about?

MRS PIGGOTT:	Did you know that the Irish Sea is the most nuclear-polluted stretch of water in the world?
TESSA:	So?
MRS PIGGOTT:	Just thought you might be interested.
TESSA:	(Looking at the waves) But this isn't the Irish Sea!
MRS PIGGOTT:	That's all right then.

A short silence. The dog is having a good time though.

TESSA:	I saw Deirdre... oh, what's her name now... de Groot in the surgery, she looks sixty!
MRS PIGGOTT:	Well, she has got cancer.
TESSA:	Oh shit.
MRS PIGGOTT:	Your father thinks she'll recover, though...
TESSA:	(Bitter) Does he?
MRS PIGGOTT:	He spotted her symptoms straight away; the consultant thinks they may have caught it in time...
TESSA:	I hope so.
MRS PIGGOTT:	He's a very good doctor.
TESSA:	I used to think he was a wonderful man.
MRS PIGGOTT:	He may well be; he does wonderful things for other people. He just happens to despise me, that's all. It happens.

24. INT. INTER-CITY TRAIN. DAY.

TESSA sits in a First Class compartment. She has "Campaign" plus all the heavy daily papers spread around, and she's marking up job ads with her

Shooting the Pilot

	Lamy fountain pen. She underscores one particular smallish ad. Then she gets her cellular phone from her handbag, and dials a number.
TESSA:	Hello, I'd like to speak to Diane Warburg, please... Tessa Piggott, we used to be at Oxford together... (To herself) I think... Yes, I'll hold...
	Then the train roars into a tunnel and she's cut off.
TESSA:	Bugger!

25. INT. TESSA'S DRAWING ROOM. DAY.

	TESSA and MALCOLM are packing up her things into tea chests. The sign outside the house says "Sold."
TESSA:	... You remember Alan Wallington?
MALCOLM:	No...
TESSA:	Of course you do, he was always on Question Time!
MALCOLM:	Oh, you mean the Labour man with the hairy tweed suits?
TESSA:	Yes, well he became Chief Executive after he lost his seat in '87... anyway, according to Diane, he's left them in a terrible state, balance sheet in the red, office full of seething lefties, projects mismanaged, three pregant field workers in Gabon...
MALCOLM:	You're serious, aren't you?
TESSA:	She really thinks I stand a chance...
MALCOLM:	A chance!? They ought to walk over broken glass...
TESSA:	Thank you fans...
MALCOLM:	But a charity!

Love Hurts

TESSA: Yes...

MALCOLM: You'll take an enormous drop...

TESSA: Probably... the advert says "salary neg."

MALCOLM: "Neg" for negligable... you'll be lucky to get more than twenty K.

TESSA: I'm sure you're right...

MALCOLM: But who can live on 20k?!

TESSA: Plenty of people get by on a lot less...

MALCOLM: Name one.

TESSA: Mrs Philpott.

MALCOLM: Who?

TESSA: Your cleaning lady!

MALCOLM: You know what I mean.

TESSA: And my brother's a deputy head, and he doesn't earn eighteen thousand... Anyway, the mortgage will be much lower on the flat, and I won't be running a car...

MALCOLM: Mmm, will you tell them about your impending drink drive conviction?

TESSA: Only if they ask.

26. INT. VICTORIAN HOUSE. DAY.

TESSA is climbing the stairs of a large Victorian pile. She reaches a landing. On the door is the sign "LIFE SUPPORT - A REGISTERED CHARITY." She enters.

27. INT. BOARDROOM. DAY.

TESSA faces an interview panel of three people. DIANE WARBURG, an attractive Jewish woman of about 40, is Chairwoman, and she is flanked by BOB PEARCE, a staff representative, and LORD GODFREY, a black Labour peer of the Gaitskellite tendency and a Yorkshire accent. BOB PEARCE is in a wheelchair.

TESSA: ... I've spent almost all my working life in marketing, media management and corporate relations, and those skills can help carve out a bigger market share for Life Support.

BOB PEARCE: Market share?! We aren't a sausage factory! We're a project based development agency!

LORD GODFREY: And a registered charity...

TESSA: Yes, but what is Life Support's raison d'etre, Mr Pearce? After all, there are Oxfam, Christian Aid, dozens of organisations carrying out the same sort of work, so why another one?

BOB PEARCE: Who's interviewing who here?!

DIANE: It's a fair question, Bob. Miss Piggott, Life Support is a very old charity — until 1986 we were the Imperial Fund For Colonial Relief — and we adminster several trust funds and bequests...

LORD GODFREY: But obviously we're not going to make much of an impact on Third World problems until we...

BOB PEARCE: Sorry to butt in, Jeff, but we did pass a resolution not to refer to the undeveloped South as the Third World any longer, it implies a hierarchical perception...

LORD GODFREY: Oh, not more claptrap...!

DIANE:	Not right now, gentlemen... Tessa, perhaps you'd like to explain how you see the role of Director?
TESSA:	Well, obviously I'm not an expert at the technology and politics of development, but I am an expert at media management... (BOB PEARCE snorts). I hadn't heard of Life Support until I saw your advert, and neither had seventeen of the twenty people I stopped in the the street outside this building this morning.
BOB PEARCE:	We've always been low profile...
LORD GODFREY:	No sodding profile you mean!
BOB PEARCE:	Why don't we just get Saatchi and Saatchi in then?!
LORD GODFREY:	I would if they'd do the job for sixteen grand...
TESSA:	Sixteen thousand...?!
	TESSA looks accusingly at DIANE, who smiles apologetically.
DIANE:	The salary is negotiable...

28. INT. HUGH MARRINER'S OUTER OFFICE. DAY.

TESSA enters the office where HUGH'S PA, HARRIET, works. HARRIET is very surprised.

HARRIET:	Tessa! How...?
TESSA:	Did I get in? I bribed the doorman.
HARRIET:	No, I mean, how are you? You look wonderful...
TESSA:	Is Hugh in?
HARRIET:	He's on the telephone...
TESSA:	I'll wait.
HARRIET:	He has appointments all day.

TESSA: I haven't.

TESSA sits on the guests' sofa. A few seconds pass. She picks up a copy of Management Today. HUGH comes out of his office. He doesn't immediately see who is behind the magazine. TESSA puts it down.

TESSA: Mr Marriner, do you think you could spare me five minutes?

HUGH jumps.

29. INT. HUGH'S OFFICE. DAY.

It's a huge office, as you'd expect. HUGH looks ill at ease behind his desk.

TESSA: ... And Marshall Baumblatt didn't say anything about your sordid little secret?

HUGH: No, I imagine he decided senior executives are entitled to their private lives.

TESSA: Or perhaps I changed my mind about sending that letter. (Produces envelope)

HUGH: Oh God, not blackmail! How utterly pathetic.

TESSA: I don't want much, Hugh. I just thought you might just want to help me in my new job. You know, a leg up rather than a leg over...

30. TESSA'S OFFICE AT LIFE SUPPORT. DAY.

TESSA sits behind an old wooden desk. Most of the furniture looks begged or borrowed. The incongruous digital clock says 15.07. TESSA is watching a video of scenes of devastation somewhere in Mozambique. A JOURNALIST in a safari suit is doing his bit to camera. TESSA is watching with horrified attention.

JOURNALIST:	Three days ago this was a flourishing village. There were crops in the fields, and several workshops, run by the small British charity, Life Support, were helping to train the villagers in carpentry, building, basic engineering... Then the night before last, South African backed rebels attacked...
	TESSA's door opens, and DIANE enters. She has a carrier bag from a Marks and Spencer food hall. TESSA freeze-frames the video.
DIANE:	What is it?
TESSA:	The Massona project. Twenty seven dead including five field workers.
DIANE:	Oh God!
TESSA:	Do you think we should show this tonight?
DIANE:	No, there's enough people who think there's no point in giving money, they're all savages. They forget Europe can still teach Africa a few lessons in mass murder... Have you had lunch?
TESSA:	(Shakes head fiercely) No!
	DIANE gets a packet of chicken legs out of her carrier bag.
DIANE:	Have a Marks and Spencer chicken leg...
TESSA:	Did my mother send you?
DIANE:	Go on – I bet you haven't had lunch.
TESSA:	How can I?
DIANE:	Anorexia in England does not solve starvation in Africa. As chairperson of the trustees, I insist.
	TESSA reluctantly bites into a chicken leg. So does DIANE.

TESSA: Isn't this your family's dinner we're consuming?

DIANE: It's all right, I'll get the kids some Kentucky Fried instead. Alex will be delighted, he's crazy about their lemon clean-up towels.

TESSA: It suddenly occurs to me, why are you still Diane Warburg?

DIANE: Instead of Mrs Simon Lucas, you mean? Because by the time I got married I already had a career in my maiden name.

TESSA: Oh, I see... Do you know, I don't actually know what you do. I suppose I thought with the kids and the charity work...

DIANE: No, I do have a job. A very interesting job. Unfortunately it involves working weekends...

TESSA: You're a football referee?

DIANE: I'm a rabbi.

TESSA: You're not!

DIANE: I am! I know I haven't got a long white beard, but the North London Progressive Alliance is very tolerant.

TESSA: A rabbi! Jesus Christ!!

DIANE: Yes, like Him, only not as charismatic.

31. INT. TESSA'S HALL. DAY.

The hall of her "new" flat in Wandsworth. A stack of free papers and a lot of junk mail on the mat. The front door pushes open against the junk. TESSA enters, with an evening dress wrapped in dry-cleaner's polythene over her arm. She collects the mail and walks through into the...

32. INT. KITCHEN. DAY.

The kitchen is shabby and unfinished, but with DIY units. TESSA enters, flicking through the mail. She puts the electric kettle on, and proceeds to the...

33. INT. BATHROOM. DAY.

Quite large, horrible wallpaper. There's an old sink but an incongruously new garish pink corner jacuzzi-bath. TESSA enters, still with dress, and turns on the jacuzzi taps, and goes through to her...

34. INT. BEDROOM. DAY.

TESSA enters, and drops all the mail in the bin by the door. The bedroom again is unpleasantly decorated, with a wall of ugly DIY fitted wardrobes. TESSA strips the polythene from the evening dress. There's one of those infuriating tags through the label. She looks on her dressing table for scissors, can't find them, so bites through the tag. She lays the dress on the bed and starts to undress.

35. INT. BATHROOM. DAY.

TESSA returns, in bathrobe. She has a mug of tea. The bath is nearly full. She turns the taps off. Nothing happens.

TESSA: Shit.

TESSA turns the knob that operates the "pop-up waste." The waste does not pop up.

TESSA: God, no! Not tonight!

TESSA rolls up a sleeve, and plunges her arm into the water. It's hot. She tries to get the waste out manually, but just succeeds in breaking a nail.

TESSA: Bastard...!

TESSA empties her tea into the hand basin, and starts bailing out the bath with the mug. After a few seconds, she realises the futility of this. She dashes out...

36. INT. KITCHEN. DAY.

TESSA charges in, collects a saucepan, her cordless phone and the Yellow Pages from a pile of phone books on the floor.

37. INT. BATHROOM. DAY.

TESSA charges in. The bath fills inexorably. She starts bailing out into the wash basin, using the saucepan. Simultaneously, she looks up plumbers in the Yellow Pages. She dials one.

TESSA: Hello? Triple A Plumbers? Look...

ANSWERPHONE VOICE:
Hello, there's no one here right now...

TESSA slams down the phone and tries another number.

TESSA: Drain Surgeons? Three years ago?! No, I don't need a minicab!

She hangs up in disgust, and looks at the date on the Yellow Pages. It's 1983.

38. EXT. PLUMBER'S YARD. DAY.

Elsewhere in Wandsworth. FRANK and MAX, both in blue overalls, are looking over a ramshackle yard full of radiators, bits of pipe and the like.

MAX:	Christ, what a dump! There must be gear here from before North Sea Gas!
FRANK:	I remember this boiler! We took it out of a rooming house in Fulham in nineteen fifty something... Still, it's a good location.
MAX:	Bollocks, it's the wrong side of the one way system. You just want it to make up for all the humiliation you suffered here as an apprentice, don't you?
FRANK:	Yeah, all right, it was my ambition to buy this place. And why not? You could do with a bit of ambition yourself...
MAX:	I got ambition.
FRANK:	What, to get up the pub before seven o'clock?
MAX:	You've read my mind.

39. INT. TESSA'S BEDRROM. DAY.

TESSA is rooting frantically through the litter bin. She finds a card from a plumber. She dashes out.

40. EXT. PLUMBER'S. DAY.

FRANK and MAX are on the pavement outside the old fashioned shop. FRANK is locking up. The telephone inside rings. FRANK hesitates.

MAX:	Let it ring.

FRANK starts to unlock.

FRANK:	Is that what you'd do?
MAX:	Course.
FRANK:	That's why you work for me.

41. INT. STAIRWELL OF FLATS/TESSA'S LANDING. DAY.

FRANK comes up the stairs of TESSA'S flats. He comes to her landing, rings her bell. The door is opened by a very flustered TESSA.

TESSA: Thank God!

TESSA rushes back to the bathroom. FRANK enters the flat.

42. INT. BATHROOM. DAY.

TESSA is back bailing as FRANK enters. He appreciates a glimpse of leg through the gap in her bathrobe.

TESSA: It won't turn off, the pop up waste thing's stuck as well, the whole flat's a disaster, I bought it from a do-it-yourselfer with the mechanical aptitude of a subnormal prawn...

FRANK: We never installed this, love.

TESSA: What do you mean?

FRANK: You said you bought it from us. I've been going through the inventory all week, and I know we never stocked this. You fibbed, didn't you? (FRANK makes to leave)

TESSA: No! Look, all right, I'm desperate, yes, I lied, you're the only plumber who answered the phone! I've got a reception at the Grosvenor House in an hour with three minor royals, The Lord Mayor of London, half the CBI, Sir Harry Secombe and two cabinet ministers !

FRANK: What, they're reforming The Goons for the occasion? All right, you get dressed, I'll sort this out. I don't suppose you know where your stopcock is?

TESSA: I've only been here a month. Sorry.

FRANK: Par for the course love.

43. INT. BEDROOM. NIGHT.

TESSA is dressed, and is applying her make up in front of the dressing table mirror. There's a tap on the door.

TESSA: Yes?

FRANK: It's your knight in shining boiler suit. Can I come in?

TESSA: Yes, all right.

FRANK enters.

FRANK: You look very nice.

TESSA: (Cool) Thank you.

FRANK: That dress must have cost a packet – Bruce Oldfield, isn't it?

TESSA: How do you know?

FRANK: I know his style. Seeing what you must have paid for that, I don't have to feel guilty about this.

FRANK hands her a bill. Her eyebrows soar.

TESSA: You're joking?!

FRANK: It's all itemised, love. Fifty quid is the emergency call out charge, yeah? Forty quid is the fee per hour or part thereof, yeah? Thirty quid is the fine for fibbing about who installed that heap of pink plastic garbage, and fifteen pee is the price of the washer. Plus VAT equals £138.17, so let's call it a round hundred and forty.

TESSA: No, let's call it a rip-off! Fifty pounds call out from Wandsworth to Wandsworth?! What did you come in? Concorde?

FRANK: Look, love, if you don't like it, I can give you your flood back.

TESSA gets a cheque book and writes the cheque.

TESSA: Here you are, and it's quite immoral.

FRANK: (Takes cheque) No it ain't love, it's simply the beauty of capitalism at work. What went through my mind when you were in your bathrobe, now that I'll admit was immoral!

TESSA: (Leaps up) Get out!

FRANK: (Backing out) All right, all right, no offence, only most posh girls like a bit of the old working class badinage.

TESSA: Just piss off!

FRANK: Very good, love, the vernacular to a tee.

44. INT. PUB. DAY.

It's starting to get dark. FRANK sits at a window seat in a pub over the road from TESSA'S flats. He drinks a half pint of proper beer, and waits. He sees TESSA coming out of her flats. She waits on the pavement, glancing at her watch impatiently.

45. EXT. STREET. DAY.

TESSA is getting very cross.

TESSA: Bloody Yellow Pages!

A smart car slows. TESSA looks hopefully at the driver. The driver slows down and rolls down his window and smiles back.

DRIVER: You working?

TESSA: (Horrified) What?!

DRIVER: Sorry. (Speeds off)

>   FRANK ambles towards her from the pub. He has a big smile.

FRANK: Think you were on the game, did he?

TESSA: Go away.

FRANK: Never had to pay for it, myself...

TESSA: Yes, I'm sure the world is full of undiscriminating women who can't wait to succumb to your grimy embrace...

FRANK: Minicab stood you up, has it?

TESSA: Brilliant guess.

FRANK: Want a lift?

TESSA: Thank you, but I don't want to drive down Park Lane in a rusty transit van – though at your prices it's probably a turbo charged transit van with compact disc player and a mattress in the back.

FRANK: A mattress! Why didn't I think of that?

TESSA: Please just disappear!

FRANK: If you're sure you don't want a lift.

TESSA: I've never been so sure of anything in my life.

>   FRANK grins, strolls off. TESSA waits some more. A tatty car stops nearby. The driver beeps his horn. TESSA'S spirits drop further. She goes over to him.

TESSA: Minicab for Piggott?

MINICAB DRIVER: Yeah, sorry I'm late, got lost.

TESSA: I ordered an executive limo...

MINICAB DRIVER: 'S'right...

Then a beautiful Aston Martin glides up. The window glides down. It's FRANK.

FRANK: You sure you don't want a lift?

TESSA takes a fiver from her purse, gives it to the minicab driver, and gets into the Aston.

46. INT. RECEPTION HALL. NIGHT.

A large crowd of journalists, business people, "movers and shakers", stands around with glasses of champagne. On the platform are TESSA, DIANE and the other LIFE SUPPORT BIGWIGS, plus several BUSINESS TYPES, including HUGH MARRINER. The platform is professionally draped with banners and promotional material plugging - "LIFE SUPPORT PRESENTS SERIOUS MONEY."

TESSA: ... and it seemed to me, a newcomer to the voluntary sector, that while we've had Bandaid, and Comic Relief, and Shop Assistance, we've never seen the people with real money putting their hands in their family vaults. No doubt there isn't a single millionaire in Britain who doesn't give at least ten thousand a year to Charity... so why are they all so coy about it? After all, how is capitalism going to thrive and expand unless markets grow? And we won't sell to the starving, the destitute and dying, will we?

On the platform, everyone looks keen except BOB PEARCE, who looks very anti.

TESSA: But who could Life Support find to build this bridge to the business community? Fortunately I was able to turn to my erstwhile colleague and very good friend, Hugh Marriner... (She exchanges smiles with HUGH) Managing Director of Baumblatt UK plc, who has helped us set up this new appeal, which we have called "Serious Money." Hugh.

TESSA motions HUGH to the microphone.

HUGH: Thank you. Actually, "Serious Money" was Tessa Piggott's brilliant idea, I only became involved because I knew I'd enjoy twisting arms throughout the City in a good cause. (Laughter from floor). So Tessa, please accept this cheque for a hundred thousand pounds, as the first instalment in an ongoing relationship between the business community and LIFE SUPPORT.

Much applause and popping of flashguns. HUGH puts his hand over the microphone and whispers sweetly in TESSA'S ear.

HUGH: Now can I have that bloody letter!?

TESSA smiles sweetly and passes him an envelope.

47. EXT. GROSVENOR HOUSE STEPS. NIGHT.

Later. It's raining. GUESTS wait for their cars or compete for taxis. TESSA and DIANE come out of the building.

DIANE: I'd give you a lift, but the babysitter...

Suddenly MALCOLM emerges from the crowd, and presses a cheque into TESSA'S hand.

TESSA: Malcolm!

MALCOLM: You were brilliant! Look, let's go and have a quiet drink somewhere, it's ages since...

TESSA: Not tonight, Malcolm. I'm shattered.

MALCOLM: Let me drive you home then...

TESSA: But it's out of your way...

Then FRANK, now in a smart suit, materialises out of the crowd, eclipsing MALCOLM.

FRANK: Great speech, love, very moving. Ready to go?

DIANE: Who's your friend?

FRANK: Hello, Frank Carver, pleased to meet you.

TESSA: He's not a friend, he's just a presumptuous plumber with an Aston Martin. All right, come on.

TESSA links arms with FRANK, and they head for the door. A PHOTOGRAPHER stops them.

PHOTOGRAPHER: Hold on Tess, one for luck. (Flash)

48. EXT. LONDON STREETS. NIGHT.

The Aston Martin hurtles through the night. Traffic lights turn from amber to red, but the car goes straight across.

TESSA: (V/O) Have you got some sort of death wish?!

FRANK: Me?! I'm immortal love!

49. INT. TESSA'S LIVING ROOM. NIGHT.

FRANK prowls the room, looking at TESSA'S books and pictures. Then he sits at her piano and plays Chopsticks. TESSA comes in with a couple of coffees and a plate of sandwiches. FRANK stops playing.

TESSA: I was too nervous to eat before...

FRANK reaches for a sandwich. TESSA snatches the plate away.

TESSA: Let's see the colour of your money.

Love Hurts

FRANK: What?!

TESSA: It's all for charity, hundred pounds a ticket, plus voluntary donation.

FRANK: Is that why you invited me up?! Blimey!

TESSA: I'll take a cheque.

FRANK: It's all right...

FRANK takes out an expensive wallet and peels off a couple of fifties.

TESSA: Plus a voluntary donation.

FRANK: When you say "voluntary"...?

TESSA: ... I mean compulsory.

FRANK gives her several more banknotes. TESSA passes him the plate of sandwiches.

FRANK: Mind if I take two, under the circumstances? (Does so) So what are you doing tomorrow night?

TESSA: I don't know. Why?

FRANK: I thought you might like to come out for dinner. I know a very nice little three star restaurant, just fractionally cheaper than your sandwiches.

TESSA: Oh, you mean a date?

FRANK: That's right. A date, yeah?

TESSA: No, I don't think so, thank you.

FRANK: Why not?!

TESSA: I don't go out with men.

FRANK: You're not a lezzie, are you?! I haven't lashed out three hundred pounds on a dyke?!

Shooting the Pilot

TESSA: No, not a dyke. Possibly a well.

FRANK: (Puzzled) What?

TESSA: A well. You know, a hole in the ground from which poor people get water. We're digging several hundred in Africa, we'll name one after you for an extra five hundred.

FRANK: You're a real bloodsucker!

TESSA: I'll take that as a compliment, coming from a plumber.

FRANK: What about the weekend? You free Saturday?

TESSA: No! I've renounced men, they're more trouble than they're worth, which isn't much.

FRANK: You don't know what I'm worth.

TESSA: I don't really care.

FRANK: Then why did you let me bring you home?

TESSA: Because you offered, you have a very nice car, it was raining and there was a queue for taxis.

FRANK: That's it? But you invited me up?

TESSA: I was going to make some coffee. I thought it was only civil to offer you a cup.

FRANK: You're just a prick teaser, then!?

TESSA: If you're just a prick. I think I'll go to bed now. Thanks for the lift, thanks for the donation, goodnight. (Ushers him into hall)

50. INT. TESSA'S HALL. NIGHT.

TESSA easing FRANK towards front door.

TESSA: You know where the door is, don't you?

FRANK: The bedroom door?

TESSA: The front door.

FRANK: And suppose I don't want to go?

TESSA: Mr Carver, you aren't the sort of man to force himself on a woman who isn't interested.

FRANK: How do you know?

TESSA: Otherwise you wouldn't spend so much money on the trappings of male sexual display. The car, the watch, the clothes...

FRANK: You really think you know all about men, don't you?

TESSA: Not all men. But I've got your number...

FRANK: No, that's just the new shop, my personal line....

TESSA: I've heard your personal line. It's very predictable. (Opens front door for him) Goodnight.

FRANK: How about a quick beer, Sunday lunchtime?

TESSA: All right, I'll have a quick beer Sunday lunchtime, and while I'm drinking it I'll think about you. Goodbye, Frank.

FRANK: All right, all right, you win... but before you chuck me out...

TESSA: What?

FRANK: Can I use your lav?

51. EXT. EMBANKMENT. NIGHT.

FRANK'S Aston Martin crosses Battersea Bridge. A couple of girls in a Peugeot 205 stop next to him at a set of lights. The passenger smiles. He smiles back, then has to be first away from the lights.

52. EXT. CHELSEA HARBOUR. NIGHT.

FRANK parks his car and heads for the lift.

53. INT. LIFT. NIGHT.

FRANK travels to an upper floor...

54. INT. CORRIDOR. NIGHT.

FRANK walks to his front door and lets himself in.

55. INT. FRANK'S FLAT. NIGHT.

A large modern open-plan living area. Expensively decorated and furnished, obviously by a professional. Great views across the river from the large windows. It's quite dark. FRANK tiptoes across the room, heading for his bedroom, when the lights go on to reveal JADE, a very attractive 20 year old in an outsize tee-shirt and nothing else. She's angry.

JADE: What kind of time do you call this?!

FRANK: Give up, what's the answer?

JADE: It's past midnight!

FRANK: So? I am 49 next birthday...

JADE: Fifty...

FRANK: (Ignores this) I'm allowed out after dark.

JADE: Where were you?

FRANK: At the new shop. Max and me were stocktaking and I had this emergency call out...

JADE: At half past six...

FRANK: Says who?

JADE: I phoned Max. It was a woman, wasn't it? I can smell her perfume.

FRANK: It's my aftershave!

JADE: Coco by Chanel?

FRANK: All right, I was with a bird... a woman. We were just talking. She's very interesting, runs this big charity.

JADE: And no doubt you slipped her a small donation?

FRANK: Not so small, five hundred quid! And all I got off her was a cheese and tomato sandwich! Bloody hell, anyone would think we were married!

JADE: I do live here, don't I? Don't I deserve a bit of consideration?

FRANK: Course, but...

JADE: We were meant to be going to see "Another Woman"...

FRANK: Oh, bloody hell! Sorry, completely forgot! We'll go tomorrow.

JADE: It finished tonight. Honestly, dad! Mum always said you were an unreliable bugger, and I used to defend you!

JADE storms back to her room. FRANK follows at a distance.

FRANK: I don't know what all the fuss is about, it's out on video!

56. INT. TESSA'S OFFICE. DAY.

TESSA is totting up some figures, and drinking a coffee. Her phone rings. She answers it.

TESSA: Tessa Piggott... Hello Mum, how are you? What, a picture in the Yorkshire Post?! You'll have to go straight down to Marks and Spencer's food hall and show everyone! No, he's nobody, just a plumber...

57. INT. ROLLS ROYCE/EXT. M4 MOTORWAY. DAY.

FRANK, in expensive suit, sits in the back of his Rolls. MAX, in grey suit, shirt and tie, drives.

MAX: I don't know what all the fuss is about Rollers, it's no fun to drive...

FRANK: It's designed for my pleasure, not yours...

MAX: I mean, try taking a corner in this at seventy five...

FRANK: And to impress the impressionable.

MAX: Like the owner of Matlock Hall?

FRANK: It worked, didn't it? And it's not every day a public school comes on the open market...

The Rolls Royce comes off the motorway and we follow it to a car rental site.

58. EXT. CAR RENTAL SITE. DAY.

FRANK and MAX get out of the Rolls and go into the office. A few seconds later they come out of the office and walk to where FRANK'S Aston Martin is parked.

MAX: Can I take this stupid tie off now?

59. EXT. TESSA'S ROAD. DAY.

TESSA gets off a bus. She has shopping bags. She walks toward her flat.

60. EXT. FRANK'S OFFICE. DAY.

A small modern office block with car parking. The Aston pulls in, FRANK driving. FRANK and MAX get out.

FRANK: See you tomorrow, Max.

MAX: Can I take the Aston, got a hot date tonight.

FRANK: If she's that hot, the Escort'll do.

MAX sighs, and gets into an old Ford as FRANK goes into the building.

61. INT. OFFICE BLOCK. DAY.

FRANK enters, passes a board that shows "The Carver Group of Companies" is on the second floor, and runs up the stairs. He reaches his office and enters.

62. INT. OUTER OFFICE. DAY.

FRANK comes in. His secretary, MARILYN, is at her word processor. She looks up.

MARILYN: How did you get on?

FRANK: Bought it. Half a million.

MARILYN: That's a steal, Frank!

FRANK: I don't know, I mean who can put a price on education? Though I think we'll put the fees up next term. Any calls?

MARILYN: Plenty... but not from her.

FRANK: She'll phone.

MARILYN: Bet she doesn't.

FRANK: How much?

63. INT. TESSA'S KITCHEN. DAY.

TESSA comes in. Dumps her shopping and fills the kettle. Then she goes to the loo and shuts the door behind her.

64. INT. FRANK'S PRIVATE OFFICE. DAY.

FRANK is on the phone to his bank manager.

FRANK: So if you'll transfer the money across... and if any of your customers are thinking of sending their little darlings away to school, there will of course be something in it for whoever recommends Matlock Hall, progressive yet disciplined education for the leaders of tomorrow.

MARILYN comes in, holding a tenner.

MARILYN: Here's the tenner I owe you.

FRANK: Got to go, Alan, my young lady's on hold. (Presses a button) Hello love.

INTERCUT WITH...

64. INT. TESSA'S HALL. DAY.

TESSA stands in the hall with the cordless phone. She is livid.

TESSA: What the hell did you do to my toilet?!

FRANK: Won't it flush then?

TESSA: You know bloody well...!

FRANK: I'll be round in half an hour.

TESSA: No...! Just tell me what's wrong!

FRANK: It's your ballcock.

TESSA: How can you be sure?

FRANK: Just an educated guess.

65. INT. TESSA'S FLAT. NIGHT.

TESSA is viciously stripping wallpaper in the empty spare bedroom. There's a ring on the doorbell.

66. INT. HALL. NIGHT.

TESSA dashes to the door, still holding the stripping tool. She opens the door to FRANK, still in his suit, with his bag of tools.

TESSA: You sabotaged my toilet, didn't you?!

FRANK: Who me guv?

TESSA: You sod!

FRANK opens the bag and removes a long gift wrapped thing in an Asprey's bag.

TESSA: Look, I'm not interested in your corny courtship routines. I want my flush back!

FRANK: Just open it, love.

TESSA: God...!

FRANK: Yeah, but you can call me Frank.

TESSA angrily rips open the package, revealing a new ballcock.

FRANK: A new ballcock; I've got a shrewd suspicion some joker's bent your old one right out of shape.

TESSA: Just fix it!

FRANK: Hold on, first we got to discuss my fee.

TESSA: Your what?!

FRANK:	I got to make a living, but as you're a valued customer...
TESSA:	I know what's coming next. Here...
	TESSA gets her bag and removes her cheque book.
FRANK:	No, I don't want money...
TESSA:	No, you want a date. I'd rather pay you, thanks all the same.
FRANK:	You're no fun.
	FRANK goes into the loo and fixes it, chatting awhile.
FRANK:	Here, you see that picture of us in the paper, my secretary reckons we make a lovely couple...
TESSA:	I don't want to know...
FRANK:	Made an impression on the Reverend Wormwold an' all.
TESSA:	Who?
FRANK:	The owner of Matlock Hall, established 1845.
TESSA:	(Sarky) Your old school?
FRANK:	No, my new school – I only bought it this morning...
TESSA:	You bought a school? I thought you were just a plumber?
FRANK:	I were... I am, but you got to have more than one string to your bow. Course, the Reverend was a bit worried he might be selling his college to some Sarf London asset stripper, but when I showed him our photo out the paper, and he realised my fiancee is a big noise in the charity game... (Pulls chain) Perfect. (Comes out of loo).

TESSA: (Apoplectic) Your what?!

FRANK: You all right? You gone a funny colour. Come in the kitchen and I'll make you a nice cup of tea.

67. INT. TESSA'S KITCHEN. NIGHT.

TESSA and FRANK drinking tea.

TESSA: If you analyse it, the whole thing is actually quite bizarre.

FRANK: Yeah? Seems perfectly natural to me.

TESSA: For a teenager, perhaps, but you're... how old?

FRANK: It's rude to ask a girl's age.

TESSA: I'm forty one. Your turn.

FRANK: Forty eight.

TESSA: Old enough to know better then.

FRANK: Look, all I want is to take you out for dinner or something.

TESSA: I know. But why? Why are you interested in me?

FRANK: You're a very attractive lady.

TESSA: I know that, so what? Let's recap. You came round to fix the jacuzzi...

FRANK: Having been summoned on false pretences...

TESSA: You spent at least half your time trying to look up the gap in my bathrobe...

FRANK: Oh, you noticed...

TESSA: And then you started this absurd pick up marathon. And to what end? All right, suppose I did go out with you, and suppose we had a reasonable time, no doubt you'd expect to get the normal sexual quid pro quo...

FRANK: I love it when you talk dirty.

TESSA: Which, needless to say, you would not obtain...

FRANK: You don't do it on the first date?

TESSA: I don't do it on any date. I've decided to become a virgin.

FRANK: Oh come on...!

TESSA: Look, Mr Carver. I haven't always been in the charity game. I joined Life Support as part of a conscious change of lifestyle.

FRANK: Really? What did you do before then?

TESSA: I was a high class prostitute. And when I joined the charity and took a seventy per cent salary drop, I also decided that men would play no further part in my life. So it's all quite pointless, isn't it? Especially as the only reason you're interested in me is that I'm not interested in you, and your totally conventional male ego is fighting to reassert itself...

FRANK: There's nothing wrong with my ego...

TESSA: No? You sure? It seems pretty fragile to me if it can't cope with the occasional rebuff...

FRANK: So that's it, then? You know exactly what I'm thinking, you understand the inner workings of my mind better than I do, you know beyond the shadow of a doubt that I'm only interested in you as an object of conquest rather than because you're actually quite an interesting bird, which casts a bit of a doubt over your ego if you ask me...

TESSA: All right, all right, look, there's only one way to settle this...!

FRANK: Absolutely. Saturday, eight o'clock?

TESSA: No, Sunday at 7.30.

FRANK: Why?

TESSA: Why not?

68. INT. FRANK'S BEDROOM. DAY.

Sunday. FRANK is packing his football kit into a holdall. The shirt has a logo on it "The Carver Group." JADE comes in.

JADE: I'm doing lunch for half one, ok?

FRANK: It's a bit early, you know I got to buy the lads a drink after...

JADE: A drink?

FRANK: You know. After all, I do sponsor the team...

JADE: Only because you're too old to get a game otherwise... Looking forward to tonight?

FRANK: What? Yeah, course... (thinks) When did I tell you?

JADE: Tell me what? I bought the tickets weeks back! You've forgotten, haven't you?!

FRANK: No...

JADE: You have! You sod!

FRANK: Hang about, I'm your father!

JADE: When Chris packed me in, you said "never mind, love, he wasn't good enough for you anyway, and if you're ever stuck for a date, I'll always be around"! Liar!

FRANK: Normally I am around, but...

JADE: But what?! Come on, you're supposed to be good at thinking on your feet!

FRANK: It's that school deal, there's a problem with the head lease...

JADE: Bollocks, dad! Why don't you just admit you've got some bird lined up!?

JADE storms out.

69. INT. TESSA'S FRONT ROOM. DAY.

TESSA is relaxing at home with the Sunday papers, coffee and croissants.

70. EXT. FOOTBALL PITCH. DAY.

FRANK's team is playing on a public pitch. FRANK is having trouble keeping up. MAX is also playing. He passes the ball to FRANK, but he is too slow to get to it.

MAX: Come on, grandad!

71. INT. TESSA'S FRONT ROOM. DAY.

TESSA still relaxing. Her phone rings. She picks it up.

72. EXT. FOOTBALL PITCH. DAY.

Play has stopped. A group of people stand around a prostrate FRANK, who is clutching his groin and groaning.

MAX: Don't hold 'em, count 'em.

PLAYERS laugh.

73. INT. TESSA'S BEDROOM. DAY.

TESSA, dressed, is packing lightweight clothes into a small suitcase. She finishes, and exits.

74. INT. TESSA'S FRONT ROOM. DAY.

TESSA comes in, picks up her Filofax, and looks through it for FRANK'S card. He'd scribbled his home number on the back. She dials.

75. INT. FRANK'S FLAT. DAY.

The phone rings in an apparently empty room. Then JADE appears and answers it.

JADE: Yes? No, he's on Clapham Common playing football, trying to recapture his lost youth. Fine, I'll tell him... Me? I'm his wife. Hello, hello? (Hangs up) That'll teach him.

76. EXT. TESSA'S FLAT. NIGHT.

FRANK drives up in the Aston. He gets out. He's brought flowers. He goes in.

77. INT. TESSA'S LANDING. NIGHT.

FRANK rings TESSA'S bell. No answer. He rings again and again. He bangs on the door. He shouts through the letter box.

FRANK: Tessa! You aren't still in the bath are you? Tessa!!

78. EXT. TESSA'S FLATS. NIGHT.

FRANK emerges angrily, opens the car door and gets his carphone. He presses a pre-programmed button and dials her number, keeping an eye on her window.

79. INT. TESSA'S FRONT ROOM. NIGHT.

The room is empty. The phone rings three times. Then TESSA's answerphone clicks on.

TESSA'S VOICE: Thank you for calling Tessa Piggott. Unfortunately I've had to go to Somalia at short notice. Please leave your mess... (It goes beep. She mistimed her message.)

80. EXT. TESSA'S FLATS. NIGHT.

FRANK is gobstruck.

FRANK: Somalia!? I said Langan's!

81. INT. HOTEL RESTAURANT IN MOZAMBIQUE. DAY.

An "International" hotel, but obviously in Africa, judging by the staff and the customers. TESSA is breakfasting with LUCAS JAMA, of the United Nations.

LUCAS JAMA: And then there is the question of local commissions...

TESSA: You mean bribes?

LUCAS JAMA: No! Look, Miss Piggott, if you want to import Somali crafts, you have to pay the merchants...

TESSA: The merchants aren't supplying me, the co-operatives are supplying me...

LUCAS JAMA: But the merchants don't like the co-operatives...

TESSA: But why can't we just bypass the merchants!?

LUCAS JAMA: Cut out the middle man, as you say?

Suddenly FRANK (in a cotton suit) materialises, having heard the end of the exchange.

FRANK:	You can't cut out the middle man, he's the one makes the world go round!
TESSA:	What are you..?!
FRANK:	I thought we had a date?! What time is it?
LUCAS JAMA:	Eight twenty five a.m.
FRANK:	Right. (To WAITER) Fetch me some shredded wheat. (Sits) Well, ain't you going to introduce me?
TESSA:	Of course. Lucas Jama, United Nations Relief Agency, Frank Carver, jumped up plumber who thinks just because he flew all the way from England I'll be impressed enough to let him get his leg over. Well, he's wrong. Come on.

TESSA sweeps away from the table, followed by a puzzled LUCAS JAMA.

LUCAS JAMA:	Leg over?

THE WAITER brings FRANK a plate of about five shredded wheat and no milk.

<u>THE END</u>

5
Goodnight Sweetheart

As soon as we stumbled upon the idea of writing a time-travel sitcom, we were excited and intrigued. Had it been done before? We didn't think so; not in this country anyway. Time travel was a staple component of many sci-fi movies, not least the brilliant *Back to the Future*, but as far as UK television was concerned, there was only *Doctor Who*, and that wasn't supposed to be funny.

The inspiration for *Goodnight Sweetheart* was a stray observation of Laurence's that there were streets in London's East End that had survived the Blitz and had hardly changed since the war. That set us off on a sort of logical progression: if these streets seem unchanged since 1940, then what if in those streets it is *still* 1940? What would happen if someone from today found himself in those streets? What would he do? Who would he meet? Who would he tell?

Once we'd answered those questions, we were more than halfway to creating *Goodnight Sweetheart*. But there was one more question to answer. What sort of protagonist would be repeatedly drawn back to the most dangerous era of the twentieth century? Answering that led us to create our hapless but loveable hero, Gary Sparrow. Gary felt like a strong and original character: a sympathetic philanderer in love with two women, divided by half a century.

Added to Gary's unique dilemma we had the vivid backdrop of World War II providing a deep well of storylines. This wasn't the first time we'd conceived of a series with an inbuilt timeline. *Shine On Harvey Moon* was set against the post-war rebuilding of Britain; *The New Statesman* harvested the absurdities of the Parliamentary calendar, and *Birds of a Feather* featured two sisters whose husbands were serving long prison sentences. In all of those shows, the timeline provided dynamism, as well as a supply of story ideas. We knew *Goodnight Sweetheart*, set against the daily drama of World War II, could run for at least as long as the war had, the sort of long-running potential that's very appealing to broadcasters.

At this point some readers might protest that like many of our ideas, the concept of *Goodnight Sweetheart* isn't intrinsically funny. They're right. The shows we're proudest of have dramatic rather than comedic roots because we don't look for overtly "funny" situations involving "comical" characters in "hilarious" situations. Instead we try to put credible individuals in realistic and challenging situations.

Gary's ability to travel in time may be a thing of fantasy, but the dilemmas he faces in the past are matters of life and love and death, for a fantasy must convey psychological truth. We knew we couldn't have Gary blithely sauntering into 1940, unafraid for his life. Luckily, we had found on a visit to the Blitz Museum a fascinating set of books detailing every single air raid on London. We realised that Gary too would find these books invaluable, so we bought them for him. Now he could check on Luftwaffe activity before nipping back to the past to flirt with Phoebe and claim another Beatles' song as his own.

A few critics of the show thought Gary should raise his horizons, get to Winston Churchill, and use his historical knowledge to help shorten the war. But Gary isn't an idiot, he knows he'd get shot, or locked up in a lunatic asylum. No, he keeps going back to blitzed London because he's met a vivacious barmaid there who thinks he's the bee's knees.

Any writer creating a new show knows that sooner or later he or she or they must stop discussing how cool the idea is and get down to actually writing the bloody thing. To say this isn't always easy is a considerable understatement. Pilots are tricky because they must work on so many levels. The script must set up and underpin the series, with a strong story that introduces a host of characters and settings never before seen. In less than thirty minutes it must convince the audience they want to tune in next week and the week after and the week after that. Yet from the viewers' perspective, once transmitted the pilot is dispensable, like the booster stage of a space rocket. It must be powerful enough to get its payload – the series – into space but once its work is done it falls into the sitcom sea, burnt out and forgotten.

Unlike some of our projects, the pilot script of *Sweetheart* came together remarkably quickly, in a rented office managed by a pleasant lady called Mrs Deadman. We asked her if she minded our borrowing her surname? She didn't, and PC Reg Deadman was born, the dimmest copper in wartime London.

Before we could take Gary back to the Forties, we had to establish that he is dissatisfied with his life in the present day, so we decided to open on his thirtieth birthday party, organised by his ballsy wife Yvonne, who has put herself in charge of the nibbles and the music and the guest list. Though she is barely in the first scene, her absence dominates. We see enough to realise that while she may love her husband, she doesn't respect him. But then Gary doesn't seem to respect himself. He knows he's reached a milestone birthday without achieving anything, and almost envies previous generations who went to war and proved themselves. Modern life is too easy, he complains, there are no challenges left. That's why we called the pilot "Rites of Passage", because Gary complains that he hasn't had one and is never likely to.

Who does Gary complain to? Ron of course. Anyone who's watched the show knows Ron is Gary's best friend, but in fact they meet for the first time in the pilot. Why? Wouldn't a pre-existing friendship have made sense? Well, we needed to tell the audience what these two did for a living. Their jobs – Gary is a TV repairman, Ron's an experienced printer – were crucial to the plot. If they already knew each other there seemed no way to convey this important information without painful chunks of expository dialogue. Nevertheless we've always been slightly dissatisfied with this aspect of the pilot and often question if we could have established these elements in a neater way. Maybe we're too self-critical; the first scene feels overlong to us, but then we have watched it a hundred times.

Having established Gary in the present day, and met the overwhelming Yvonne, our next job was to get him into the past where most of the laughter and the tears would come, so the second phase of the pilot sees

Gary wander into 1940 while looking for a tower block where he's supposed to deliver a TV. It seemed logical – that word again – that at first he thinks the Royal Oak is a World War II theme pub. When the pretty barmaid insists beer really is sevenpence-ha'penny a pint, he assumes, logically, that he must be having a particularly interesting dream. The belief that nothing is real gives the diffident Gary the confidence to flirt with Phoebe and pass himself off as a successful songwriter.

When we worked out the details of our "scene breakdown", it was never our intention to make songwriting a major part of Gary's cover story. It was only when we were actually writing the key scene in the Royal Oak that it occurred to us that Gary might sit down at the old piano and pick out the opening notes of Elton John's 'Your Song'.

Then, as sometimes happens, the characters took over.

Phoebe says, "That's nice. Did you learn that in America?"

And Gary, who still thinks it's all a dream, replies, "What? Yeah… Well actually, I wrote it."

That was almost as much a surprise to us as it was to Phoebe, but we quickly realised that Gary's songwriting prowess would give him huge leverage in 1940, and the audience huge pleasure in 1993.

Then the air-raid siren shrieks and Gary knows that he really has trespassed into history. Suddenly everything is real and terrifying. Good. The best comedies make room for high drama and real emotion. By this stage we felt confident we would take the audience with us, for we were ourselves intensely invested in Gary's adventure. What was going to happen to him? Would he survive? Would he ever get back to the Nineties? What if he was trapped in the past forever? Who knew? We were as eager to find out as we hoped the viewers would be.

What we did know was that Gary had to be a winner in this wartime world, for he was definitely a loser in his own era. His chance comes when Phoebe's grumpy father is concussed by flying debris, namely his prized cash register, and Gary saves his life with mouth-to-mouth resuscitation, to the horror of the onlookers, who assume he's snogging a corpse. Gary saves himself, as he repeatedly will as the series progresses, by claiming that he learned this technique in America. To the Cockneys in 1940, the USA was the place where the future was already taking place. When her father regains consciousness Gary is a hero in the eyes of the lovely Phoebe, her dad, and all of the regulars.

The final scene of the pilot finds Gary back in his little house in Cricklewood. At first, he's relieved. But his experience has changed him. Everything is different. He tries to tell Yvonne about his surreal adventure, but quickly sees that she'll never believe him. He shrugs, changes the subject, and they go to bed. The end.

Well that was the end of the pilot script in this book, the version that we sold to the BBC, but between that happy day and the recording of the pilot we radically rewrote the final scene. We honestly can't remember why or when. Perhaps we realised at the first cast read-through that the ending was too much of an anti-climax.

The new scene is so much stronger. Now Gary tells Yvonne a version of the truth; that he went into an East End pub, the landlord fell down the trapdoor and concussed himself, and he, Gary, saved his life. Yvonne laughs, not unkindly. She thinks Gary's just spinning a line to justify spending the night in the pub. Gary realises he'll never be a hero in his wife's eyes, but he'll always be one to Phoebe. That's why he knows and we know he'll have to go back to 1940, because in the past he's a somebody.

GOODNIGHT SWEETHEART

Episode One: "RITES OF PASSAGE"

October 1993

1. INT. THRU LOUNGE. NIGHT 1.

A NEAT, RATHER UNDER-FURNISHED ROOM IN A NEWISH HOUSE ON AN ESTATE. THERE IS A THREE PIECE SUITE PUSHED AGAINST THE WALL, AN IKEA COFFEE TABLE WITH BOWLS OF CRISPS, NUTS, AND TWIGLETS, AND A COUPLE OF AMERICANISH POSTERS IN CLIP FRAMES ON THE WALL. THERE'S A VERY GOOD HI-FI SYSTEM ON ONE OF THOSE BLACK MESH RACKS, PLAYING "THAT'S WHAT I CALL MUSIC - VOLUME 92" - IT'S AS AWFUL AS ONLY TOP OF THE POPS MUSIC CAN BE WHEN YOU TAKE AWAY THE VIDEOS. OBVIOUSLY A PARTY IS IN PROGRESS, BUT THE ROOM IS EMPTY EXCEPT FOR GARY, A MOROSE LOOKING MAN IN JEANS AND SWEATSHIRT, WITH A PINT OF LAGER, NOT HIS FIRST OF THE NIGHT. HE'S LOOKING THROUGH THE RACK OF OLD FASHIONED L.Ps. SOUNDS OF JOLLITY FROM ELSEWHERE IN THE HOUSE. THEN RON AMBLES IN, A BIG BLOKE WITH A PINT OF BEER, NOT HIS SECOND OF THE NIGHT. HE CROSSES TO THE COFFEE TABLE, PICKS UP THE ENTIRE CONTENTS OF THE TWIGLET BOWL IN ONE HUGE HAND, AND PUTS THEM IN HIS MOUTH. THEN HE AMBLES OVER TO GARY.

RON: (INDISTINCT, MOUTH FULL) What a 'king awful party.

FORTUNATELY, AS HIS MOUTH IS FULL OF TWIGLETS, WE ONLY GET THE GENERAL GIST OF HIS SPEECH. UNFORTUNATELY, GARY GETS MOST OF THE TWIGLETS SPRAYED OVER HIS CHICAGO BEARS SWEATSHIRT.

RON: (MORE DISTINCTLY) Sorry mate.

GARY:	It's all right, you got to expect spillages at parties, what with all the people surging excitedly from room to room. (LOOKS POINTEDLY AROUND THE EMPTY ROOM)
RON:	They're all having a blinding time in the kitchen.
GARY:	Where else? Remember that Jonah Louie record – (SINGS) "You will always find me in the kitchen at parties..."
RON:	Yeah... wonder what became of Jonah Louie?
GARY:	Probably still in the kitchen. Why is it that every time you go to a party there's a completely empty living room, and the kitchen's like the Black Hole of Cricklewood...?
RON:	I think you mean Calcutta.
GARY:	Yeah, I know. But I said Cricklewood because, you know, this is Cricklewood... it was by way of being a joke.
RON:	Oh, only there is a lot of Indian food in the kitchen and I thought that's what you might be alluding to. Chicken tikka nuggets, I ask you! My fingers look like I'm on 60 Capstan Full Strength a day!
GARY:	I know... What happened to the party food of yesteryear? Sausage rolls, ham sandwiches, pickled onions? I'm even growing nostalgic for cheese and pineapple hedgehogs!
RON:	I'm growing nostalgic for proper music! I mean, compared to this, Boney M were talented.
GARY:	They have got some decent stuff here though. Look...

>   GARY HAS SELECTED A BLACK BLUES ALBUM – JOHN
>   LEE HOOKER OR SUCHLIKE. HE SHOWS IT TO RON WHO
>   NODS APPROVINGLY. HE CAREFULLY PUTS IT ON THE
>   TURNTABLE, DELICATELY LOWERS THE ARM AND
>   SWITCHES THE AMP FROM CASSETTE TO PHONO.
>   ELECTRIC BLUES FILLS THE ROOM. RON GIVES GARY
>   THE "THUMBS UP". GARY TURNS UP THE VOLUME. THEN
>   THE DOOR OPENS AND YVONNE BUSTLES IN. SHE'S AN
>   ATTRACTIVE BUT RATHER INTENSE 30 YEAR OLD
>   WOMAN IN FIGURE-HUGGING PARTY WEAR. SHE RUSHES
>   OVER TO THE HI FI AND PRESSES THE TAPE BUTTON.
>   TECHNO-GARBAGE REPLACES BOTTLE NECK GUITAR.

YVONNE: Gary, people want to dance!

> YVONNE BUSTLES OUT AGAIN.

GARY: What people? I see no people! Do you want to dance er...?

RON: Ron. And no thank you Gary, I think I'll sit this one out... In fact I think I'll give this whole lousy party a miss. I only got dragged along cos my Stella's on the same psychology course as our hostess, whom I presume that was?

GARY: Yeah, that's Yvonne.

RON: Right, nice tight little bum I thought...

GARY: Yeah, I noticed that.

RON: Though she did strike me as a bit of a madam.

GARY: Yes, I noticed that too.

RON: Anyhow, I took the precaution of sussing out where the nearest real ale hostelry is, and I think I shall repair thence. Fancy a good drink?

GARY: Love to Ron, but I can't really leave.

RON: Why not?

Shooting the Pilot

GARY: It's my party.

RON: No! Tell me you're kidding?! I'm sorry... I'm so sorry... So Yvonne...

GARY: ... With the tight little bum....

RON: Is your... your...

GARY: My wife, yes.

RON: What I said about her was completely out of order.

GARY: Indeed it was Ron, though perfectly accurate on both the madam and bottom fronts.

RON: But if it is your birthday, her bottom not withstanding, why didn't you put your foot down and insist on John Lee Hooker and pork pies?

GARY: I tried, but ever since she started doing this Open University degree she's become so adept at manipulating me I can't get a thought in edgeways. And when I complain, she says don't I want her to get her degree and get promoted to deputy personnel manager and get a big pay rise? And I can't say – no, I preferred it when you were a wages supervisor and we used to go out every night and have a laugh.

RON: I don't really mind Stella doing this course; it's better than when she went out every night, boozing and getting into fights.

GARY: The trouble is women always know how to make men feel like little boys. It'd be different if I'd ever killed anything.

RON: How so?

GARY: I mean, what we men lack in society today is a rite of passage. Our fathers for example did National Service. Their fathers fought in the War.

	Experiences which marked their shift into manhood. In "A Man Named Horse" Richard Harris was suspended by his nipples in order to be accepted as a Sioux.
RON:	I'd bloody sue if they did that to me.
GARY:	Whilst in Africa, the Masai have to go out and kill a lion, armed only with a spear...
RON:	You'd think they'd at least give the Masai boy the spear...
GARY:	And then you have your apprenticeship system. When my grandad completed his five years as a cooper...
RON:	Learning to make barrels.
GARY:	The very trade; they marked his entry into manhood by coating him in brewers malt, shutting him in a barrel and rolling him down five flights of factory steps then into the Thames. A moment ripe with symbolism. All right, he was so badly injured he was never able to ply his new trade... but the principle...
RON:	I fully comprehend, Gaz. I suppose that's why I feel a man. I was one of the last people to do the old hot metal print apprenticeships. Following which I was covered head to toe in printers ink and projected stark naked into the ladies toilet.
GARY:	Sounds better than being a cooper.
RON:	Happy days. What do you do then?
GARY:	I'm in televisions.
RON:	What, you're not famous are you? You been in anything I'd have heard of?
GARY:	Depends. You heard of Rumbelows?

RON: Sorry pardon?

GARY: Televisions, plural. I repair them. At least I used to. They seldom go wrong these days. And since The Who stopped touring you don't even get to fix the ones they threw out of hotel windows.

RON: But wasn't your apprenticeship capped with some satisfyingly pseudo-tribal ceremony?

GARY: No, the nearest we came to a rite of passage was being forced to watch "Blankety Blank".

<u>2. INT. GARY & YVONNE'S BEDROOM. NIGHT 1.</u>

IT IS ABOUT TWO A.M. GARY COMES INTO THE BEDROOM, A ROOM THAT IS CLEARLY ALL YVONNE'S TASTE. GARY WEARS A HOODED LONSDALE BOXERS' DRESSING GOWN OVER BOXER SHORTS. HE'S MOVING NICELY ON THE BALLS OF HIS FEET, HARRY. SITTING UP IN BED, IN A TEE-SHIRT IS YVONNE. SHE IS WATCHING A VIDEO OF AN OPEN UNIVERSITY LECTURE FROM BBC2. LIKE ALL O.U. LECTURES IT WAS ORIGINALLY RECORDED IN 1973 BY A WOULD-BE TRENDY ACADEMIC WITH TERRIBLE LONG FRIZZY HAIR AND AWFUL WIDE LAPELLED JACKET IN PINK CRUSHED VELVET. HE DRONES ON IN AN ANNOYING LOYD GROSSMAN ACCENT.

GARY: Did people really wear jackets that colour in the Seventies?

YVONNE: He's a brilliant psychologist. You can't expect him to have dress sense too.

LECTURER: ... It has now become the accepted subtext of even the crassest of popular fiction that the fundamental motivating factor in male psychological development is the urge to kill the father and impregnate the mother....

GARY: I'm really glad we paid extra for the porno channel.

Goodnight Sweetheart

YVONNE PRESSES THE PAUSE BUTTON ON THE VIDEO.

YVONNE: Gary, I'm already falling behind with my course. I have to watch this.

GARY: Yeah, but tonight of all nights. It's my birthday.

YVONNE: Not really, your birthday was yesterday, remember? I gave you an expensive Mont Blanc rollerball and you said, in that sulky little boy voice you do so well, "just the job to sign me work sheets with".

GARY: I'm sorry Yvonne, but I was disappointed. When you promised me something sleek, black, and German, I was expecting a BMW.... or at least a date with Boris Becker's girlfriend.

YVONNE: Don't you want me to get my psychology degree? Don't you want me to get promoted? Don't you want us to be able to move off this estate of starter homes into a house where when the neighbours pull the chain your shower water doesn't run cold?

GARY: All I know is you'll never get a psychology degree if you lack the insight that on his birthday your husband expects a shag.

YVONNE: At the risk of sounding conventional, is sex all you think about?

GARY: Yes, except when I'm actually doing it: then I think about John Selwyn Gummer, I find it helps me last longer.

YVONNE: John Selwyn Gummer, eh? Very interesting.

GARY: (GETTING INTO BED) So it's Open University and closed legs, is it? Well goodnight.

YVONNE: (SOFTENS HER TONE) Look darling, as soon as this is finished, I promise to give you such a thorough seeing-to that for the rest of the month you'll

	be hard pressed to erect as much as a satellite dish. Just be patient. I don't demand physical gratification in the middle of the Super Bowl, do I?
GARY:	All right. (CLOSES HIS EYES) If I fall asleep, wake me up before you go-go.
	GARY STARTS TO NOD OFF. YVONNE PRESSES THE PLAY BUTTON ON THE REMOTE. NOTHING HAPPENS. THEN SHE NUDGES GARY.
GARY:	That was quick. Okay, let's do it!!
YVONNE:	No, the video's on the blink again.

3. EXT. WHITECHAPEL/INT. GARY'S VAN. DAY 2.

LATE AFTERNOON. GARY'S RUMBELOWS VAN IS PARKED AT THE KERB IN A BUSY STREET. INSIDE, GARY IS PEERING INTO HIS A-Z.

GARY:	Why is it everywhere you want to find in the A to Z is always in the crease?
	HE TAKES HIS SLIMLINE MOBILE PHONE FROM A POCKET IN HIS OVERALLS AND DIALS BASE.
GARY:	Hello, who's that? Yeah, this is Gary, look, this address you've given me, I can't... What? No, can't hear you, you're breaking up... Oh sod it!
	GARY THROWS THE PHONE DOWN ON THE FLOOR OF HIS VAN, AND GETS OUT. HE LOOKS AROUND, SEES A MIDDLE AGED POLICEMAN PASSING. HE IS P.C. DEADMAN.
GARY:	'Scuse me, I'm looking for Hugh Gaitskell House, got to deliver a telly...
P.C. DEADMAN:	Ah yes, Hugh Gaitskell House... always admired Hugh Gaitskell, great shame he died so young, would have made a wonderful Prime Minister,

	might have changed the course of British history...
GARY:	I'm sure, but where's his house?
P.C. DEADMAN:	Yes, course, sorry, always do tend to go off on tangents, that's what they said the last time I failed my sergeant's interview... Hugh Gaitskell House, best thing to do is go down Ducketts Passage over there, then take your first left, second right and you can't miss it. But if you do miss it ask at the Duke of Marlborough.
	DEADMAN POINTS OUT AN ALLEY ABOUT FIFTY YARDS DOWN THE ROAD.
GARY:	Cheers.

GARY GETS BACK IN HIS VAN, AND DRIVES ALONG TO THE ALLEY. WHEN HE GETS THERE HE SEES, TO HIS FRUSTRATION, THAT BLACK CAST IRON BOLLARDS PREVENT HIM DRIVING DOWN THE ALLEY. HE GETS OUT OF HIS VAN, LOCKS IT, AND SETS OFF DOWN THE ALLEY TOWARDS A PUB HE CAN SEE. AS GARY EMERGES FROM THE ALLEY THERE MIGHT BE A SUBTLE CHANGE OF LIGHT, A SEPIA OVERTONE SUFFUSING THE COLOURS. GARY FINDS HIMSELF IN A STREET OF OLD GRUBBY TERRACED HOUSES, AND IN FRONT OF THE PUB HE SPOTTED, A DRAB PLACE CALLED THE DUKE OF MARLBOROUGH. HE DOESN'T NOTICE ALL THE WINDOWS IN THE STREET ARE CRISS CROSSED WITH BROWN STICKY TAPE. HE ENTERS THE PUB.

4. INT. PUB. DAY 2.

<u>OCTOBER 1940.</u>

GARY ENTERS THE PUBLIC BAR OF THE DUKE OF MARLBOROUGH. WOODEN FLOOR, HARD BENCHES, BROWN PAINT, BEER HANDLES, AND GAS MANTLES. THE DIRTY WINDOWS HAVE BROWN STICKY TAPE ON THEM.

Shooting the Pilot

>HEAVY BLACK CURTAINS ARE OPEN AT THE WINDOWS. THERE ARE A FEW ELDERLY MEN IN THE PUB; A COUPLE OF THEM PLAY CRIB, ONE AT THE BAR, ANOTHER ALONE READING THE DAILY HERALD. THEY ALL HAVE HALF PINTS IN FRONT OF THEM AND SMALL BROWN CARBOARD BOXES – CONTAINING THEIR GAS MASKS – NEAR AT HAND. THERE IS NO ONE BEHIND THE BAR, BUT A DOOR TO A BACK PARLOUR IS AJAR. THE VOICE OF AL BOWLLY ON A WIRELESS CAN BE FAINTLY HEARD. THE REGULARS ALL LOOK UP AS THE OVERALLED GARY WALKS UP TO THE BAR. HE ACKNOWLEDGES THEM WITH A NOD.

GARY: (GENERALLY) Afternoon... (TO THE MAN AT THE BAR) 'Scuse me, I'm looking for Hugh Gaitskell House...

> THE OLD TIMER LOOKS AT HIM BLANKLY.

GARY: (GENERALLY) Hugh Gaitskell House anyone? Your starter for ten?

> THE OTHERS REGARD HIM ODDLY. THEN PHOEBE COMES OUT OF THE PARLOUR. SHE'S AN ATTRACTIVE YOUNG WOMAN, ABOUT 25, VERY 1940s IN HAIR, MAKE UP, AND CLOTHES. THE PENNY DROPS FOR GARY.

GARY: Oh, it's a theme pub, isn't it? Course it is. (LOOKS AROUND) Very convincing.

PHOEBE: Hello, haven't seen you in here before. What can I get you?

GARY: Actually I just came in for directions. Hugh Gaitskell House...

PHOEBE: Sorry, means nothing to me. You sure it's round here?

GARY: I asked a copper and he said it was just round the corner.

Goodnight Sweetheart

PHOEBE:	Sorry... dad might know though, he knows everything, he thinks.

THE TRAP DOOR TO THE CELLAR IS OPEN BEHIND THE BAR. PHOEBE CALLS DOWN.

PHOEBE:	Dad...!
ERIC:	Half a mo, I'm coming up.

ERIC, THE LANDLORD, APPEARS WITH A CRATE OF BROWN ALE. HE'S A WIRY BLOKE OF ABOUT 55.

ERIC:	What is it?
PHOEBE:	This gentleman wants to know where Hugh Gaitskell lives...
ERIC:	Hugh Gaitskell? Don't ring a bell with me. (TO PHOEBE) Is this Hugh Gaitskell a regular?
GARY:	No, not Hugh Gaitskell, Hugh Gaitskell House. It's a tower block.
ERIC:	A what? (BEAT) Here, why do you want to know anyway? You're not from round these parts, are you?
GARY:	No, I'm from Cricklewood as luck would have it.
ERIC:	(SUSPICIOUSLY) Cricklewood. That's not south of the river, is it?
GARY:	No... why, have we declared war with South London or something?
ERIC:	Don't you cheek me you young pup! I was in both Battles of the Somme, I'm entitled to ask. We got to be careful. Careless talk costs lives.
GARY:	Oh, sorry, got you! Have to stay in period!
ERIC:	Eh?

Shooting the Pilot

GARY: Though I have to say you could be taking this 1940s theme a bit far. For starters, it doesn't look like it's been much of a hit with the crucial 18 to 25 D1 & 2s.

ERIC: Eh?

GARY: I mean, where are the younger generation?

ERIC: Where are they? I'll tell you where the bloomin' younger generation are! They've have taken the King's shilling.

GARY: (AMUSED) Oh dear, what's the King going to do when his gas goes out?

ERIC LEANS ACROSS THE BAR AND GRABS GARY BY THE FRONT OF HIS OVERALLS.

PHOEBE: Dad, calm down! (TO GARY) I'm all for a laugh myself, and that Jimmy Handley's a real tonic. But dad takes it all very seriously...

ERIC: Seriously!? Britain stands alone, girl. The Hun is poised to invade! Adolf's Panzers are gunning their engines even as we speak! Course I take it seriously! (TO GARY) And I'd like to know why you're not in blinkin' uniform?

GARY: (BELIEVING HE IS ENTERING INTO THE SPIRIT) I'm afraid I'm not at liberty to divulge that information. Careless talk and all that. (TAPS THE SIDE OF HIS NOSE)

ERIC: Oh really? (MORE RESPECTFUL) Right you are, son. Mum's the word.

ERIC GOES BACK DOWN THE CELLAR.

GARY: I got to say it, he's bloody convincing, your dad, does he do amateur dramatics?

Goodnight Sweetheart

               EVERYONE IS SHOCKED AT GARY'S "BLOODY". THE OLD
               CODGER AT THE BAR GLARES ANGRILY AT HIM.

CODGER: Oy, ladies present!

GARY: Sorry... Well, since I'm here, I think I'll have a drink... I don't suppose you do lager?

PHOEBE: Do what?

GARY: No, course you don't. All right, give me a pint of best.

PHOEBE: Sorry, only allowed to serve halves for the duration.

GARY: Righty ho, a half then. And how much will that be, pray? Sixpence ha'penny?

PHOEBE: Where do you think you are, The Ritz? It's threepence three farthings...

GARY: Happy hour is it?

PHOEBE: Happy?! When it went up from threepence ha'penny there was nearly a riot!

GARY: No come on, be serious, how much?

               BUT PHOEBE RINGS UP 3¾d ON THE TILL. FOR THE
               FIRST TIME A SHADOW OF DOUBT CROSSES GARY'S
               FACE.

GARY: Would you excuse me a moment?

               GARY GOES TO THE DOOR, OPENS IT, AND STEPS
               OUTSIDE.

               <u>5. EXT. PUB. DAY 2.</u>

               CONTINUOUS. GARY LOOKS UP AND DOWN THE ROAD,
               SEEING IT PROPERLY FOR THE FIRST TIME. IT
               SHOULD BE AS 1940 AS POSSIBLE WITHOUT GOING
               OVER THE TOP. TAPED UP WINDOWS, PIG BINS IN THE

Shooting the Pilot

STREET, A SIGN POINTING TO A BRICK SHELTER AT THE END OF THE ROAD, A BOMBED OUT HOUSE A FEW DOORS AWAY, AND AN ANTI-AIRCRAFT GUN SANDBAGGED IN AT THE OTHER END OF THE ROAD. A CARTHORSE IS DRINKING FROM THE HORSE TROUGH. AND A BARRAGE BALLOON FLOATS OVERHEAD, ITS CABLE DISAPPEARING BEHIND THE STREET. OH YES, AND THE STREET LAMPS ARE GAS. (PAUSE FOR THE DESIGNER TO HAVE AN ORGASM.)

GARY: Jesus..!

THEN GARY SEES CONSTABLE DEADMAN COMING DOWN THE ROAD. GARY RECOGNISES HIM, AND LOOKS RELIEVED. THERE MUST BE SOME SIMPLE EXPLANATION. GARY DOESN'T NOTICE P.C. DEADMAN WEARS AN OLD FASHIONED UNIFORM, BUTTONED TO THE NECK, AND HAS HIS BROWN CARDBOARD GAS MASK BOX OVER HIS SHOULDER. DEADMAN APPROACHES, AIMING FOR THE PUB.

GARY: Hello again.... Look, is the whole street in on this theme lark?

P.C. DEADMAN: (A WEE BIT CONFUSED) Theme? You all right, son?

GARY: You told me to ask in here about Hugh Gaitskell House, remember? And they all blanked me. Are they frightened I'm a spy from the brewery, or something, trying to catch them out of character?

P.C. DEADMAN: I sincerely hope you're not a spy, son! (WITH A CHUCKLE) Now who was it you were asking after? Hugh Gaskell was it?

GARY: Look, you gave me directions not half an hour ago...!

P.C. DEADMAN: Must have been another Bobby, son. Half an hour ago I was doing a bandaging demonstration for the A.R.P. in the Christadelphian Hall... Standing room only, though that might have been due to the appeal of Mrs Hardcastle's rock cakes.

P.C. DEADMAN GOES INTO THE PUB WITH AN AVUNCULAR CHUCKLE. GARY LOOKS VERY PUZZLED. THEN A SMILE BREAKS OUT.

GARY: Of course! It's not a theme pub, it's a dream! I'm asleep, that's all right then... Wonder if I'll get my leg over that barmaid, or will she turn into Auntie Enid like they normally do. I wonder what's the significance of that?

HE GOES BACK INTO THE PUB.

6. INT. PUB. DAY.

GARY RETURNS JAUNTILY INTO THE PUB. HIS HALF OF BITTER WAITS FOR HIM, AS DOES PHOEBE WITH A QUESTIONING EXPRESSION. ERIC, MEANWHILE, IS SERVING P.C. DEADMAN.

GARY: Sorry I rushed out like that, but I thought I saw Vera Lynn walking down the road with Winston Churchill, but it turned out to be an off-duty Polish airman with a roll of lino over his shoulder. Easy mistake to make. (HE DRINKS HALF HIS BEER AND MAKES A FACE)

ERIC: I hope you aren't babbling in order to convince us you aren't all there, so I'll forget you owe me threepence three-farthings?

GARY: Course not. (PATS HIS POCKETS) Oh, I seem to have left home without any coppers on me... no offence Constable. (TAKES OUT HIS NEW MONT BLANC) Would you take a cheque...? (REACHES INTO POCKET FOR HIS CHEQUE BOOK)

ERIC: You cheeky Arab, who do you think you are?!

Shooting the Pilot

GARY: (UNTROUBLED, HE KNOWS IT'S A DREAM) If that's a "no", I'll have to write you an I.O.U...

HE TWISTS THE SHAFT OF THE PEN AND THE ROLLERBALL EMERGES.

ERIC: (AMAZED) Where did you get that?!

GARY: It was a birthday present.

ERIC: (TO CONSTABLE DEADMAN) Here Reg, ever seen anything like this before?

P.C. DEADMAN: No I have not, and as a policeman I flatter myself I am on more than nodding terms with pens pencils and other writing implements. (TAKES THE PEN AND LOOKS AT IT) Where does the ink go then?

ERIC: (EXAMINES THE PEN IN TURN, THEN READS WHAT IS WRITTEN ON THE GOLD BAND) "Made in Germany"?! I think you've got some serious explaining to do Sunny Jim!

GARY: (FEELING THREATENED FOR THE FIRST TIME) It was given to me in America.

ERIC: America! And I've just come back from the Moon! Arrest him, Reg. He's a spy. Stands to reason, no money, German pen, asking after some bloke no one's ever heard of...

PHOEBE: Don't be silly dad...

ERIC: Don't you talk to me like that! You'll feel the back of my hand, young lady!

PHOEBE: But if he was a spy, would he be drawing attention to himself like this? Of course not. He'd have English money, an indelible pencil, and he wouldn't keep going on about this Harry Gaskett...

ERIC: Who asked you?! You should be in the kitchen getting my tea!

Goodnight Sweetheart

PHOEBE EXITS THROUGH A DOOR TO THE PARLOUR.

P.C. DEADMAN: She has got a point, Eric.

ERIC: It could be a double bluff though. Only one way to find out...

P.C. DEADMAN: You mean...?

ERIC: Precisely.

ERIC GETS A PIECE OF PAPER AND WRITES ON IT WITH GARY'S MONT BLANC. GARY TRIES TO SEE WHAT HE'S WRITING, BUT ERIC SHIELDS IT WITH HIS OTHER HAND.

ERIC: All right, read this... Fritzy.

GARY: (WONDERING WHAT IT MEANS) Worcestershire beat Warwickshire by ten wickets.

ERIC AND P.C. DEADMAN EXCHANGE GLANCES.

P.C. DEADMAN: Sorry we doubted you son.

GARY: (CONFUSED) What did I do right?

P.C. DEADMAN: Everyone knows the Krauts can't pronounce their "Ws". If you were a German spy you'd have said "Varvickshire" and "Vorsestershire". I think you owe him an apology, Eric.

ERIC: Unless he was born in Germany, educated in England, then went home to join the Nazis. There was a flick like that up the Regent...

P.C. DEADMAN: Eric, just say sorry.

ERIC: All right... But he still owes me for the beer.

GARY: I know, thing is, that's why I was looking for Hughie Gaitskell, he owes me two quid, from before I went to the States.

Shooting the Pilot

P.C. DEADMAN: Two quid, that's a lot of money. Have you told the police?

ERIC: He just told you!

P.C. DEADMAN: Right you are.

GARY: Look, it's not a police matter.

ERIC: It will be if you don't pay for your beer.

P.C. DEADMAN: Tell you what, why don't you sell me your Yankee pen? I'll give you half a dollar for it.

GARY: Half a dollar!?

ERIC: I'll give you three bob.

GARY: It cost over £30!

P.C. DEADMAN: A month's wages!? Pull the other one! Three and a tanner.

ERIC: Four bob.

GARY: I never said it was for sale!

P.C. DEADMAN: Four and (GETS ALL HIS CHANGE FROM HIS POCKET) sevenpence ha'penny.

ERIC: (SMUGLY) Four and eightpence.

GARY: Oh, all right... (SIGHS. S/V) What do I care, it's only a dream.

ERIC: Right. Half a crown, three and six, four bob, four and threepence, fourpence... farthing. I took for the beer.

GARY: I thought you might.

A COUPLE OF SOLDIERS COME IN, FROM THE ACK-ACK BATTERY. ERIC GOES TO SERVE THEM. P.C. DEADMAN TAKES HIS DRINK OVER TO THE TABLE WHERE THE CRIB PLAYERS SIT, LEAVING OUR GARY AT THE BAR

	FINISHING HIS DRINK. HE NOTICES AN OLD UPRIGHT PIANO. HE CROSSES TO IT AND STARTS TINKERING. HE CAN PLAY A LITTLE. HE STARTS PICKING OUT THE NOTES OF "YOUR SONG" BY JOHN/TAUPIN (OR A SIMILAR WELL KNOWN CLEARABLE POP CLASSIC) AND SINGS ALONG. PHOEBE COMES OUT.
PHOEBE:	That's nice. Did you learn that in America?
GARY:	What? Yeah... Well, actually I wrote it.
PHOEBE:	You never!? You written any others?
GARY:	One or two. (PLAYS AND SINGS THE FIRST FEW BARS OF "MY WAY") "And now the end is near and so I face the final curtain..."
ERIC:	'ey, 'ey, 'ey, none of them defeatist songs in my pub if you don't mind!!
PHOEBE:	Leave him alone dad, he's talented. You could be on the wireless. "And now, live from the Cafe de Paris, the tinkling tunes of...." What's your name?
GARY:	Gary. Gary Sparrow.
PHOEBE:	Phoebe Bamford.
	THEY SHAKE HANDS.
PHOEBE:	What do you do for a living?
GARY:	Television repair man.
PHOEBE:	Times must be hard for you then?
GARY:	Why?
PHOEBE:	Cos there hasn't been any telly since the war started, has there? Dad was really browned off, he'd bought one to follow the fighting on.
GARY:	Well naturally, during the hostilities, I've switched to other things, you know, radar...

Shooting the Pilot

PHOEBE: What's that when it's at home?

GARY: It's a radio system used for tracking enemy.... (HE CAN SEE SHE HAS NO IDEA) Ooops, forget I spoke. (TAPS THE SIDE OF HIS NOSE)

PHOEBE'S IMPRESSED.

ERIC: (CALLS OVER) Oy Phoebe, he's not the only customer, and you're a married woman.

PHOEBE: (CALLS BACK) We're only chatting.

ERIC: Make sure that's all you do.

GARY: So where is your old man then?

PHOEBE: Last letter I had, he was in Tunisia... Been gone over six months now.

GARY: Bet you miss him?

PHOEBE: Course. We used to go dancing, pictures, I never get out now...

GARY: I'll take you dancing if you like. I've got a car, we could go up West...

PHOEBE: You cheeky so and so! We'd have to sit out the slow numbers.

BUT SHE IS MORE FLATTERED THAN OFFENDED. THEN ERIC COMES OVER WITH A NEW SUSPICION.

ERIC: Where's your gas mask then?

GARY: What?

ERIC: Reg, he ain't got a gas mask!

P.C. DEADMAN: (COMING OVER) I think we got a spare one up the station.

ERIC: That's not the point! Why hasn't he got one? It's all very suspicious...

GARY:	I don't have a gas mask cos I'm a claustrophobic, all right?
ERIC:	Oh, so now he's claiming he's from a neutral country!
GARY:	What? No, claustrophobia is a fear of confined spaces, not a place!
ERIC:	Is he telling the truth Reg?
P.C. DEADMAN:	He is Eric...
ERIC:	I'd still ask him for his papers if I was you...
GARY:	(GETTING UP) I'm getting really bored with this now...
ERIC:	(GETTING BETWEEN GARY AND THE EXIT) Unless he hasn't got any papers.
GARY:	Of course I got papers. We German spies never go anywhere without a copy of Mein Kampf, a signed photograph of Adolf Hitler, and a packet of dehydrated sauerkraut.
ERIC:	Cheeky bugger!
CODGER:	Oy, ladies present.
P.C. DEADMAN:	Leave him alone, Eric. This isn't a police state, anyone can see he's true blue.
GARY:	(GERMAN ACCENT) Zenk you, officer, vould you permit me to buy you a schnapps?
P.C. DEADMAN:	Very amusing. Very amusing...
ERIC:	Well I ain't laughing. I knew he was the Hun!
P.C. DEADMAN:	Oh shut up Eric! (TO GARY) Now I shouldn't be seen drinking on duty... let's go into the Snug.
	BUT THEN THE AIR RAID SIREN GOES OFF.

PHOEBE: Hermann's early tonight.

                     THEY ALL START MOVING TOWARDS THE STREET DOOR.
                     THEN THERE'S AN EXPLOSION VERY NEARBY. GARY
                     JUMPS.

GARY: What was that! Jesus Christ!

ALL EXCEPT PHOEBE:
                     Oy, ladies present!

P.C. DEADMAN: That was too close for comfort.

ERIC: We'd better all get down the cellar...

GARY: (BEING CARRIED ALONG) But I really am
                     claustrophobic!

                     THEY ALL DISAPPPEAR DOWN THE CELLAR STEPS. THE
                     TRAP DOOR IS CLOSED. THEN WE HEAR A SCREAM OF
                     CLAUSTROPHOBIC TERROR FROM GARY.

                     ### 7. INT. PUB CELLAR. DAY 2.

                     A GLOOMY PUB CELLAR LIT BY KEROSENE LAMPS, A
                     MAKESHIFT SHELTER, WITH ALL THE PEOPLE FROM
                     PREVIOUS SCENE THEREIN. HOWEVER, WE START ON A
                     TIGHT CLOSE UP ON GARY, WHO HAS PASSED OUT AFTER
                     HIS CLAUSTROPHOBIC PANIC. TO THE AUDIENCE IT
                     SHOULD LOOK AS IF HE COULD BE ASLEEP AT HOME IN
                     BED. HE IS MUMBLING IN HIS HALF CONSCIOUS STATE.

GARY: Let me out, I can't stand it... Please...

                     A HAND WAVES SMELLING SALTS UNDER HIS NOSE. HE
                     JERKS TOWARDS CONSCIOUSNESS.

GARY: Ohh... I was having this brilliant dream, I was
                     chatting up this gorgeous little bird, she was
                     dying for me to give her one, and then this air
                     raid siren...

Goodnight Sweetheart

BUT BY NOW HE IS COMPLETELY AWAKE. WE PULL BACK. HE LOOKS ROUND. EVERYONE IS STARING AT HIM. HE AND THE AUDIENCE REALISE IT WASN'T A DREAM. THE GROUND SHAKES AS BOMBS FALL NEARBY.

GARY: Oh my God it's real!!

GARY LOOKS UTTERLY DAZED. PHOEBE GETS A BOTTLE OF BRANDY FROM WITHIN THE DEPTHS OF THE CELLAR, UNDOES IT AND GIVES GARY A SWIG FROM THE BOTTLE.

ERIC: Not so fast, I'm saving that 'til the Tommies march into Berlin.

PHOEBE: (EXASPERATED) Oh Dad... Feeling any better Gary?

GARY: Yeah, I'm all right now, the panics sort of come and go. I don't like it down here though...

ERIC: Oh, I'm so sorry, if I'd known you were coming I'd have had the painters and decorators in!

P.C. DEADMAN: Look, why don't we all just keep calm and have a nice sing song? How about "Run Rabbit Run? "Run rabbit run rabbit run run run..."

THERE'S A RAGGED RENDITION OF THE FIRST VERSE.

PHOEBE: Gary writes songs.

GARY: Well, not really...

PHOEBE: Yes you do, lovely songs... Do that one, you know, it's a bit funny...

GARY: You sure?

P.C. DEADMAN: Go on son...

GARY: All right. (STARTS TO SING IN A CRACKED VOICE) "It's a little bit funny this feeling inside..."

8. EXT. STREET. NIGHT.

THE STREET OUTSIDE THE PUB IS EMPTY. WE HEAR BOMBS AND SIRENS, THE SOUND OF ANTI AIRCRAFT FIRE AND EMERGENCY SERVICE BELLS. WE SEE SEARCHLIGHTS, MAYBE STOCK FOOTAGE OF AERIAL DOGFIGHTS. A BIT OF CAMERA SHAKE AS THE BOMBS DROP NEARBY.

9. INT. CELLAR. NIGHT.

SOME TIME LATER, THEY ALL KNOW THE SONG NOW.

OMNES: ... "I hope you don't mind, I hope you don't mind, I put down the words, how wonderful life is now you're in the world".

THE SONG FINISHES. ALL APPLAUD.

P.C. DEADMAN: That was really morale lifting son. Well done.

ERIC: Not bad, I suppose... but I still say Words and World don't rhyme... unless they rhyme in German...

EVERYONE IGNORES ERIC. GARY GETS UP, MAYBE BANGING HIS HEAD ON THE LOW CEILING. HE CROSSES TO WHERE PHOEBE PUT THE BRANDY BOTTLE.

GARY: (TO HIMSELF) It really is 1940, isn't it? My van's parked in 1993 and I'm in 1940! (HAS ANOTHER SWIG OF BRANDY)

ERIC: I saw that! That's a tanner... (THEN SUDDENLY) Phoebe, did you bring the till tray down with you?!

PHOEBE: No, I thought you did!

ERIC: Oh no! You stupid girl!

PHOEBE: It ain't my fault, you never let it out of your sight usually!

Goodnight Sweetheart

P.C. DEADMAN: Calm down Eric, who's going to nick your takings during an air raid?

GARY: Ah, but haven't you heard of Goering's crack 15th Airborne Petty Cash Brigade? Highly trained Luftwaffe paratroopers whose mission is to steal small amounts of loose change.

ERIC: All right, clever dick! And suppose there's a bomb and it blows the till to kingdom come? Listen, I think they're going away...

EVERYONE IS SILENT. THE SOUND OF BOMBS AND AERIAL BATTLE DOES SEEM TO HAVE MOVED AWAY.

ERIC: I'm going upstairs to check the till...

P.C. DEADMAN: You got to wait for the all clear...

ERIC: It's my pub, I can do what I like!

AND ERIC'S OFF UP THE STAIRS. HE PUSHES OPEN THE TRAP DOOR AND CLIMBS THROUGH. THE SIGHT OF FREEDOM EXCITES GARY AGAIN.

GARY: Got to get out of here!

GARY STARTS UP THE STAIRS TOO.

ERIC DISAPPEARS THROUGH THE TRAP DOOR. THEN JUST AS GARY REACHES THE TOP, THERE'S A HUGE EXPLOSION, SOUND OF BROKEN GLASS, AS A BOMB DROPS YARDS FROM THE PUB.

PHOEBE: (SCREAMS) Dad!

DUST SWIRLS IN THE TRAP, OBSCURING VISION. PHOEBE MAKES FOR THE STEPS.

P.C. DEADMAN: Now now, love, wait 'til the all clear!

PHOEBE: But my dad...!!

P.C. DEADMAN:	If he's copped a packet, makes no sense you copping one too!

PHOEBE STARTS TO CRY, P.C. DEADMAN TRIES TO COMFORT HER, THEN THE ALL CLEAR SOUNDS. EVERYONE RUSHES FOR THE STAIRS, PHOEBE IN THE LEAD.

10. INT. PUB. NIGHT.

THE PUB IS FULL OF DEBRIS, THOUGH NOT BADLY DAMAGED. IT'S GLOOMY, THE ONLY LIGHT BEING A SEARCHLIGHT IN THE STREET, POINTED AT THE SKY. WE CAN DIMLY SEE GARY KNEELING OVER AN UNCONSCIOUS ERIC, GIVING HIM THE KISS OF LIFE. PHOEBE AND P.C. DEADMAN AND THE OTHERS EMERGE FROM THE CELLAR, ILLUMINATED BY P.C. DEADMAN'S LAMP. THEY ARE HORRIFIED TO SEE GARY APPARENTLY SNOGGING AN UNCONSCIOUS OR DEAD PUBLICAN.

PHOEBE:	What are you doing!?
P.C. DEADMAN:	You animal!

P.C. DEADMAN DRAGS GARY OFF ERIC.

GARY:	No...!
PHOEBE:	(KNEELING BY HER DAD) He's not breathing! Dad! Dad!
P.C. DEADMAN:	(HOLDING ON TO GARY) They had a case like this over Dalston in '33. Chappie used to break into morgues and interfere with...
CODGER:	Oy, ladies present!
GARY:	Don't be stupid, I was giving him the kiss of life.
P.C. DEADMAN:	The what?
GARY:	Mouth to mouth resuscitation! I learned it in America!

PHOEBE:	Let him! Don't die, dad!
	P.C. DEADMAN RELUCTANTLY LETS GO OF GARY, WHO RETURNS TO KISSING ERIC. AFTER TEN LONG SECONDS, ERIC STARTS TO BREATH AGAIN. THEN HE STARTS TO COME ROUND.
P.C. DEADMAN:	You got to hand it to them, when it comes to kissing they know a thing or two these Yanks.
	A DELIGHTED PHOEBE BENDS DOWN AND HUGS HER FATHER.
ERIC:	What happened?
PHOEBE:	What happened was, this German spy just saved your life!
ERIC:	How?
P.C. DEADMAN:	Don't ask.
ERIC:	Why not?
GARY:	It was brilliantly resourceful but not very manly.
ERIC:	Blimey, my head's killing me.
GARY:	I'm not surprised, look what hit you. (PICKS UP DENTED TILL DRAWER)
P.C. DEADMAN:	Gary, son, you know you're a hero.
	P.C. DEADMAN SHAKES HIS HAND. PHOEBE KISSES HIM.
ERIC:	(GETTING TO HIS FEET) Nip down the cellar and get that brandy, Phoebe, we may as well finish it off. (ERIC SHAKES GARY'S HAND)

12. EXT. DUKE OF MARLBOROUGH. NIGHT.

THE STREET IS QUIET. BLACKED OUT. FROM INSIDE THE PUB WE CAN HEAR A SING-SONG LED BY GARY ON

Shooting the Pilot

                    THE PIANO... SOMEWHAT DETUNED BY THE LUFTWAFFE. SOMETHING PERIOD LIKE "WE'LL MEET AGAIN". THE SONG FINISHES.

ERIC: (O.O.V.) Don't go, Gary, sing us another one of them tunes you wrote...

                    THE DOOR OPENS A CRACK. GARY APPEARS IN IT, HIS BACK TO US.

GARY: No, honestly, I'll miss my last tram...

P.C. DEADMAN: (O.O.V.) Don't be a stranger, come back and see us soon...

PHOEBE: (COMES TO THE DOOR) I'll walk to the tram stop with you if you like?

GARY: No, don't put yourself out...

PHOEBE: You saved my dad's life! Besides, you got lost coming here in broad daylight.

GARY: Just come to the end of the street then...

                    THEY WALK SLOWLY DOWN THE STREET. SHE SLIPS HER ARM INSIDE HIS.

PHOEBE: Do you s'ppose you ever will come up this way again?

GARY: It's not on my usual route.

PHOEBE: (DISAPPOINTED) Oh... So when you said about going dancing were you just taking the Mick?

GARY: But you're married, and this isn't 1993.

PHOEBE: Eh? What you talking about?

GARY: Nothing. Only I was reading this book set in the future where women get up to all sorts of things whether they're married or not.

PHOEBE:	Well it's 1940, my husband's overseas, God knows when he'll come home, and I just thought it would be nice to go dancing with someone who wasn't going to try and take advantage...

THEY'VE NOW REACHED THE ALLEY.

GARY:	Well of course, there is still the two nicker Hugh Gaitskell owes me.

DELIGHTED, PHOEBE KISSES HIM ON THE CHEEK, LEAVING A LIPSTICK MARK.

GARY:	Go on, you get back to your Dad.

PHOEBE GOES OFF TOWARDS THE PUB. GARY LOOKS ALONG THE ALLEY.

GARY:	Right. (STARTS WALKING DOWN THE ALLEY) If there's not a "K" reg Rumbelows' van parked at the end of this alley, am I in the...

SUDDENLY THE VAN IS VISIBLE. GARY GIVES A BIG RELIEVED GRIN.

13. INT. GARY & YVONNE'S BEDROOM. NIGHT.

YVONNE IS LAYING IN BED WATCHING THE SAME CANADIAN OPEN UNIVERSITY LECTURER. GARY ENTERS WARILY AND WEARILY. HE DOESN'T REALISE HOW DIRTY HIS CLOTHES, HANDS, FACE, AND HAIR ARE. NOR DOES HE REALISE THERE'S A TRACE OF RED LIPSTICK ON HIS CHEEK. HE STOPS IN THE DOORWAY. IT FEELS LIKE A DEJA VU EXPERIENCE.

YVONNE:	Where the hell have you been? What time do you think it is?
GARY:	I was going to ask you that question.
YVONNE:	It's half past eleven...
GARY:	What year?

Shooting the Pilot

YVONNE: What are you talking about!? And look at the state of you!

HE SITS HEAVILY ON THE BED.

YVONNE: Are you all right? Has there been an accident?

GARY: Yeah. What happened was I was in this pub, having a quiet half...

YVONNE: Half? You always say only poofs drink halves!

GARY: And the landlord tripped and fell down this open trap door into his cellar, banged his head and stopped breathing.

YVONNE: And you gave him the kiss of life?!

GARY: No, I helped out behind the bar until he felt better. God, I'm done in. (COLLAPSES ON THE BED)

YVONNE: Gary, get those dirty overalls off first!

GARY STAGGERS TO THE LITTLE EN SUITE SHOWER ROOM, AND STARTS TO TAKE OFF HIS OVERALLS. HE LOOKS AT HIS DUSTY FACE IN THE MIRROR AND SEES PHOEBE'S LIPSTICK. HE REACTS AND RUBS IT OFF WITH HIS HAND. YVONNE SWITCHES OFF THE BEDSIDE LIGHT.

YVONNE: (O.O.V) 'Night love...

GARY: Goodnight sweetheart.

"GOODNIGHT SWEETHEART" BY AL BOWLLY FADES UP.

WE FADE OUT.

<u>CREDITS.</u>

<u>THE END.</u>

7
Lady Ottoline Pierpoint's Guide to Intimate Behaviour for Gentlewomen

THIS BOOK DISCUSSES the pilot scripts of six of our most successful series. Here is a bonus track for you – the "one that got away".

Some history:

At the start of the 1990s we signed an exclusive deal with the BBC. This exquisite arrangement obliged the BBC to commission a new series from us every year. It didn't quite work out that way, because *Birds of a Feather* and *Goodnight Sweetheart* both had marathon runs. We still created a healthy handful of original BBC comedies during the decade, but in 2001 our deal was nearing its end. We still owed the BBC one more series. We wanted it to be a smash hit. We wanted to go out with a bang.

As we have explained elsewhere, new ideas do not just drop from the heavens, but we felt we had a good 'un in *Lady Ottoline*. Again, the source material was unearthed by Laurence in a junk shop. Not the London junk shop where he found the magazine that led to *Shine On Harvey Moon*; this time he was in a Parisian flea market, where he stumbled on a tatty old book, *The Trompe l'Oeil Bible*, which featured extraordinary *trompes l'oeil* found in seemingly ordinary homes. (In case you don't know, *trompe l'oeil* is a French phrase meaning "deceives the eye", used to describe paintings that create the illusion of a real object or scene.)

We were drawn to one particular painting, of a woman sitting in a striped deckchair in her manicured garden, reading a book. Her clothing, her demeanour, her hair and her spectacles led us to believe she belonged in the 1920s. There was definitely something Virginia Woolf-ish about her, and we found ourselves wondering – suppose somebody bought a flat in an old house, stripped the wallpaper and found this *trompe l'oeil*? And what if she came to life? Now that felt like an exciting idea and certainly something to play with.

Judy, our heroine, who has just moved into this flat, is the only living person who can see this, well, what, *ghost*? Is Judy frightened? Perhaps, for a moment. But she's mesmerised too. Especially when Lady Ottoline turns out to have written a best-selling book on how to meet eligible bachelors and is happy to accompany and advise Judy as she tries to negotiate London's social jungle.

We were anxious that we might be treading in the footsteps of *Goodnight Sweetheart*. Wasn't Lady Ottoline just another time-travelling fantasy, this time in skirts? But the contrast between the mores of the new millennium and the decorous behaviour described in *Lady Ottoline Pierpoint's Guide to Intimate Behaviour for Gentlewomen* seemed to offer considerable comedic potential, though we did briefly wonder whether the idea had legs hidden beneath Lady O's long dresses. Perhaps it was more suited to the stage?

However, the BBC's head of comedy, the late and much missed Geoffrey Perkins, was tickled by our proposal. We wrote a script and he loved it. He enthused about its originality and never once compared it to *Goodnight Sweetheart*. We were delighted, but then we did have an excellent relationship with the BBC. We presumed we would write a first series of six or seven episodes, the BBC would transmit it, and as long as it was well received, a second series would follow. That's how the BBC worked, especially for writers with a proven track record.

But this was the brave new millennium. All that had happened in the twentieth century was irrelevant. Now we had a twenty-first-century BBC with a scientific approach to commissioning. We became dimly aware that all was not well as the weeks went by and Geoffrey hadn't phoned up to commission the series. We trooped into his office at the BBC, where he was forced to admit that Peter Salmon, the Controller of BBC1, had decreed that he wouldn't 'green-light' any series simply on the strength of the script. There had to be a big star attached. We asked Geoffrey if there were any big stars Peter wanted to get on his channel? Not really, Geoffrey replied morosely.

Never mind. We were used to working with stars. As we've noted elsewhere, several of our shows were cast before they were written. We gave the script to our favourite casting director, Susie Parriss, and asked her to compile a shortlist of possible Lady Ottolines – after all, hers was the title role. Susie as ever produced a stunning list for us. At the top was Judi Dench. We contacted the great lady, who said she loved the sound of our new project, but sadly she was preoccupied with nursing her very sick husband.

Next on the list was Celia Imrie, who we'd enjoyed working with before on *The New Statesman*. She was keen too. Very. We told Geoffrey about Celia, and he agreed she was a terrific idea. He was also excited about Emma Chambers, who had been such a success in *The Vicar of Dibley*. He felt she was ripe to lead her own series and would make a perfect Judy. Emma and Celia: what was there not to like?

The script was duly sent to Emma. She was very taken with the part of Judy, so we met for tea at Brown's Hotel, the sort of establishment of which Lady Ottoline would surely have approved. Emma really "got" Judy, and was excited about how she would interact with Lady O.

Then she said, "We're not doing it in front of a studio audience, are we?"

We had every intention of playing our new comedy in front of an audience. We were and are fans of that sort of show, with its theatrical atmosphere reinforced by live laughter. Most of our hit shows had been recorded in front of a studio audience, as had *The Vicar of Dibley*. Nevertheless, Emma believed that studio audiences were passé. Maybe she was right.

We passed Emma's reservations on to Geoffrey Perkins who told us that under Peter Salmon's new BBC protocols, all sitcom must be played before a studio audience, otherwise he couldn't assess whether the show is funny or not. We were in a pickle. We wanted Emma Chambers, but she simply wasn't interested in an audience show. Then all of a sudden Emma became the least of our problems.

Our good friend Greg Dyke became Director-General of the BBC. We thought this was fantastic news. He'd shake the place up. One of the first things Greg did was decree that Channel Controllers like Peter Salmon shouldn't get involved in deciding which comedies and dramas to commission. It wasn't their area of expertise. We couldn't have agreed more. Instead Greg initiated what he called the "double tick" system. Now there would be so-called "genre commissioners", who would have to approve a project before it went to the Channel Controller. If he or she liked it as well, then bingo, two ticks! We couldn't have agreed less.

The foremost problem was that neither of these ticks originated with Geoffrey Perkins, a man who had commissioned, written, performed and produced dozens of hit comedies. No, there were two new tickers. Peter Salmon moved across to a new post in sport, to be replaced by Lorraine Heggessey, previously Head of Daytime and Children's TV. The other tick belonged to Danielle Lux, whom we had never met. We were told that she too was a Head of Children's programming at Granada and London Weekend Television, so both tickers seemed to possess scant experience of narrative comedy.

How did this new arrangement go down with Geoffrey? Not well. He sat behind his TV Centre desk with his head in his hands. How do we know? We were there, sitting opposite him. He asked us what was the point in being "Head of Comedy" if he couldn't recommend what was to be made and what wasn't? We didn't have an answer.

But we did have a question. "What is going to happen to *Lady Ottoline*?"

"I don't know what to say," admitted Geoffrey. "I can commission a second script if that helps...?"

"But what about a series commission?" said Laurence.

"It's out of my hands," said poor old Geoffrey.

We decided that until Ms Lux and Ms Heggessey got their ticks together we would put Lady O aside and focus on our first theatrical project, for the legendary Sir Alan Ayckbourn, who didn't need two ticks: he understood comedy. Laurence – striking lucky again – had bumped into Sir

Alan at a literary dinner and the great man had asked why we hadn't attempted theatre before. Suddenly a new career path seemed to beckon, one that led to Broadway, via Sir Alan's theatre in Scarborough.

We said adieu to *Lady Ottoline* and consigned her to a metaphorical bottom drawer – well, an old-fashioned floppy disk to be precise – until we retrieved the poor dear to show you that not every script gets what it deserves.

Geoffrey Perkins left the BBC to join an independent production company that appreciated him. Danielle and Lorraine moved on too, as BBC executives always do, but the accursed "double tick" system survived for many years. We haven't written a new comedy for the BBC since. We're too impatient to wait over a year to hear whether the double tickers think it might be appropriate to have a semi-rehearsed reading in a church basement to hear if our work is any good.

We're often asked, "Have you got anything in your bottom drawer that you'd like to revive?"

We always say, "We would rather do something new."

But having reread *Lady Ottoline* after two decades, we're almost convinced it could still work as a comedy of manners for our times… on stage. Until then, Lady O can recline in her deckchair and work on the new edition of her *Guide to Intimate Behaviour for Gentlewomen*.

LADY OTTOLINE 2001

by

LAURENCE MARKS & MAURICE GRAN

Episode One: "BACK ON THE HORSE"

Second draft - March 2001

SCENE ONE. EXT. THE HOUSE/INT. THE FLAT. DAY 1.

ABOUT 5PM. ESTABLISH A BIG OLD VICTORIAN HOUSE IN SOUTH TOTTENHAM. BOTH HOUSE AND STREET HAVE SEEN BETTER DAYS.

WE GO THROUGH THE FRONT DOOR ON A TRACK, AND INTO THE HALL. WE APPROACH A CLOSED DOOR TO A FLAT.

JUDY: (OOV) Don't give me a hard time, I'm stripping as fast as I can!

CUT TO

SCENE TWO. INT. THE LIVING ROOM. DAY 1.

THE LIVING ROOM OF A RENTED FURNISHED FLAT. IT'S A BIG ROOM, WITH A WINDOW AND A KITCHEN CORNER.

THE FURNITURE IS IN THE MIDDLE OF THE ROOM, UNDER DIRTY DUST SHEETS. JUDY (29) AND LAURA (24), THEIR HAIR TIED UP, ARE DECORATING. JUDY IS STRIPPING PAPER OFF ONE WALL WITH A SCRAPER. LAURA IS SPLOSHING WHITE EMULSION ON ANOTHER WALL. THE THIRD WALL IS COVERED BY DISGUSTING HESSIAN PANELS ON A BAMBOO FRAME.

JUDY: I wish we hadn't started this! It's all that Laurence Llewellyn Bowen's fault, he makes it look easy!

LAURA: It'll be great when it's finished.

JUDY: Yes, all we need's a couple of spotlights, a few scatter cushions and a pound of semtex.

JUDY FINGERS THE HESSIAN WALL.

JUDY: What are we going to do about this... sacking?

LAURA: It's hessian...

JUDY RAISES AN EYEBROW.

LAURA: Sonia's Nan has it, it was big in the Seventies...

JUDY: So was Gary Glitter.

JUDY BANGS THE HESSIAN AND DUST FLIES UP. SHE SNEEZES.

JUDY: I bet there's all sorts of disgusting things living in there... (BEAT) I must stop fixating on Gary Glitter.

JUDY INSERTS HER SCRAPER BETWEEN A PANEL AND THE WALL, AND PRIES IT AWAY. THEY PULL THE PANELS RIGHT OFF – TO REVEAL A HUGE TROMPE L'OEIL OF A 1920-STYLE GARDEN, FEATURING A VIRGINIA WOOLF DRESS-ALIKE SITTING IN A GARDEN CHAIR WRITING HER JOURNAL. HER FACE IS HIDDEN BY THE SHADOW OF HER HAT.

LAURA: Eugh, creepy old lady! (PICKS UP HER PAINT ROLLER)

JUDY: Don't you dare! I like it, and I always wanted a garden flat.

JUDY TAKES A COUPLE OF STEPS BACK TO BETTER APPRECIATE THE PICTURE, AND BUMPS INTO A COVERED BOOKCASE, WHICH COLLAPSES WITH A SAD

CREAK. JUDY ROLLS HER EYES, PULLS BACK THE DUST SHEET, AND WE SEE A BIG PILE OF BOOKS AND A DECONSTRUCTED BOOKCASE.

JUDY: I resign!

JUDY STOMPS OVER TO THE FRIDGE AND GETS OUT A LITRE BOTTLE OF WHITE WINE, THREE QUARTERS FULL. SHE FINDS A COUPLE OF TUMBLERS ON THE DRAINING BOARD AND FILLS THEM BOTH. SHE TAKES A BIG DRINK.

LAURA: Hold on... (RAISES GLASS) Here's to our new lives in London!

JUDY: (UNENTHUSIASTIC) Cheers.

LAURA: For God's sake Judy! We're going to have a laugh down here! All the fanciable guys are in London.

JUDY: Let me remind you – I'm off men.

LAURA: You can't let Colin ruin the rest of your life.

JUDY: It's not Colin, he was just the last in a string of duds.

LAURA: I quite liked him.

JUDY: As you demonstrated last Christmas.

LAURA: You can't count Christmas, there was mistletoe everywhere.

JUDY: Not down his boxers.

LAURA: I didn't know it was him, it was dark in that cupboard! Anyway, it was well after he... you know...

JUDY: Dumped me.

LAURA: I didn't want to say it.

> JUDY FINISHES HER WINE AND REFILLS HER GLASS. THEN SHE STARTS PICKING UP BOOKS AND STACKING THEM NEATLY OUT OF HARM'S WAY. SHE LIKES BOOKS.

LAURA: Just because it didn't work out with Colin, there's plenty other fish...

JUDY: I never wanted another fish, I'm a one fish woman! We were going out since college...

LAURA: Exactly. Don't you think seven years was a bit like... long to be with one man? Hence the itch?

JUDY: Of course he itched, he was a louse! Look, I said I don't want to talk about Colin, and all we do is talk about Colin. The subject is now closed.

> A BOOK CATCHES JUDY'S EYE. IT'S AN OLD HARDBACK, IN A TOOLED LEATHER COVER, WITH THE TITLE ON THE SPINE IN GOLD LEAF.

JUDY: Is this yours? (SHOWS LAURA)

LAURA: "LADY OTTOLINE PIERPOINT'S GUIDE TO INTIMATE CONDUCT FOR GENTLEWOMEN" Duh – I don't think so. The last tenant must have left it.

> JUDY FLICKS THROUGH THE PAGES, AND SMILES.

JUDY: Listen; "Love making On The Dance Floor."

LAURA: It was Ibiza, I was drunk.

JUDY: (POSH VOICE) "No matter how Mr A and Miss B feel about each other, if they are unable to resist kissing in full view of their fellow guests, then serve them right if their hostess never invites them again."

LAURA: Horn-ey! When was it written?

JUDY: (CHECKS TITLE PAGE) 1927.

LAURA: It must have been so boring back then!

JUDY: But at least women knew where they stood, and it wasn't on a crowded bus with four bags of shopping because all the men are too uncouth offer you a seat...

LAURA: Speaking of shopping, what do you fancy for tea?

JUDY: We ought to eat that Skirton and Eckersley pork pie mum sent...

LAURA: She's mental.

JUDY: She cares.

LAURA: Then why does she keep sending us edible heart attacks? One of the reasons I came south was to get away from all them fattening pies. I fancy something a bit more organic.

JUDY: Kentucky Fried Chicken?

LAURA: (KEEN) Yeah!

JUDY: Go for it.

JUDY GIVES LAURA A FIVER. LAURA EXITS. JUDY FINISHES HER SECOND TUMBLER OF WINE AND POURS A THIRD. TO HER SURPRISE, THIS EMPTIES THE BOTTLE. SHE FINDS A CHAIR, SITS, AND READS.

JUDY: "While a short engagement might be considered vulgar, and a too speedy wedding may cause guests to wonder at the bride's virtue, a very lengthy betrothal casts doubt on the strength of the gentleman's ardour." Too bloody true!

JUDY FINISHES HER WINE, PUTS DOWN THE BOOK AND GRABS THE PHONE. SHE DIALS.

JUDY: Hello? Mrs Scales? It's Judy. Yes, that Judy. Is Colin there? Of course I'm not going to shout at him! If you must know I've found a PEP we bought together five years ago and he's entitled to

Lady Ottoline Pierpoint's Guide to Intimate Behaviour for Gentlewomen

half... Hello Colin. What do you mean how much is it worth? You were listening on the extension weren't you, you coward! There is no PEP! I just wanted you to know I'm in London, the new job's crap, the flat's horrible, and I'll never forgive you... Colin? Don't you want my number...?

JUDY HANGS UP. SHE'S VIRTUALLY IN TEARS. SHE GOES TO THE SINK AND SPLASHES COLD WATER ON HER FACE. WHEN SHE TURNS ROUND, SHE'S ASTONISHED TO SEE LADY OTTOLINE STANDING THERE, HOLDING THE BOOK. LADY O'S CLOTHES, GENUINELY 1920S, DON'T LOOK ABSURD, JUST QUAINT. WE DON'T PLAY UP THE FACT THAT THE TROMPE L'OEIL CHAIR IS EMPTY.

JUDY: Who are you?!

LADY OTTOLINE: I'm sorry if I startled you. The door was ajar...

JUDY: Was it?

LADY OTTOLINE: I see you've found my book?

JUDY: <u>Your</u> book?

LADY OTTOLINE: Lady Ottoline Pierpoint, how do you do?

JUDY: Judy, Judy Wemys... (PRONOUNCED WEEMS)

JUDY OFFERS HER HAND BUT LADY O. DOESN'T TAKE IT.

JUDY: Lady Ottoline? You wrote this?

LADY OTTOLINE: Yes. I lent it to a previous occupant, you see.

JUDY: Oh...

LADY OTTOLINE: And if you had read it, I doubt you would have debased yourself on the telephone just now.

JUDY IS VERY EMBARRASSED. SHE ASSUMES LADY O. HEARD FROM THE HALL. JUDY PROFFERS THE BOOK.

JUDY: Did you want it back?

Shooting the Pilot

LADY OTTOLINE: I think your need is the greater.

JUDY: So... You must be from upstairs?

LADY OTTOLINE: (VAGUE) Upstairs? I suppose I am. I lived in this house for an awfully long time. A very, very long time... it was a very refined neighbourhood once...

JUDY: I suppose you've seen some changes?

LADY OTTOLINE: Oh yes, I remember when we first got a telephone; a tremendous boon, although it did ring the death knell of the social visit.

JUDY LOOKS PUZZLED. SHE WONDERS EXACTLY HOW OLD IS LADY O.? THEN THE FRONT DOOR SLAMS AND IN COMES LAURA, WITH A KFC CARRIER BAG. SHE GIVES IT TO JUDY.

LAURA: I chatted up the bloke behind the counter and he threw in some coleslaw!

LADY O LOOKS DISTRESSED AT THE THOUGHT OF FLYING COLESLAW.

JUDY: Laura, this is...

LAURA: Won't be a tic, dying for a pee!

LAURA DARTS OUT AGAIN. JUDY STARTS REMOVING THE BOXES.

JUDY: Sorry about her, she wasn't so much brought up as spewed out.

LADY OTTOLINE: It was always hard to get good servants.

JUDY: She's my cousin...

LADY OTTOLINE: Ah... well, one can't choose one's family. May I sit down? Sometimes I feel quite faint. (SITS)

	LADY O HAS BECOME A LITTLE TRANSPARENT, BUT JUDY DOESN'T NOTICE.
JUDY:	(BRANDISHES THE BUCKET) Would you like a piece of...?
LADY OTTOLINE:	I'm sure it's delicious but – no thank you...
	JUDY EXTRACTS A BAG OF CHIPS FROM T'BUCKET. SHE EATS SOME.
JUDY:	I'll be covered in spots tomorrow, but it's worth it.
LADY OTTOLINE:	(MUSING) When did cutlery become obsolete?
LAURA:	(RE-ENTERS) He's really nice, Jude...
JUDY:	Who?
LAURA:	Mehmet, the bloke at KFC! Bit of a hunk.
LADY OTTOLINE:	"Mehmet" doesn't sound very English?
JUDY:	He's probably Turkish...
LAURA:	That's what I thought! Anyway, he's having a bit of a party over the shop after they close: loads of booze, and all the nuggets you can eat, subject to a last minute rush.
LADY OTTOLINE:	Sounds rather vulgar.
JUDY:	(TO LAURA) I ought to introduce you to Lady Ottoline...
LAURA:	Lady Ottoline?
LADY OTTOLINE:	How do you do.
JUDY:	She lives upstairs.
LAURA:	Oh, of course. I didn't know her name, but we met last night, didn't we?

Shooting the Pilot

LADY OTTOLINE: Did we?

LAURA: On the stairs, she was coming out of the loo. Nice old dear... Hang on, Lady Ottoline? You're not telling me <u>she</u> wrote that book?

JUDY: Exactly!

LAURA: Well bugger me sideways.

JUDY: Laura, please!

LAURA: So what about tonight? Mehmet's got a friend who's a body builder, you could do with a few muscles on you. (TUCKS IN)

LADY OTTOLINE: She isn't suggesting you venture unchaperoned into the apartment of an unknown Turk? Do you want to end up in a harem?!

JUDY: (SLIGHTLY OFFENDED) My best friend at school was Turkish!

LAURA: That's why I knew you'd like them!

LADY OTTOLINE: I strongly advise you against this "party". If they are gentlemen, your attendance will only cheapen you in their eyes.

JUDY: I don't know, we don't want them thinking we're a couple of Northern slappers.

LAURA: It's only a bit of a laugh!

JUDY: Lady Ottoline's right. We're not going to meet stockbrokers if we hang around with chicken batterers.

LAURA: Snob! (BEAT) What do you mean, "Lady Ottoline's right"?

JUDY: (PUZZLED) Are you okay?

LAURA:	I'm okay. You're the one who just stopped making sense.
LADY OTTOLINE:	(GENTLY, TO JUDY) My dear, I don't think she knows I'm here.
JUDY:	What do you mean?
LAURA:	I mean you're talking rubbish!
JUDY:	(TO LADY O) I don't understand?
LAURA:	What's to understand? We've pulled! Finish your tea and go and shave your bikini line!
LADY OTTOLINE:	It's simple. You can see me, you can hear me, but she can not. It's a question of sensitivity. She has none.

JUDY IS AGHAST.

LAURA:	What's up Jude? You look like you've seen a...?

JUDY STANDS. SHE FEELS WEIRD. SHE HEADS FOR THE DOOR. LAURA LOOKS PUZZLED. JUDY EXITS. LADY O VANISHES.

CUT TO:

SCENE THREE. INT. JUDY'S BEDROOM. NIGHT 1.

JUDY ENTERS AND SITS ON HER BED.

JUDY:	What's happening to me!?

LADY O IS SITTING NEXT TO HER.

LADY OTTOLINE:	It's nothing at which to be alarmed...
JUDY:	Oh my God, you! (JUMPS UP) Either I'm going mad, or you're a ghost, and I don't believe in ghosts, so I am going mad!
LADY OTTOLINE:	I want to help you.

JUDY: Then disappear!

LADY OTTOLINE: You need me.

JUDY: How do you know?

LADY OTTOLINE: Because you found me, and then you found the book, or to be more precise, the book found you...

JUDY SHIVERS INVOLUNTARILY.

LADY OTTOLINE: That's how I knew you need my help. And when I'm needed I... seem to... (TAILS OFF)

JUDY: Seem to what?

LADY OTTOLINE: I'm not really sure, it's quite puzzling.

JUDY: Oh great, she's puzzled!

LADY OTTOLINE: One thing is clear: You're an intelligent, presentable young lady, on the brink of her fourth decade, with a conspicuous lack of jewellery on her wedding finger.

JUDY: That's because I gave Colin his quarter carat Argos easy-terms solitaire back, and good riddance.

LADY OTTOLINE: Quarter carat? You made the right decision. I'm sure we can do better than that, Miss Wemys.

CUT TO:

SCENE FOUR. INT. THE LIVING ROOM. DAY 1.

LAURA IS STILL EATING. JUDY COMES BACK IN.

LAURA: You okay? I was just coming to see if...?

JUDY: I'm fine.

LAURA: So you on for this party tonight?

JUDY: Laura, raise your sights! If we're going to go out, let's go somewhere new, somewhere special, somewhere that's really London!

LAURA: You're on!

LAURA LEAPS INTO ACTION. SHE PUTS THE REMAINING FOOD IN THE FRIDGE, WHIPS OFF THE DUST SHEETS, AND STARTS MOVING FURNITURE INTO PLACE.

JUDY: What are you doing?

LAURA: If I pull, I'm not bringing him back to a building site! Come on, help us...!

JUDY ROLLS HER EYES AND TIDIES AWAY THE PAINTING THINGS. LADY O IS IN HER CHAIR IN THE PICTURE. IS SHE SMILING?

CUT TO

SCENE FIVE. BAR BROBDINGNAG. NIGHT 1.

ABOUT 7.30. JUDY, LAURA AND LADY OTTOLINE ENTER A BUSY TRENDY BAR, NAMED AFTER GULLIVER'S LAND OF GIANTS. ALL THE FURNITURE AND FITTINGS ARE TOO BIG. WHEN YOU SIT YOUR FEET DON'T TOUCH THE FLOOR, AND THE BAR IS CHEST HIGH.

THE CUSTOMERS ARE THE AFTER-WORK CROWD: SMART SUITED YOUNG MEN AND WOMEN, WITH A SMATTERING OF HIGH FASHION TYPES. JUDY AND LAURA HAVE DRESSED UP – LADY O HASN'T CHANGED. JUDY'S CLOTHES ARE FAIRLY FASHIONABLE BUT QUITE RESTRAINED. LAURA IS A BIT OF A FASHION VICTIM.

LAURA: Why is all the furniture so big?

LADY OTTOLINE: Bar Brobdingnag is obviously named after the Land of Giants in Gulliver's Travels.

JUDY: Bar Brobdingnag is obviously named after the Land of Giants in Gulliver's Travels.

LAURA: You and your books.

JUDY: Let's see if the drinks are equally huge.

LAURA: And the men!

THE GIRLS GO TO THE BAR. JUDY TRIES TO CATCH THE BARKEEP'S EYE.

LAURA: I read Madonna drinks vodka and cranberry juice.

JUDY: Well she'd know.

JUDY STAYS AT THE BAR, TRYING TO GET SERVED, WHILE LAURA LETS HER EYES ROVE. AN ELEGANT CHAP IN A CITY SUIT (PAUL, 28), ALSO AT THE BAR, CATCHES THE BARKEEP'S EYE.

PAUL: Jools...

THE BARKEEP FINALLY COMES OVER.

JUDY: Excuse me, I was first!

PAUL: But you weren't having very much success... What would you like?

JUDY: I'll buy my own drinks thank you.

PAUL: Of course. (SMILES AND MOVES AWAY)

JUDY: Two vodka and cranberry juices please...

THE BARKEEP POURS THE DRINKS.

BARKEEP: Ten pounds.

JUDY: I didn't want doubles!

BARKEEP: You're not getting doubles.

JUDY PUTS A TENNER ON THE BAR, AND GIVES LAURA HER DRINK.

LAURA: That fellow at the bar was nice.

JUDY: He was a posh pompous git! Let's sit down.

LAURA: You can, I'm going for a recce...

JUDY SEES LADY O PERCHED IN AN ARMCHAIR BIG ENOUGH FOR TWO. JUDY CROSSES TO HER AND SITS.

JUDY: I feel so out of my depth here. I mean, we have bars in Eccles, with bouncers and everything, but this!? I don't know anyone, I don't know how to act, what to say...

LADY OTTOLINE: Are you sure you should be speaking to me so openly? People might think...

JUDY: They'll just assume I'm on my hands free phone. Look around.

HALF THE PEOPLE IN THE PLACE ARE BABBLING INTO ALMOST INVISIBLE TELEPHONE PICK UPS.

LADY OTTOLINE: Fascinating. People go out for company, then spend their time talking to people who aren't here?

JUDY: True – though strictly speaking, you're not here. So, do you see any suitable men?

LADY OTTOLINE: You can tell a gentleman by his well kept shoes. Now, that's a pair of nicely polished brogues.

JUDY: Where?

LADY OTTOLINE: It's rude to point. At the bar, reading the financial pages.

JUDY: Him!?

Shooting the Pilot

LADY OTTOLINE: That's right, the man who committed the heinous crime of offering to buy you a drink. Even in my day...

JUDY: Will you shut up now?

LADY OTTOLINE: You know I'm right.

THEY SEE LAURA STEAM OVER TO PAUL.

LAURA: (TRYING TO SOUND POSH) Hello... If it isn't too much of a cheek, could I just check my shares in your paper?

PAUL: Be my guest. (HANDS HER THE PAPER)

LAURA: (GLANCING AT THE CITY PRICES) Fantastic! You're looking at one rich bitch. I'm Laura Breadalbane, by the way...

PAUL: Paul Miller.

THEY SHAKE HANDS.

LAURA: Can I get you a drink?

PAUL: Thanks, but no, I'm driving later.

LAURA: You're a cheap date!

PAUL: Not if there's caviar on the menu.

LAURA LAUGHS A SILVERY LAUGH. JUDY AND LADY O EDGE INTO EARSHOT.

JUDY: (GRUDGINGLY) I hate to admit it, but she's good.

LADY OTTOLINE: Good? She's a forward little minx!

JUDY: Same difference.

LADY OTTOLINE: It's a little like Pride and Prejudice, isn't it? You form a hasty bad judgement of the gentleman, and spend the next five years...

JUDY GETS OUT HER PHONE AND PRESSES A PRESET. LAURA'S PHONE RINGS.

LAURA: Excuse me Paul, my broker. (INTO PHONE) Yes?

JUDY: (INTO PHONE) I saw him first!

LAURA: (LOWERS VOICE) And you said he was a pompous git! (LOUDER) Sell French Connection, buy Marks and Spencers. (HANGS UP) Sorry about that...

PAUL: It's okay. (BEAT) I'm afraid I have to go...

LAURA: Must you? The night's so young it's still in nappies.

THEN JUDY SAUNTERS OVER.

JUDY: Hello, I'm Judy. We're cousins. Sorry I was offhand before, but we've only just arrived in London, and my mother warned me about good looking men in well polished shoes.

JUDY OFFERS PAUL A BIG SMILE AND A HANDSHAKE.

LAURA: (MOUTHS) You bitch!

PAUL: I'm Paul...

PAUL SHAKES JUDY'S HAND WARMLY. HE PREFERS HER TO LAURA, FOR SURE.

LAURA: Unfortunately Paul was just saying he has to go. Back to the wife and kiddies is it?

PAUL: I'm not married. No, it's a charity thing, you're welcome to come along...

JUDY: That depends. Is it the first night of a smash hit Broadway musical, or bungee jumping?

CUT TO:

Shooting the Pilot

SCENE SIX. INT. GRAND DRAWING ROOM. NIGHT 1.

PAUL USHERS JUDY AND LAURA INTO A FABULOUS DRAWING ROOM IN A REGENCY MANSION IN REGENT'S PARK. THERE ARE ABOUT 80 GILT CHAIRS SET OUT IN FRONT OF A PERFORMING SPACE, WHICH HAS FOUR EMPTY CHAIRS, AGAINST ONE OF WHICH LEANS A CELLO. MANY POSH TYPES MILL AROUND, WHILE WAITERS HAND ROUND CANAPES AND CHAMPERS. AT A CARD TABLE, LATE ARRIVALS ARE BUYING TICKETS FROM A DEBBY LOOKING GIRL. ANOTHER DEBBY TYPE IS GOING ROUND SELLING BOOKS OF RAFFLE TICKETS. LAURA LOOKS AROUND OPEN MOUTHED.

JUDY:	This place is absolutely incredible!
PAUL:	It's one of the finest private houses in London.
LAURA:	Someone lives here?! I thought it was a museum!
JUDY:	I hope he's got a big family?
PAUL:	He would have, but all wives keep leaving him.
LAURA:	He lives on his own?!
JUDY:	That's obscene! There's thousands of homeless people, yet one man...!
LADY O & LAURA:	Shh!
JUDY:	Well...!

PAUL SEES THE TICKET QUEUE HAS GONE.

PAUL:	Don't go anywhere...

PAUL CROSSES TO THE TABLE AND SPEAKS BRIEFLY TO THE DEB.

LAURA:	Is this real champagne?
JUDY:	How the hell should I know?

Lady Ottoline Pierpoint's Guide to Intimate Behaviour for Gentlewomen

LAURA:	I wonder if the bloke who owns it is married at the moment.
LADY OTTOLINE:	I don't like this wallpaper. The last time I was here, it was...
JUDY:	(HISSES AT LADY O) Not now!
LAURA:	I only said...

PAUL RETURNS WITH 2 TICKETS.

PAUL:	I used my influence to get you some freebies.
JUDY:	I'd rather pay my way thanks. How much are they?
PAUL:	A hundred pounds each.
JUDY:	(QUICK AS A FLASH) How much are the raffle tickets?
PAUL:	A pound.
JUDY:	I'll have two.

PAUL GRINS AND BECKONS OVER THE RAFFLE TICKET CHAP. JUDY HANDS OVER A £2 COIN, AND GETS HER TICKETS.

PAUL:	If you give me your 'phone number, I'll fill out the counterfoils for you...
LAURA:	Good pick up technique!
JUDY:	It's... I can never remember my mobile...
LAURA:	0702 881 935...
JUDY:	That's your mobile!
LAURA:	Oops.
PAUL:	Give it to me later.

THE LIGHTS DIM. MOST OF THE AUDIENCE HAVE TAKEN THEIR SEATS.

Shooting the Pilot

PAUL: Time to do my party piece.

PAUL GOES TO THE FRONT OF THE ROOM, AND TAPS HIS GLASS WITH HIS PEN. NOISE SUBSIDES.

PAUL: My Lords, Ladies and Gentlemen...

LAURA: (SV) There are lords here...!

PAUL: It's my pleasure to welcome you to Montgomery Lodge, generously made available tonight by Lord Fulcrum, and to thank you for your continued unstinting support. We all know how hard it is to maintain fundraising momentum the year after a general election. But it is vital that the Party keeps the cash flowing in, so we can face the future in the black and not in the red.

A LITTLE LAUGH GOES ROUND THE ROOM, BUT JUDY ISN'T LAUGHING.

JUDY: (TO LAURA) I don't believe it, he's conned me into supporting the Tory Party!

LAURA: You only bought two raffle tickets!

PAUL: But you haven't come here to listen to me, but to the delightful and very talented Bartholdy quartet.

THE YOUNG QUARTET COME ON TO APPLAUSE. JUDY DOESN'T SIT.

LAURA & LADY O: Judy! Sit down.

JUDY: Stop ganging up on me!

LAURA: What?

JUDY: I'm going!

LAURA: I'm staying. You heard, there are lords!

JUDY: Suit yourself. (EXITING)

LADY OTTOLINE: But I haven't been to a recital since 1935!

JUDY: Stay then!

LADY OTTOLINE: If only I could.

JUDY GOES, GETTING SOME FUNNY LOOKS. LADY O GOES TOO PERFORCE. THE MUSIC STARTS.

CUT TO

SCENE SEVEN. EXT. LORD FULCRUM'S PLACE. NIGHT 1.

JUDY HURRIES OUT. SHE HAILS A PASSING CAB, BUT IT'S FULL. SHE STRIDES OFF, LADY O IN ATTENDANCE. PAUL COMES OUT OF THE HOUSE.

PAUL: Judy!

JUDY KEEPS WALKING. PAUL CATCHES UP WITH HER.

PAUL: Wait!

JUDY STOPS UNWILLINGLY.

PAUL: What's wrong?

JUDY: I just don't appreciate being conned into some fat cat's house full of other fat cats!

PAUL: Conned? You picked me up in a bar!

JUDY: Fine, it's my fault. Of course it is. Typical bloody Tory. I demand my two pounds back!

PAUL: Actually, I'm New Labour.

JUDY: What?!

PAUL: Check the raffle tickets. You're probably confused because I left me whippet and flat cap at home.

JUDY: Well, you look like a Tory.

PAUL: (ULTRA POSH VOICE) I'm most frightfully sorry.

JUDY CAN'T BUT LAUGH.

CUT TO:

SCENE EIGHT. INT. TOILET. NIGHT 1.

JUDY WASHES HER HANDS. LADY O WATCHES, BUT IT'S ONLY JUDY IN THE MIRROR.

LADY OTTOLINE: I think you're being most unfair! I haven't been out to dinner in sixty five years.

JUDY: I don't need you here all night, telling me which fork to use!

A MIDDLE AGED WOMAN COMES IN TO ADJUST HER MAKE UP. JUDY DOESN'T NOTICE HER.

LADY OTTOLINE: It's quite simple, you start from the outside...

JUDY: Just go home!

JUDY SEES THE WOMAN LOOK AT HER ODDLY.

JUDY: (TO THE WOMAN) You heard! Go!

THE WOMAN RUNS. JUDY TOSSES HER HEAD A LA MISS PIGGY.

CUT TO:

SCENE NINE. INT. TRATTORIA. NIGHT 1

A NICE HOMELY TRATTORIA. JUDY REJOINS PAUL, AND HE RAISES HIS GLASS TO HER. THEY DRINK.

JUDY: Still no sign of our mains?

PAUL: He's refilling his pepper mill, it takes time.

JUDY: So - you've heard my life story; how about you? You're not an MP are you?

PAUL: Me, you're joking! No, I'm a doctor.

JUDY:	(DOUBTFUL) Really? What sort of doctor?
PAUL:	Of gyroscopy.
JUDY:	You mean you're a spin doctor? Then why can't you just say spin doctor? Silly question, because you're a spin doctor.
PAUL:	I'm sorry...
JUDY:	Really sorry, or is that more spin?
PAUL:	You're quick!
JUDY:	But I'm not fast.
PAUL:	I'm not in a hurry.
JUDY:	Neither's our waiter.
	PAUL REFILLS HER GLASS. THE WAITER APPEARS.
PAUL:	At last.
	THE WAITER GIVES THEM THEIR FOOD. IT LOOKS GOOD. THE WAITER GOES. THEY EAT. IT TASTES GOOD.
PAUL:	How does it compare to the food in Eccles?
JUDY:	Let's just say back home, people throw themselves down the stairs to qualify for hospital catering.
	THE WAITER COMES BACK WITH A TINY WOODEN PEPPER MILL. JUDY BURSTS OUT LAUGHING.
JUDY:	(TO WAITER) Sorry, I know size isn't everything...
	THE WAITER GOES WITHOUT GRINDING. HE'S PUT OUT.
PAUL:	So where exactly do you live?
JUDY:	South Tottenham.
PAUL:	Where even the crack dealers go round in pairs?
JUDY:	And just when you'd stopped annoying me...

PAUL: Sorry, it's just I've never been to Tottenham...

JUDY: What makes you think you're going to?

PAUL: (SMILES) A gentleman always sees a lady home.

CUT TO:

SCENE TEN. INT. THE LIVING ROOM. NIGHT 1.

THE ROOM IS DARK. THE DOOR OPENS. JUDY AND PAUL ENTER. SHE PUTS THE LIGHT ON. THE ROOM IS ROUGHLY TIDIED AS THE GIRLS LEFT IT, WITH THE WALLS HALF PAINTED AND THE HESSIAN PANEL LEANING AGAINST ONE OF THE WALLS. LADY O. IS BACK IN HER TROMPE L'OEIL.

JUDY: (APOLOGETICALLY) I'm in the middle of painting...

PAUL ADMIRES THE PICTURE.

PAUL: You did this?!

JUDY: Yes, just after I finished the Laughing Cavalier. Do you like it?

PAUL: It's fantastic!

JUDY: I used to like it, but the woman in it gets on my nerves. Coffee?

PAUL: Double decaff espresso please...

JUDY: In your dreams.

PAUL CROSSES TO THE CD PLAYER AND THE SMALL PILE OF DISCS. JUDY PUTS ON THE KETTLE. LAURA COMES IN. SHE'S WEARING HER MANCHESTER UNITED PYJAMAS. SHE GOES OVER TO JUDY IN THE KITCHEN CORNER. SHE DOESN'T NOTICE PAUL.

LAURA: Where did you get to?!

JUDY:	Just went for something to eat... What time did you get home?
LAURA:	Ages ago. I wasn't going to stay there on my own, plus they didn't play one song I recognised!
JUDY:	Shame.
LAURA:	You know Paul left about half a minute after you?

TEXAS'S GREATEST HITS COMES ON. LAURA SPINS ROUND AND SEES PAUL. SHE'S MORTIFIED. HE JUST SMILES.

LAURA:	(S.V., ALMOST JOKING) I hate you!
JUDY:	(S.V.) I tried to get rid of him... I'm just making him coffee so he doesn't fall asleep driving home. I'd make you a cup, but you've got an early start tomorrow, haven't you, the Stock Exchange opens at 7 o'clock. Night night, don't let the bed bugs bite.
LAURA:	Why not? It's the only excitement I'm going to get. (EXITS)

PAUL SITS, KICKS OFF HIS SHOES, AND FINDS LADY O'S BOOK ON THE COFFEE TABLE. JUDY SPOONS INSTANT COFFEE INTO TWO MUGS. LADY O IS THERE NOW.

LADY OTTOLINE:	Do you realise what you're doing?
JUDY:	(SV) I haven't got any proper coffee.
LADY OTTOLINE:	I leave you alone for an hour, you bring a strange man home and let him take his shoes off!
JUDY:	I thought you liked his shoes?
LADY OTTOLINE:	Exactly, and you're compromising yourself!
JUDY:	Get back in the picture before he notices.

Shooting the Pilot

LADY OTTOLINE: You shouldn't have let Laura go to bed, she was your guarantee of respectability.

JUDY: Laura? Respectable?

PAUL: Where did you get this book? It's fantastic!

LADY OTTOLINE: Thank you.

PAUL: "In accepting an escort, a young lady must exercise common sense. She should never let a man she does not know well conduct her home. If the man owns a car and offers her a lift, she will be doubly reprehensible if she accepts." Oh smack my wrist.

JUDY: It was written a long time ago by a very eccentric lady.

LADY OTTOLINE: It is as relevant today!

PAUL: "He may be well spoken and have nice eyes, but at the very least her reputation will be compromised, if not blemished." (A SNORT OF DERISION) This is the 21st Century!

JUDY: It hasn't reached Eccles...

JUDY BRINGS THE COFFEE, AND SITS NEXT TO PAUL.

PAUL: Men and women are equals, and if there's a connection...

JUDY: Connection? We don't agree on anything!

PAUL: That's what's I like about you. Most of the women I meet don't have opinions, except about handbags and shoes.

JUDY: I expect they've got opinions about you, but they're too polite to voice them.

PAUL: Sorry – and that's not spin.

PAUL PUTS AN ARM ROUND HER SHOULDER.

LADY OTTOLINE: Judy! This is going too far, and too fast.

JUDY: Biscuit? (GETS UP)

PAUL: Not allowed biscuits in New Labour.

LADY OTTOLINE: Just tell him to go!

JUDY: (STILL STANDING) Can I say something?

PAUL: You have the floor.

JUDY: You know how when you go shopping for shoes, and you really like the first pair you try on? But you go into some other shops, just in case, and when you get back to the first shop, either the shoes have gone, or your feet have swollen up and they don't fit any more?

PAUL: Are your feet hurting?

JUDY: No, what I'm trying to say is... meeting new people is like buying new shoes.

PAUL: I'm with you now, it's a girl thing! So which shoes am I?

JUDY: I don't know yet.

PAUL: You worried I'll be too large, give you blisters?

JUDY: (SPIRITED) More likely be too small...

PAUL: Touché. Come on, sit down.

JUDY: Don't tell me what to do, this is my flat.

PAUL: Sorry.

JUDY: I'll sit because I want to. (SITS)

THEY LISTEN TO THE MUSIC FOR A FEW MOMENTS. JUDY RELAXES.

PAUL: In my experience, the most important thing about shoes is making sure the tongue is comfortable...

PAUL GOES FOR THE SNOG. JUDY GOES FOR IT TOO. WE CLOSE UP ON LADY OTTOLINE.

LADY OTTOLINE: Judy, no! This is very ill advised! Stop it! Judy...!

CUT TO:

SCENE ELEVEN. INT. JUDY'S BEDROOM. DAY 2.

EARLY SATURDAY MORNING. JUDY IS IN BED. PAUL IS PERCHED ON THE EDGE, HE IS DRESSED.

PAUL: I'd love to stay, but I've got this meeting...

JUDY: (TEASING) On a Saturday...?

PAUL: Spinning's a 24-7 kind of job. I'll phone you tonight...

JUDY: (COOL) You don't have my number.

PAUL: That's right. Have you remembered it yet?

JUDY: 07809 536599. (BEAT) Aren't you going to write it down?

PAUL: I won't forget your number.

JUDY: What is it then?

PAUL: (SMOOTH) 07809 536599.

THEY KISS TENDERLY. PAUL GOES.

MIX INTO...

SCENE TWELVE. INT. JUDY'S BEDROOM. DAY 3.

CAPTION: "THREE DAYS LATER AND STILL NO PHONE CALL"

MONDAY 8AM. JUDY'S IN BED, LADY OTTOLINE IS PERCHED ON THE EDGE, IN AN ECHO OF THE PREVIOUS SCENE. LADY OTTOLINE HAS BEEN TELLING HER OFF.

JUDY: ... I know, I know, I know...

LAURA ENTERS, DRESSED IN TODAY'S FASHION.

LAURA: You sure you're okay?

JUDY: No, but you get off to work anyway. Just phone my office and tell them my malaria's flared up.

LAURA: You can't stay in bed for the rest of your life just because a guy didn't ring you!

LADY OTTOLINE: Exactly what I said!

JUDY: It's not just Paul. It's me. I'm 29, I've got a university degree, why am I so naïve?

LAURA: Give up, why are you?

JUDY: You fancied him too!

LAURA: For a bit of fun, not a white wedding and a joint mortgage.

JUDY: I swore I wouldn't be taken in by the next smooth talker who bought me a drink...

LADY OTTOLINE: You were only too ready to be taken in.

LAURA: It could have happened to anyone. It's a jungle down here, there's ten single women for every straight, available, tattoo-free man with a job that doesn't involve onion rings.

JUDY: Life was so much simpler in Eccles. At least if a bloke dumps you, you can go round his house and break his windows.

LAURA: It was you!

JUDY: In London, Paul can have his evil way, then vanish into the darkness.

LAURA: That book's really got to you, hasn't it?

JUDY: If I followed Lady Ottoline's advice, I wouldn't be lying here in bed with malaria.

LADY OTTOLINE: And "lying" is the word, isn't it?

LAURA RUFFLES JUDY'S HAIR, AND GOES.

JUDY: What am I going to do?

LADY OTTOLINE: Stay in bed until you lose the use of your limbs?

JUDY: It's an option.

THE PHONE RINGS IN THE LIVING ROOM. JUDY RUSHES OUT.

LADY OTTOLINE: A miraculous recovery.

CUT TO

SCENE THIRTEEN. INT. LIVING ROOM. DAY 3.

JUDY DASHES IN, IN TIME TO HEAR A MESSAGE BEING LEFT ON THE PHONE BY HER MUM.

JUDY'S MUM: Judy, it's mum here... (JUDY CHOOSES NOT TO PICK UP) I expect you've left for work, but for God's sake, don't touch the pork pie, Eccles is in the grip of an E Coli epidemic! (RINGS OFF)

LADY OTTOLINE: I take it you thought it was Paul?

JUDY: No, I thought it was British Gas asking me if I'm happy with my electricity supplier! That's stumped you, hasn't it?

LADY OTTOLINE: (STICKING TO HER LINE) And if it had been Paul, what would you have done? Given him a piece of your mind, or agreed to another night of tangled sheets?

JUDY: I'm not ashamed I slept with him, I'm angry he didn't call.

LADY OTTOLINE: You see no connection? When you wish to sell a motor car, do you give the keys and the log book to the first person who responds to your advertisement – and crank his starting handle to boot? If you do, you can't be surprised when he drives off and you never see him or the car again.

JUDY: I liked him! I thought he liked me!

LADY OTTOLINE: I liked David Lloyd George, but I didn't go to bed with him.

JUDY: You were in a very small minority.

LADY OTTOLINE: That's what he said.

JUDY: What do you think I should do?

LADY OTTOLINE: You could sue him for breach of promise. Chapter eleven tells you how to go about it.

JUDY: I didn't expect a proposal on the strength of a one night stand!

LADY OTTOLINE: But he's taken something very precious.

JUDY: I was hardly a virgin.

LADY OTTOLINE: I meant your self respect. You need to restore it.

CUT TO:

SCENE FOURTEEN. INT. LABOUR PARTY HQ. DAY 4.

JUDY, WITH OTTOLINE, ENTERS THE MILLBANK LOBBY. IT'S ALL VERY CLASSY AND GLASSY, WITH LABOUR PARTY CORPORATE I.D. IN VIEW. SOME SMOOTH POLITICOS COME OUT OF A LIFT AND HEAD FOR THEIR CHAUFFEURED CARS. JUDY GOES TO THE RECEPTION DESK, WOMANNED BY THE DEBBY TYPE WHO WAS SELLING TICKETS AT THE RECITAL.

JUDY: Hello, we met at the recital; I'm here to collect my raffle prize from Paul Miller. (BRANDISHES HER TICKET) It's a waffle maker, as used by ministerial speech writers.

LADY OTTOLINE: Very witty.

JUDY: Thank you.

THE GIRL LOOKS CONFUSED. WHY IS JUDY THANKING HER?

CUT TO

SCENE FIFTEEN. INT. ROOM 429. DAY 4.

PAUL'S OFFICE ISN'T VERY BIG, BUT AROUND HIS TABLE SIT PAUL AND SIX OTHER PRESS OFFICERS – DIFFERENT COLOURS AND GENDERS, BUT ALL VERY MIDDLE CLASS.

PAUL: We must not deviate from the message that the Minister had no idea the donation came from a man wanted for currency offences in seven countries…

THE DOOR OPENS AND IN COME JUDY AND LADY O. PAUL REACTS.

JUDY: Excuse me, is this the right room for bullshit?

PAUL: Not now, Judy…

JUDY: Why "not now"? It was "yes, now!" on Friday night, wasn't it? And on Saturday morning.

PAUL:	Everybody, I think this would be a good time to break for lunch...

NO ONE MOVES.

PAUL:	The Milky Bars are on me?

NO ONE MOVES. PAUL CROSSES TO JUDY AND PUSHES HER OUT INTO THE CORRIDOR.

CUT TO:

SCENE SIXTEEN. MILLBANK CORRIDOR. DAY 4.

CONTINUOUS. PAUL, JUDY, AND LADY O. COME OUT OF HIS ROOM.

PAUL:	Are you some sort of crackpot bunny boiler?!
LADY OTTOLINE:	Crackpot bunny boiler?
JUDY:	You promised you'd phone.
PAUL:	Is that what this is about? I meant to...
JUDY:	What's my number?
PAUL:	Er... (HE'S CLEARLY FORGOTTEN IT)
JUDY:	And now you needn't bother. All that "it's so unusual to meet someone like you these days". You meant someone gullible and accommodating! Why say it Paul?
PAUL:	Couldn't help it, that's my technique.
JUDY:	(WITH CONTEMPT) What are you scared of?
PAUL:	Snakes, and being out of my depth in the sea?
JUDY:	I feel sorry for you. You're not capable of a proper relationship, you're frightened of commitment, you don't even like women!

Shooting the Pilot

                    JUDY GETS A ROUND OF APPLAUSE FROM LADY OTTOLINE AND FEARFUL LOOKS FROM SPINNERS GAWPING IN THE DOORWAY.

PAUL: Okay, that's all, get to it.

                    PAUL'S TEAM LEAVE HIS ROOM. HE DARTS INSIDE, SLAMS THE DOOR, AND ILLUMINATES THE "DO NOT DISTURB" SIGN.

JUDY: That cheered me up.

LADY OTTOLINE: And what will you do next time you meet a presentable man wearing decent shoes?

JUDY: Consult you before making a fool of myself.

LADY OTTOLINE: Do you mean that, or is that just spin?

JUDY: You're a fast learner for a disembodied spirit.

LADY OTTOLINE: Shall we go?

JUDY: Hold on, I think I can hear the cavalry.

                    A WORKER APPEARS PUSHING THE TEA TROLLEY. SHE SEES PAUL'S SIGN, AND LEAVES A CUP OF TEA AND A PLATE OF SANDWICHES OUTSIDE HIS DOOR. OFF GOES THE TROLLEY. JUDY GRINS. SHE OPENS HER BAG, TAKES OUT THE PORK PIE, REMOVES THE SANDWICHES, AND PUTS THE PIE ON PAUL'S PLATE. LADY O LOOKS STARTLED.

JUDY: I actually brought it to throw at him.

                    JUDY AND LADY O WALK OFF. PAUL'S DOOR OPENS A CRACK AND HE PULLS IN HIS LUNCH TRAY.

                    <u>THE END</u>

Afterword

I'M NOT IN THE HABIT of watching our shows when they pop up on obscure satellite channels, so it's been many years since I've revisited most of these projects. That must be why rereading these old scripts triggered such a range of responses, including pride, amazement, gratitude, and a degree of embarrassment.

To deal with the embarrassment first, I realised long ago that *Holding the Fort*, our breakthrough script, was too desperately full of jokes for its own good. In our defence, we *were* desperate; desperate to break into television and make our mark.

We were lucky that back in 1979 the ability to make people laugh was still highly prized in comedy circles. The thinking was that if you can do funny, you can learn most of the other stuff, and so we proved over the subsequent decades.

Amazement? At the risk of sounding arrogant, I'm amazed by how quickly we matured from the juvenilia of *Holding the Fort* to the assured tone of *Shine On Harvey Moon*. We must have been fast learners, back in our early thirties. After *Harvey*, we always felt we knew what we were doing, even if we didn't always know how we were doing it. As a result, all but one of the pilots in this book made it to the screen with relatively little interference from the broadcasters, and were kindly received by critics and viewers alike.

As for pride, well yes, we're both proud that we succeeded in so many different arenas of comedy, from the outrageous satire of *The New Statesman* via the mainstream appeal of *Birds of a Feather* to the more subtle comedy-drama of *Love Hurts*. Would we have been able to create all these shows if we hadn't worked with so many supportive producers and commissioners? We very much doubt it. In those early days, Barry and Lyn Took (this book's dedicatees, if there's such a word) believed in us more than we did.

We're grateful too that we had the good fortune to work with the best: Humphrey Barclay at London Weekend Television; Vernon Lawrence at Yorkshire TV; our writer-heroes Dick Clement and Ian la Frenais; Tony Charles and Allan McKeown at our production company, Alomo Productions… I won't say the list is endless but it's a long one!

Finally, of course, we're grateful to you for buying this book. But don't stop at one copy: buy a dozen. Then you and your friends can recreate these pilots in the comfort of your own home.

Maurice Gran
January 2021